Better work together

How the power of **community** can transform your **business**

Producing Authors | Anthony Cabraal
Susan Basterfield

Preface

Douglas Rushkoff is an educator, media theorist, and author: Most recently of the book Team Human and host of the Team Human podcast. (https://teamhuman.fm/)

I receive over a hundred emails a day from people with great ideas for social change, new democratic platforms, eco-villages, and alternative currencies. Some of them have already written eloquent white papers, created gorgeous renderings, or plotted out cyclic revenue streams that seem to challenge the laws of perpetual motion. These are well-meaning people, with great educations and skills, turning their attention to the most pressing "wicked problems" of our age.

Yet almost all of their ingenious blueprints for the salvation of humanity have been conceived and generated alone, in a room, on a computer. Yes, they want to find the others now - people and organizations who share the same fundamental values, and will recognize the wisdom of their master plans. But no matter who I try to connect them to, it never quite works out. That's because they're reaching out to the other people much too late.

Solidarity is not the result of world-changingly good ideas, it is the cause. There's no paucity of solutions to our collective woes; from permaculture and the commons to consensus building and platform cooperatives. What we too often lack are the communities of people to organize and apply these solutions in the real world, from the bottom up. It doesn't have to be this way.

The Occupy movement has long been criticized as lacking substance or purpose. As if it were just a bunch of idealistic college students and dropouts with great motives but no plan. But to me, this was precisely their strength: a willingness to gather together with no particular expectation other than to forge solidarity, and model a new approach to social change. Less a demand or a eschatological goal than a process: a new normative state, and a new way of occupying reality. This may not have been Adbusters' intent when they called for a protest against Wall Street; it's simply what happened when people came together with a determination to engage in the long game of social change, one collaborative step at a time.

No, Occupy didn't achieve some landmark concession from government or the corporate sector. But it did set in motion a new approach to collective action, governance, and trade. Or maybe it just retrieved some lost approaches, from the General Assembly of Ancient Greece, to the commons of pre-industrial Europe. These mechanisms were not part of some master plan, but rather emerged in response to the needs of people engaging differently. And as the needs of the people in the park and streets changed, different experts rushed into the scene to provide food solutions, technology, WiFi, and more. Each solution generated from the bottom up, in an occasionally ad hoc but always organic way.

Enspiral may have predated Occupy by a year, but it arose in the same way and for some of the same reasons, asking the same questions: How can a business, organization, or society itself work without bosses? How can a group take everyone's opinion into account, and still get anything done? How can a company make money for its stakeholders without extracting needed funds from somewhere or someone else?

The collective's solutions and now-thriving initiatives were as much responses to its own challenges as they were bright ideas for the world. Loomio, a consensus tool modeled on Occupy's General Assembly meeting style, helps groups agree on difficult issues. Instead of promoting winner-takes-all, polarizing outcomes of traditional debate, it seeks to minimize total discomfort with group choices. And yes, solving this problem for themselves gave Enspiral a tool that was applicable as far and wide as the Podemos movement in Spain or local government in the United Kingdom. Similarly, Enspiral's Experience Agency organizes and facilitates events and retreats - but only because its founders needed to develop this expertise to facilitate their own meetings and workshops on open source.

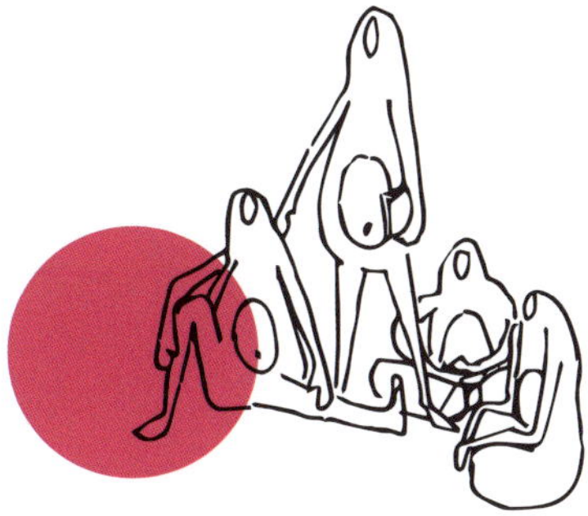

The efforts grow, for sure, but they don't "scale" in the way Silicon Valley may think of growth. These are not the one-size-fits-all Industrial Age solutions now being distributed through digital networks. These initiatives spread because they are techniques that can be modeled by others, and then adapted to particular circumstances. They are not products but processes. They are less services than offerings.

Because the problems engendered by the monolithic solutions offered by industrial capitalism aren't countered by more big solutions but by many different local responses. Enspiral's methodologies are more fundamental than any fully realized rendering of an eco-village or white paper for another blockchain. Like the service offered by Enspiral's companies, these are not answers to your challenges so much as recipes for finding and developing your own.

The work itself - the process of collaboration - ends up as important as whatever product or service is being delivered. It's less of a final solution that can be thought up, written down, and emailed to the world than it is a commitment to engaging honestly, openly, and transparently from the beginning.

Here's how that happens.

Douglas Rushkoff
New York, November, 2018

"If you are sincere in your desire to make the world a better place then your personal success is our number one priority."

~ enspiral.com/recruitment 2010

Thank you for your attention.

As a species we have never been so powerful.

New tools, unprecedented levels of resource, and our ability to mobilise enables we humans to rewrite the rules of how life can be. As individuals we are smarter, healthier and more connected. Together, we have harnessed our collective creativity to build systems that make us more powerful and effective than at any point in history, on any planet we know of.

With this power we're changing things.

The world we've built is changing dramatically. How we control information, money and power, how we connect with each other, share, and create together is changing fundamentally. Our businesses, markets, financial systems, and nations are being transformed.

We are reaching limits we haven't encountered before.

Our collective footprint has never been so heavy on the Earth. There have never been so many of us demanding so much from the planet. The impact of our individual and collective decisions has never been so strong. Every side effect, every externality, every waste product we create lands hard on a planet that once felt infinite, and has quickly become smaller and more fragile.

What do we do?

Disruption, collapse, reimagination, transformation, revolution. These are the times we are living in. As individuals, as agents of change, community builders, entrepreneurs, parents, employers, leaders, followers, citizens, (whatever the hats we wear), as participants on Planet Earth we must navigate this time of immense challenge and opportunity together.

The fundamental natural systems that support stable life on this planet are shifting with our weight. Technology is making our wildest imaginings more possible every day. The future is our hands - right now. We have the potential (and the urgent need) to change everything.

Where do we start?

What is this book about!?

This book speaks from a community, not on behalf of a community; the words are written by many voices, and not all of them agree. It is it not intended to be 'the Enspiral story' or an answer to the ongoing question "what is Enspiral?"

There is much work still to be done, innumerate angles yet unexplored, work that has not been surfaced, and plenty of space to continue to expand the frame of this conversation. Depending on where you are right now, this could be...

- A book about building teams and successful companies, to grow livelihood and support new ways of working together.
- A book about challenging the way things are and creating alternative systems for a radically different world.
- A book about committed action, persistence and the first steps of progress on a very long journey to answer some big questions.
- A book about big ideas to change the world, and what happens when the right people find one another, and something remarkable happens.

If the essays, guides and reflections in this book point toward one thing, it's an urgent need for conscious attention.

Regardless of what kind of world we want to build, or the lives we want to lead, perhaps the most powerful starting question we can ask ourselves is: Where do we choose to put our attention?

Our attention is so valuable.

It is fleeting and difficult to control. With effort we can focus it, but we cannot acquire more of it. We can protect it but it cannot be stored or transferred. It is constantly demanded, always under threat and yet we give it away freely as we move through the world.

Our attention silently determines how we choose to build our livelihoods, look after ourselves, and make decisions about what is important to us.

The world that will exist 10 years from now, 20 years from now, 30 years from now is being built today. It is our conscious attention, put into action, that is building that future.

Our attention is our power. It is the invisible, constant force that ultimately determines our individual and collective potential.

This book is an exploration of what happens when our conscious attention is turned to how we choose to work. What is the most important work of our lives? What is right work for us as individuals? As groups and teams and organisations? What is good work? What is better work?

What does **better work together** look like?

How to read this book

The book has been designed to be read front to back, or back to front, middle to end or picked up and browsed spontaneously.

You'll find short essays written by 10 co-authors that speak deeply to expertise developed through practice, alongside guides, provocations and reflections from dozens of contributors.

Some questions to keep in mind might be:

- *Might these provocations start much bigger conversations?*
- *Do these ideas shift your thinking?*
- *Which processes might you experiment with?*
- *Are there practical resources here you can use?*
- *Are there tools you can adopt?*
- *Are there mistakes you can avoid?*
- *Are there assertions that you can challenge?*

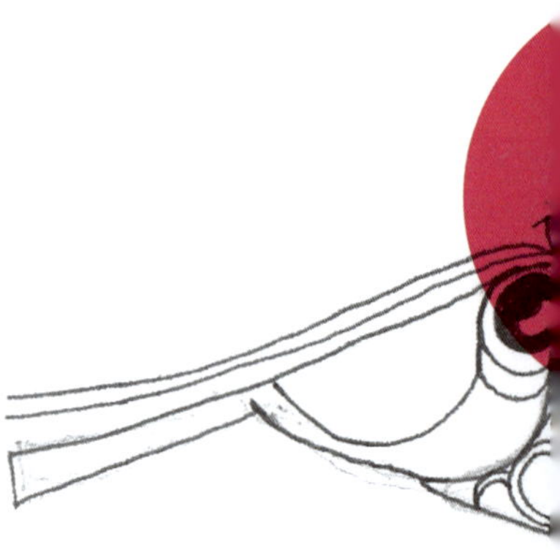

Ultimately, we hope these pages challenge you and open you to opportunities that bring more attention and action towards a future that will work better for all of us.

Thank you for your attention.

Anthony Cabraal & Susan Basterfield
Producing Authors

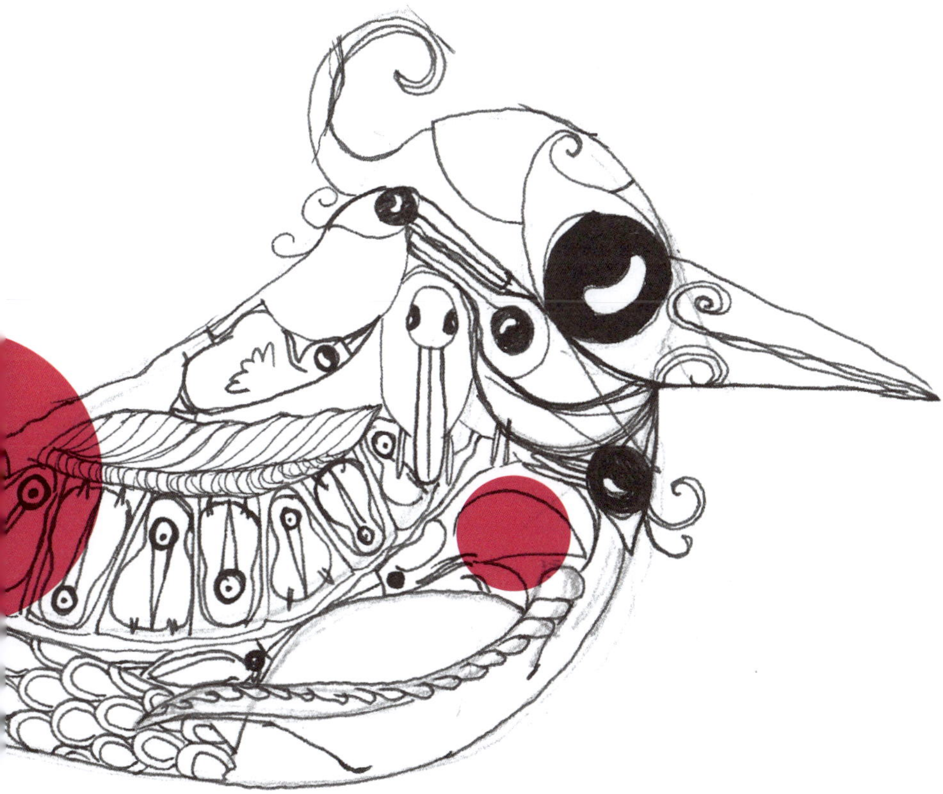

Better work together

essay.One

More people working on stuff that matters

by Joshua Vial

It all started with a story

In February 2011 Enspiral was just about to turn 1 year old. A handful of us had moved into a shared office a few weeks before. This email showed up in my inbox:

"Hi Joshua, I'm really interested to learn about what Enspiral is doing right now and how I might collaborate with you guys. I've been programming for a long time, launched a startup, and I'm now working on a new venture focusing on rest homes. So, If you think I'm the right kind of person for Enspiral, or there are opportunities to talk about, please let me know. Kind Regards, Rob"

We organised a time to meet, and I shared the Enspiral story. Shaped by hundreds of conversations, it wasn't just my story, but I was the main story-holder at the time. It went something like this:

More people working on stuff that matters

There is a growing awareness of some big problems in our society—climate change, extreme poverty, ecological collapse and gender inequality, to name a few. It feels like core systems in society are fundamentally broken and our current political and economic systems are not adequately responding. Often, the knowledge and resources to provide solutions are there, they just aren't pointing in the right direction.

A growing number of people are becoming aware of these big problems and are deciding to do something about it. Our strategy is help those people connect with peers and help each other succeed.

I don't care what you work on, whether it's climate change, global poverty, self management, social enterprise, planting trees, gender equality, decolonisation, or steady state economics. If your primary mission is to make the world a better place, your personal success is the reason Enspiral exists.

There is a trickle of human energy going into the most important issues of our times. Enspiral exists to help turn that trickle into a river.

We organise differently

Most organisations in the world look like pyramids. Their strategy is to choose the best people they can find and centralise money, information, and control. The leaders distribute information, delegate power, and allocate resources as best they can, and those resources flow down like a waterfall. People who work in the organisation have limited ability to influence who the leaders are and what they do.

This is a very successful form of organising. Many organisations in the world use some form of hierarchical, command and control model. When the cost of transacting information is high (meetings, letters, phone calls), it makes a lot of sense. Collaboration costs can be managed and people can work together to deliver big projects.

However, as Clay Shirky would say, technology changes everything. The flood of information makes the attention economy as important as the financial one. Leaders are forced to reason about a complex world with simple abstractions, and information loss occurs as data flows up and down the pyramid. People who are conditioned by the culture of pull requests, wikis, and participatory media feel friction in a read-only world.

The revolution in communications technology and the culture it produces has opened the possibility space for how groups can work effectively together. A core hypothesis of Enspiral is that a new form of organising is not just possible, but optimal—one based on peer relationships that value individual sovereignty and consent-based decision-making. We want to exercise power with others, not over others. No one should lead all the time and everyone should lead some of the time.

We consciously decentralise money, information and power, and use rich information systems to coordinate our actions. We borrow old social technologies from cooperative organising and integrate them with modern technologies to explore new ways of working together.

Get paid well to change the world.

Many people who dream of changing the world are constrained by having to earn a livelihood doing something that doesn't contribute to their core mission. For many of us with commercially valuable skills, there are plenty of opportunities to help companies earn money, or to work for charities as an ambulance at the bottom of a cliff, or to work in the public sector wrestling with large and inefficient bureaucracies and politics.

At Enspiral, we focus on helping each other earn sustainable livelihoods that are aligned with our values. This might be through freelancing, starting a mission-driven venture, or working for another organisation. The Enspiral challenge is to get paid well to do work you love, with people you love, while working on a systemic issue you care deeply about.

It isn't easy, but it is possible. People join this community to help each other meet that challenge. Enspiral doesn't have jobs, but we've got lots of opportunities, and we find that the right people tend to hire themselves.

Rob resonated with that story, and became the 49th person to join Enspiral. That's the story we came from.

These days, there are many Enspiral stories, and no one person can hold them all. The only way to understand Enspiral is to listen to many people, which is why many of us are contributing to this book.

My Enspiral journey

Each of us have our own stories of how we found this community and what it means to us. My Enspiral journey began in 2007 at the feet of the Eiffel tower.

I had just spent two months walking the Camino de Santiago pilgrimage path through France and Spain. I don't remember what made me want to walk the Camino. I was restless and figured walking for a long time would be a good way to figure things out. But by the end, I hadn't figured out much at all; my feet were sore and my mind clear. On my last night in Europe I went for a walk through the streets of Paris.

I found myself at an art exhibition by Yann Arthus Bertrand on the banks of the Seine called 'Alive'. There were dozens of beautiful photographs of people, animals, and the planet. Alongside each photo was a fact about global systems failure: biodiversity loss, extreme poverty, climate change, and so on. Devastating data told an irrefutable story of the harm caused by humans and a small story about a group of people trying to do something positive offered a glimmer of hope.

Image after image washed over me. Some of the facts I knew, and some I didn't. Most I'd bumped into previously, and were drifting around in my subconscious under the title of 'bad things happening in the world'. As I walked away from the exhibition, I was left with a voice ringing in my head: "maybe there isn't enough time".

I started educating myself. I actively researched global issues, and the more I looked the more horrified I became. It seemed to me that the majority of human systems were fundamentally flawed. It wasn't a case of if they would collapse but when. I did some maths and figured out that, if I was lucky and had a full career, I would probably have about 80,000[1] hours in my working life. That realisation was profoundly enabling. I didn't have to take responsibility for solving massive problems; I just had to spend my time as best I could.

Over the next two years, I supported myself as a freelance programmer, which paid well and left me a lot of time to volunteer as I tried to turn my time into impact. I worked on climate change, youth leadership, a 'no plastic bags' campaign, a young professionals' network focused on sustainability, and various other projects.

Over those two years, I didn't make much impact but I learned a lot. I met many other people who were passionate about making a difference but were limited by their livelihood options. Either they were working full time on something that wasn't aligned with their purpose or they were struggling financially as they put all their energy into volunteering. It occurred to me that maybe the best way I could contribute was to help people who wanted to change the world get highly paid contract work.

And so, Enspiral[2] was born. The Alive exhibition provided the motivation, the research into global systems the conviction, and the idea of helping changemakers find great livelihoods the focus.

1 Based on 2,000 hours per year for 40 years

2 People are often curious where the name Enspiral came from. In 2003 I needed a name for a company and wasn't inspired by "Joshua Vial Contracting Limited". I spent a few hours on a long distance phone call with my mother brainstorming ideas. Spir is a latin root which means breathe and is the root of words like respiration, spirit and inspire. En means to cause or grow - encourage, enlarge, endear. Spiral reminded me of the Fibonacci sequence and golden ratios. So to me, the word Enspiral meant "to cause and grow an outward flowing of spiritual fractal energy", which seemed like a good thing. Plus the .com was available and no one was using the name. I built a placeholder website and used the company for a few contracts before leaving it dormant.

Thinking in decades

The 80,000 hours concept naturally extended my time horizon. I started to think in decades more than years.

The thing about decades is that questions start to matter a whole lot more than answers. I sought lines of inquiry likely to keep my attention for decades. The question "how can I help more people work on stuff that matters?" is still alive and present for me today, whereas I'm no longer pursuing the specific strategy of a freelancers' collective. Focusing on the deeper questions is key in the startup world, where falling in love with a problem and understanding it deeply is a prerequisite for success.

Thinking in decades also makes it a lot easier to focus on what is truly important. Early on, I realised that by far the most important thing at Enspiral was our relationships with each other. If we lose all our money and businesses but keep our relationships, then we can build it all again. If we lose our relationships then we will destroy anything we have created. Likewise, it doesn't matter how many people join the community; what matters is the quality of the relationships.

This led to a conscious strategy of "always put the relationship before the deal", which has served me well. When all parties in a negotiation are genuinely putting the relationship first, it becomes so much easier. Whether subcontracting, splitting equity, or allocating tasks, it makes the concept of exercising power over others seem odd. How can there be any quality of relationship if one person is using sticks and carrots to influence the other's behaviour?

For many people, the word 'business' implies selfish individualism. "It's just business" becomes an excuse for ignoring consequences decisions have on others. But it doesn't have to be that way. By creating a community with clear boundaries and norms, I could create a bubble where helping people unconditionally is normal. A high-trust, small-scale ecosystem takes a specific set of skills to manage, but I can't imagine working any other way.

I have found that thinking in a longer time frame can be radically disruptive. Like showing up with unconditional generosity, designing for

Around 2005, my housemates gleefully suggested that I google Enspiral and to my bemusement some folks had launched a sex toy company with the same name. This prompted me to register various other Enspiral domains, cross linking them all and taking back the first page of search results with naive search engine optimisation. It wasn't until 2008 when I started contracting that I used the company in earnest.

intrinsic motivation, or putting purpose at the heart of everything, it helps people imagine new futures and connect with what is important.

A culture of experimentation

From the very beginning, Enspiral was an experiment. None of us knew if it would work, but we hoped it would. Pretty much every successful pattern at Enspiral was inspired from somewhere else. For everything we tried that worked, we tried a dozen things that didn't. The path became littered with failed experiments.

A big cultural influence for Enspiral was open source software. As a programmer, I was very familiar with building on top of code others had written and shared freely online. I would adapt it to the problem I was trying to solve and, where possible, share code back. This led to a culture of copying ideas wherever we found them, and sharing our learnings for others to build on.

When I think back on the early days of Enspiral, what stands out is just how much stuff we tried. We ran a social enterprise internship programme, once. We ran a programming internship, once. We ran a 'Night Owls' programme for people working on startups outside of work hours for about three months. We used to have ventures give equity to the Enspiral Foundation, until we decided that wasn't a good idea and gave it all back. For a while, we experimented with the Enspiral Village, where people working on startups would meet for breakfast at 7am on a Monday morning, but that didn't last long.

We also honed in on a membership model that has stayed consistent since 2011, committed to consent-based decision making that has changed little since 2012, and formed a not-for-profit cooperative to anchor the network, which is still running today. We managed the evolution from a network of freelancers to a network of ventures, and throughout it all the purpose—more people working on stuff that matters—has never wavered.

A culture where it is normal to try new things is one of the things I value most about Enspiral. Here are three examples of long-term experiments that have been run at Enspiral, and some personal learning.

Enspiral Services

The first big experiment at Enspiral was to create a freelancers' collective. In March 2010, I took my personal contracting company and turned it into a collective vehicle for people to earn a livelihood. The initial deal was simple: 80% of revenue goes to the contractor, 20% to the collective funds, which we decide how to spend together. I started running all my contract work through the same 80/20 split and focused my volunteer time on supporting the growing community.

I had managed employees before and didn't want to do that again, so everyone worked as a freelancer. Security didn't come from having an employment contract, but from having a healthy cash buffer and the ability to find work when you needed it. Most of us had more offers for contracts than we could take up, which lead to a healthy internal referral network. People set their own contracting rates, and the plan was that we would all pitch in to run the company. The ideas were exciting and a lot of us jumped in to give them a try. As Enspiral evolved, we renamed the company Enspiral Services. For many people it was an onramp to the community.

We no longer have a freelancers' collective at Enspiral. While it worked well for a few years and was vital to Enspiral's early days, we never found a model that stuck. The premise that people could earn more than they needed with 80% of the contracting revenue and use their surplus time and money to serve the community was flawed. It worked for some of us, some of the time, but we didn't have a reliable enough source of organising and supporting energy, which created endless problems.

The core problem we didn't solve was designing a financial model that paid for people to work on the core of Enspiral. The collective worked well when a handful of us were volunteering to keep it all together but as we moved on to other projects we weren't able to replace ourselves.

We went through many iterations, but in 2017 I resumed control and transitioned Enspiral Services back to my personal consulting company, changing the name to Blackwood Systems. It was a little like hosting a party at your house and making a huge mess with your friends, only to be left with a big cleanup job the next day. I had invited the guests to the party, and I made more mess than most, so I took responsibility for the cleanup.

Enspiral Services taught me the value of just getting started. It doesn't matter that the model didn't work in the long run and we ended up closing it down after seven years. Without the momentum from the initial freelancer collective, Enspiral wouldn't exist at all. We were asking the right questions and the lessons informed much of our future direction. Our experiments in this space continue, and a group of us are now exploring how a swarm of micro-cooperatives can support people and help secure livelihoods.

Enspiral Space

A bunch of us in Wellington wanted to work in the same space, so I partnered with some other companies and rented a quarter of a large office in 2011. We eventually took over the full lease and Enspiral Space was born. It became the physical heart of Enspiral for the next four years.

We no longer have a coworking space. It turns out that while lots of people wanted a coworking space to exist, few people wanted to run one. Managing the Enspiral Space company was a constant burden. We moved the office in 2014, and wound down the company in 2015.

Enspiral Space taught me that it isn't enough to focus on a need. There also needs to be passion, ability, and a sustainable business model. We had an amazing space manager who was passionate about the physical space and facilitating meaningful interactions, but we never found someone equally skilled and passionate about running the business side of things. Many of us stepped up at different times to be that person, but it was always driven by a sense of obligation to serve the community at significant personal cost. If we'd found the other person for the team, the space would probably still exist today.

After we closed the coworking space, we experimented with the concept of multiple Enspiral Spaces. The idea was for ventures with their own offices to offer desks that Enspiral folks could use to connect with the community. This experiment is ongoing and working to some extent, but it is unclear whether it will be a long-term solution.

Retreats

A small group of us co-hosted the first Enspiral retreat in April 2011 in a large house outside of Wellington. Sixteen people attended, and we spent our time in open space[3] sessions, sharing stories, meals, and outdoor adventures. The biggest question most people came with was "What is Enspiral?", and the most common conclusion was "I still don't know, but I like the people".

Not much has changed since then. We started running retreats every six months and they became the heartbeat of our community. For the first half dozen or so, they were extremely stressful. We celebrated the first retreat we held where an organiser didn't cry, and we have slowly improved our practice on each iteration.

From our retreats, I learned about the power of bringing people together. To some degree, I feel that Enspiral only exists when we gather, and lies latent during the times in between. I also learned that as an idea evolves the experiments continue, they just get smaller. Instead of experimenting with the concept of retreats, we run little experiments about how to gather better. A few things are the same at every retreat, but there are always new experiments as we deepen our hosting practice.

Managing the cost of failure

In an ideal world, an experiment is purely for research, with a clearly defined hypothesis explored under tightly controlled conditions. There is no need to deliver anything apart from learning, and the focus is solely on discovery. Unfortunately, experiments in the entrepreneurial world do not have the same luxury.

The costs of experimenting-as-you go are real, and they are often human. We've had people leave Enspiral because of relationships damaged by broken decision-making processes. We've seen a continuous stream of people who care deeply about the community ground down when working on the core. We've had contractors walk away from clients halfway through a project without a word, leaving others to clean up after them.

Of the first 50 people to join Enspiral, only Rob and I are still active in the community. Of the next 50, who joined from early 2011 to mid 2012, about five people are still with us. Some of the early Enspiral folks are still

3 Open space is a participant-driven process whose agenda is created by people attending

good friends of the network and have just gone on to other things. Most drifted silently away, and a few left with a hiss and a roar. How much was healthy selection, and how much was unnecessary attrition?

Sometimes failure is a mistake, an error that causes harm, something to be actively avoided. Other times it is the unavoidable cost of exploring new terrain. Knowing the difference is the art of innovation. It all comes down to understanding how to manage the costs of failure. This is also the secret to overcoming the fear of failure, and one thing I know for sure is that the fear of failure kills learning.

Here are some things that I've learned that reduce the likelihood and cost of failing.

Respect the status quo

The more I see of the world, the more respect I have for the way things are. I am no less resolved in my intention to experiment, but I respect that things are the way they are for a reason.

It is critical not to be satisfied with those reasons. We must deeply understand the status quo in order to overcome it. The more widely a pattern is replicated, the more respect it is due, even if we don't like it. There are reasons people organise in hierarchies, politicians ignore climate change, and people feel more empathy for folks who look like themselves.

Trying to cause change without deeply understanding the status quo is a dangerous game that increases the likelihood of failing.

Decentralised organising is an excellent example. Optimi, an Enspiral venture that optimises business processes, is currently experimenting with self-management practices that respect the status quo. They want to organise without having a boss, so they asked themselves what a boss does. They generated a list of topics such as feedback, accountability, allocating roles, and so on. They then hold a weekly team meeting and cycle through these topics one at a time, reviewing their systems for these functions without making anyone the boss.

Copy patterns that work

Copying a pattern that works somewhere else is more likely to succeed than creating something from scratch. Things that we 'invent' draw inspiration from many sources, so actively looking for ideas in a wide variety of domains is a good strategy. Adapting a pattern to a specific environment is hard enough work without the complication of creating something completely new.

Sometimes it is necessary to create a new pattern, but it should always be a last resort. I have found that people attracted to experimenting (myself included) will have a bias towards creating new things as opposed to researching how other people solve a problem. It is similar to the way programmers will unconsciously underestimate the costs of starting from scratch because new projects are more enjoyable than building on legacy code.

Enspiral has drawn on ideas from many domains, and it's at this intersection that something interesting is created. Enspiral can be understood as a group of programmers, facilitators, entrepreneurs, activists, and designers who came together to help each other meet a challenge: get paid well to do work you love, with people you love, while contributing to a systemic issue you care deeply about. We all shared ideas from our various backgrounds, tried lots of things, and kept the stuff that worked.

Start small

Don't bet the house on a speculative idea, even if it has had success elsewhere. Try new ideas in environments where the cost of failing is small. Trying to make a whole company self-managing, or agile, or teal, or whatever, is a lot of work. Start with one team, and when they succeed share the stories honestly. If the patterns have merit, other teams will copy them.

When I had the initial idea of creating a collective of freelancers, I didn't rush out and start trying to scale. I worked with one person, then another, then another. With every person I tried to help, I learned something. Over time, the patterns that make Enspiral what it is evolved and solidified.

Just because a series of small-scale experiments yields promising results doesn't mean that longer term success is guaranteed. Both Enspiral Services and Enspiral Space were built on top of lots of small successful experiments but had deeper issues. But if we hadn't started small, we would have got nowhere at all.

Let things settle

If you are interested in running experiments in your community, it is likely that you have a higher tolerance for change than those around you. This is especially true if there are significant information asymmetries and you know more about your community than others.

One of the biggest lessons I had to learn with Enspiral was to honour the role of time.

Trying to cook a cake faster by turning up the oven doesn't work; you just burn the outside and undercook the inside. Communities aren't built: they grow, at the pace it takes people to develop shared understanding and close relationships. There are no shortcuts.

I would often get frustrated when people couldn't keep up with the rate of change at Enspiral. There was friction between people who were rapidly evolving ideas at the core and people focused on their ventures. We live in an attention economy and people's attention is a precious resource. When I started to evaluate initiatives based on how much attention they would consume to be successful, I found it naturally kept the rate of change healthy.

Failing to count the impacts on the attention economy is like failing to count any economic externality. It makes things look artificially cheap by not counting their true cost.

Deliver value early

Where possible, make sure an experiment delivers value when you test a new pattern. Sure, learning something is always useful, but if the experiment can deliver value above and beyond learning, it's much better.

This idea also ties into thinking about timescales for experimentation. When viewed from a short-term time frame Enspiral Services and Enspiral Space weren't experiments, they were ventures. Ventures that failed while creating a bunch of value and helped us learn a lot of lessons. But when zooming out to a longer term timeframe they were absolutely experiments that helped us learn.

Whichever viewpoint you take, the important thing is that the project / experiment delivered value. Learning how to deliver value through experiments even if they fail is an important part of making an experimental culture viable. When planning a new experiment I will look for ways that it can do things like strengthen relationships, provide livelihoods, help people grow and build reputation above and beyond the core purpose.

Distributing leadership

As Enspiral started to gain traction, I had a very clear goal. I wanted a community of peers to engage with in a dance of dynamic leadership and followership. I started living by the philosophy that 'no one should lead all the time and everyone should lead some of the time' early on, and it has served me incredibly well.

It's easy to say those words, but when it came to putting them into practice I found there weren't that many patterns I could copy. I found reflecting on asymmetries extremely useful. By asking where there were asymmetries of power, information, relationships, skill, reputation, money, and time, I could find small interventions to make the asymmetries smoother. I don't believe you can (or would want to) have a flat community where everyone is equal in every way. Instead, aim for a conscious community where asymmetries are spoken about and consciously managed.

When I sat down with Rob in 2011, I had selected and onboarded every member of the community personally. There was a massive relational asymmetry, so the most efficient strategy for someone to navigate the ecosystem was to talk to me directly. Over time, I supported other members to invite people in, and now plenty of folks know more people in Enspiral than I do. Without any formal decisions or big moves, the power contour became a little more balanced because the relational asymmetries reduced.

That, times a thousand, is how I became the ex-founder of Enspiral. It took about five years.

There were some formal steps on the way, but the real work was managing all the asymmetries.

Just after the first retreat in 2011, we registered a new company called the Enspiral Foundation. I chose 12 other people and we became the first 13 members of Enspiral. The Foundation is not for profit and each member has one share. With a stroke of the pen, 12 other people had the same legal powers I did to govern Enspiral.

Nothing changed overnight, but slowly the community became more balanced. I celebrated and supported every independent act of leadership, and made it a habit to discourage permission-seeking behaviour.

Through a very clear indication of intent, I encouraged other people to step up. It took lots of little interventions to get the asymmetries under control, but by 2015 I was just another Enspiral Member who happened to have a lot of context.

So that's my Enspiral story. I've spent about 20,000 hours on and in this community and I would do it all again in a heartbeat. I had lots of ideas when I began this journey, but mostly I just had hope. A blind, naive hope that there were people who wanted the same things I did, and that we could do some interesting things together.

My heart sings that this turned out to be true. I am left grateful and excited as I start imagining how to spend the the remaining 60,000 hours I (hopefully) have.

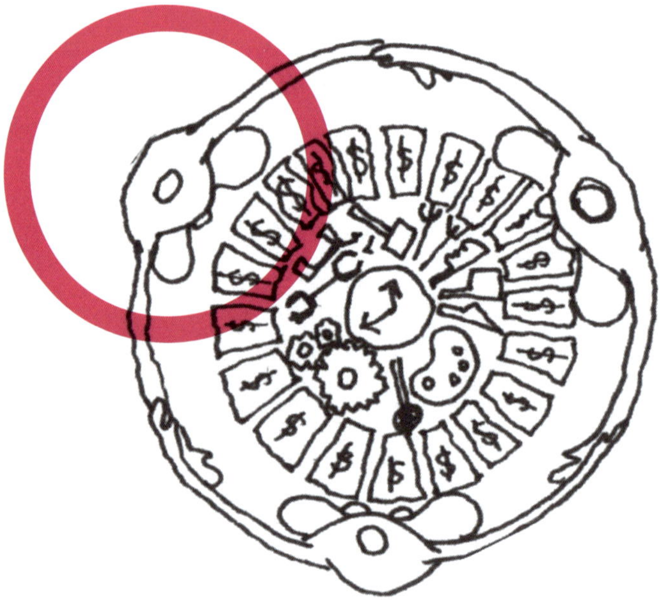

essay.Two

Evolving Enspiral

by Alanna Irving

July, 2011

"Hi Joshua. I keep running into Enspiral people at events around Wellington related to trying to make the world a better place. You must have hit on a powerful way to organize if you're attracting so many switched on and motivated people. My goal is to bring my professional life in line with my values and passions, and work with people who feel the same. If you think there's a place at Enspiral for a communicator-organizer-problem-solver type person such as myself, that would be awesome." ~ Alanna

Finding my place

I had recently arrived in New Zealand, searching for something I could not describe. I knew I couldn't go on doing "just a job", but I didn't know what was next for me. I wanted meaning and connection. I wanted to bring my whole self to work. I wanted to grow.

After living in six different countries throughout my 20s, I had a good feeling about New Zealand, and Wellington specifically.

Wellington is a compact city, where you always run into someone you know walking down the street. Close-knit communities are easy to form when everyone's within walking distance. The local business culture is very collaborative, and people help each other out. You don't come to these far-flung islands to climb over others on your way to the top.

Kiwis are, for the most part, egalitarian, and relationships are human-scale. If you want to talk to a politician or CEO, you can generally just ask them to lunch. When you call a government agency, you can expect someone to simply pick up the phone and say, "Hello, how can I help you?" (Kiwis don't even understand why people from other countries find this incredible).

As a small, isolated market with a relatively educated and open-minded populace, New Zealand is a fantastic place to incubate new ideas. You can experiment without getting immediately crushed by competitors.

You can be more idealistic in how you go about building a company.

Nature is ever-present and wilderness never far away, which keeps our interconnectedness at the front of mind. Māori culture brings an emphasis on stewardship of the land, community, and inter-generational awareness. While I won't presume to try to explain Māori culture, it has a big influence on everything in Aotearoa New Zealand, including business.

There is a much stronger social safety net here, compared to the US where I grew up, which means more people can take risks as entrepreneurs. No one has to stay at their nine-to-five for health insurance, take out huge loans to get an education, or end up on the street if their start-up doesn't work out.

At the time, I didn't know what was next, but I stayed in Wellington, knowing on some level that I would find what I was looking for.

Ever since I was a child, I've had a tendency to end up in charge of things. I'd get impatient with a lack of clarity or coordination, and next thing you know I'm organising the group. When I grew up and got hired for a corporate job, I quickly started climbing the pyramid.

But it didn't feel right. Even in corporate environments, no one laboured under the illusion that a pyramid was the best way to organise. In fact, most hated it. Yet they remained resigned, because that's just the way things were. I grew impatient with the restrictions and inefficiencies, and couldn't accept wearing a mask to work every day. I tried to make things better, but my manager told me I "had too many ideas" and "cared too much".

After not long, I looked up and realised that, no matter how high up the pyramid I climbed, it wasn't somewhere I wanted to go.

Outside work, I sought environments that weren't shaped like pyramids, instead gravitating toward circles. I lived in a housing co-op where we made decisions by consensus, and I organised egalitarian groups of volunteers. I saw the best in others, and in myself, when we coordinated as a community of peers, as our authentic selves, primarily driven by values. In that kind of environment, I could use my skills to help everyone take collective action without having to be the boss.

Jumping in

When I first arrived in Wellington, I went to a lot of networking events related to business for social good. People would hear a bit about me and say, "You have to meet Joshua". So I got in touch.

He invited me to visit the Enspiral office, and I went down on my lunch break one day. I found about a half dozen computer programmers and a few other people sharing a sunny office with wood floors and brick walls.

It was kind of like a coworking space, except they shared a brand and cooperated on projects. Kind of like an agency, except they chose their own work autonomously and had variable income. Kind of like a company, except there were no bosses, no job titles, and no receptionist. Kind of like a startup incubator, but totally ad hoc. Kind of like a business, but focused on positive social impact.

A lot of people need time to wrap their heads around all that. But to me, it felt like coming home. I immediately sensed that Enspiral was a place where having ideas and caring a lot would never be seen as weaknesses.

That's not to say everything was perfect. On that first visit, I asked an Enspiralite: "So, how do you know what projects everyone is working on?" He looked around. "Uhhh, we don't, I guess." Then, to the person on his other side, "Hey, what are you working on, anyway?"

I listened to some more conversations and asked some more questions. Apparently, information flows were a challenge. Great stuff was happening, but the stories weren't getting told, internally or externally, and opportunities were being missed.

On my walk back to my boring job that afternoon, I thought about how I had got involved in previous projects and communities that had meant a lot to me. I hadn't stood on the sidelines waiting for an invitation, and I hadn't first needed to know what I would get in return for my contributions. I just found a gap with my name on it and filled it. Enspiral needed better information flows, and I needed an excuse to get to know the network.

When I got back to the office, I wrote Joshua another email. This time the subject was: "Ready to jump in!"

Thus I began the process of joining Enspiral, following a pattern I would later recognise as common: get attracted to the vision and the people; make it through some natural filters (no set pathway, not much money, no stability); hang out, get context, and identify some needs; then hire yourself to meet them.

Doing all that on the first day might be less common, but if the shoe fits...

Getting to know the collective

A few weeks later, I sent out the first Enspiral newsletter, created during slow times at my boring office job. It had a video of Joshua explaining what Enspiral was all about, updates from nascent internal startups, articles sharing expertise of people in the network, client testimonials, and stories about ongoing projects.

As I'd hoped, gathering the content for the newsletter helped me get to know Enspiral and the people in it. Through many conversations, I came to understand how it all worked.

At the time, Enspiral was one company. There were a bunch of freelance programmers and a few designers who did work for clients autonomously, all invoicing through Enspiral. They shared office space, group software subscriptions, client leads, and personal and professional support.

When an invoice was paid by a client, the money went into Enspiral Ltd's bank account, just like any company. From there, 80% went to the freelancer who did the work and 20% was contributed to shared costs. Instead of getting a regular paycheck, freelancers were credited virtual dollars in their Enspiral account, which they could withdraw as income or spend on business expenses as they saw fit.

This way of working enabled powerful possibilities. Since everyone was already set up in the company, dynamically forming internal teams was frictionless. Money could be transferred between Enspiral accounts with the click of a button, so it was common for everyone to hire each other. People could work as little or as much as they chose, on whatever projects they chose. Everyone's work built up the Enspiral brand and generated more leads to share.

The freelancers benefitted by collectivising. We paid a lawyer to create client contract templates that everyone could use. Each person didn't have to set up their own legal entity and bank account to do business, instead using Enspiral Ltd as a common resource. Taxes were managed by a shared accountant. In some ways, it was the best of both the freelance and in-house worlds at once.

As I came to understand the back office processes, I realised that, while the genuine intention was to be a collective, behind the scenes Joshua was still the backstop. He was the one with access to the bank account, and the sole owner and director of the Enspiral LLC. He took on liability so others didn't have to, and so Enspiral could keep moving quickly.

In some ways this was awesome, and in other ways it was dangerous. Let's just say Joshua has a higher risk tolerance than admin tolerance. There was virtually no documentation, no policies, and no decision-making processes. Everything came down to "just do it" or "ask Joshua".

In the absence of policies or systems, natural filters were key. No one was offered a job, or any direction. To join, you had to be capable of generating your own income stream, but prefer to be part of a collective by choice. To get anything done, you had to be willing and able to communicate and collaborate. This generally selected for competent, trustworthy people who were more or less aligned.

Working elsewhere was much more straightforward, not to mention more lucrative, so there was no reason to get involved if you weren't committed to the values and vision. That meant trust was implicit. Since everyone was ultimately focused on positive social impact, helping each other furthered that common goal. There was a ton of generosity flowing around the system, and, while it was sometimes hard to quantify, people were getting back more than they put in.

Getting to work

When I turned up, Enspiral was growing. You can't wing it with a larger group the way you can with just a few people. The bubblegum holding everything together was beginning to stretch. Once it was no longer feasible for everyone to have a conversation with Joshua about everything, the lack of systems became more painful.

It was time for Enspiral to go through a phase change. I saw a whole class of work that wasn't getting done while everyone was busy with client contracts and their own startups. It was the 'in-between' stuff, the meta-layer, the substrate to support all the other work — a cross between operations and governance, from the details to the big picture. This bothered me.

In an environment like Enspiral, the work that bothers you most probably has your name on it.

I quit my boring job and jumped into Enspiral full time, and immediately got to work downloading information from Joshua's head, writing documentation, creating onboarding processes, cleaning up finances, chasing unpaid invoices, updating the website, improving communications, organising retreats, facilitating group decision-making, and ensuring we always had coffee in the kitchen (very important!). And I continued doing the Enspiral Newsletter every month.

Enspiral grew quickly, expanding from a few people to more than 50 over my first year. I considered myself employed by everyone at Enspiral, and I tried to serve all those employers well.

Leadership that grows leadership

When I'm inspired and excited, my natural inclination is to jump right in, not worrying about stepping on toes. This had gotten me into trouble in the past, when I bumped up against petty fiefdoms and institutional inertia. But this time, I felt welcomed as I mucked in and started suggesting changes. Part of me kept waiting for the other shoe to drop, but it didn't.

Of course, people had differing perspectives, and not all my suggestions were good ones. But I noticed a distinct lack of colliding egos. There was a shared understanding that our most precious resources were energy, attention, and motivation, so the default setting was cheering on and giving things a go, instead of shutting down new ideas. We were playing a non-zero-sum game, where more for me doesn't mean less for you, it means more for everyone.

What enabled this culture? I think a large part was thanks to a particular kind of leadership.

Meeting people trying to work in highly collaborative ways around the world, I've encountered two leader personas repeatedly. Both embody a natural ability to attract people and resources to get a vision off the ground, but they differ at the point they start to scale.

One type of leader just takes on more work, figuring out solutions as efficiently as possible, without taking much time to consult or delegate. He constructs of a house of cards around himself, becoming trapped in the centre for fear it will all fall over if he moves.

The other type of leader is overly concerned with making space for others and not taking over, leaving a vacuum. Even when she knows the way forward she doesn't claim the mandate, and momentum is paralysed.

The kind of leadership needed to build effective collaborative communities transcends both of these archetypes. It neither hangs on too tightly nor hangs back. It's confident, yet humble. It's forever optimistic about what others can contribute, while constantly insisting on moving forward. It uses accrued power to further distribute power to others. That was the kind of leadership Joshua brought, and that founding DNA attracted others who could lead in a similar way.

When I joined Enspiral and started working closely with Joshua every day, I realised our leadership dispositions complemented one another: he overflowed with ideas, while I wanted to make visions real. He went ten steps ahead while I was figuring out the first nine. Together, we worked to distribute power, money, and information throughout the network.

What? Enspiral is evolving!

As Enspiral continued to grow, we started to bump up against the limitations of being a single software development company. Our challenge was to evolve into an entrepreneurial community, where many kinds of professionals could work in different ways, without losing our values and organising DNA.

The complexity of a growing community increases exponentially, so linear change–the same as before but more–isn't enough.

One of the early systems I tried to create at Enspiral was an attempt to answer that question I'd asked on my first visit: what is everyone working on? I went around and got information about all the current projects, and put it online where everyone could see. For one beautiful moment there was actually a comprehensive view of what was going on. I was pretty pleased.

Unfortunately, the very next moment everything went out of date. That's the problem with a system like that in a network like Enspiral: everything is constantly changing, people are busy, and, while you can try to persuade people to engage, you can't compel them.

A similar thing happened with a system to track availability and skills, to make it clearer who was available to work on different projects. We built a system, and I tried poking people to update their data. I sent out lots of email reminders, but again, it was impossible.

I thought about suggesting making these boring tasks a mandatory gateway to picking up jobs or getting paid. But coercive strong-arming went completely against Enspiral's essential nature. Our strength was the free-flowing way collaborations formed, and our value was our busy, creative, independent-minded people.

In a community of peers, effective solutions have to go with the tides of energy, not against them. When you're going with the tide, there's an amazing rush of collective energy. I had to learn (and re-learn) not to try to push things upstream—even the most efficient or beautiful solutions. As someone who loves designing processes (and, ahem, never fails to action an email reminder), this took me a while to accept.

We didn't need better information tracking systems; we needed a completely new level of collective intelligence. While the first phase change was about scaling up one company, now it was time for Enspiral to evolve into a network.

Tensions were emerging. While some people wanted to take on long-term client projects, others really valued the flexibility of short-term freelancing, and still others wanted to develop their own products instead of working on other people's. Most people in Enspiral were professional and reliable, but a few instances of people falling short threatened to tarnish the brand. Quality control was a problem. With no central command, there was no good system for detecting problems before they fully surfaced, or bailing out troubled projects.

While the default revenue split—80% to the freelancer and 20% to overheads—still worked for certain contracts, we needed more flexibility. Sometimes the person who had the initial relationship with a client found themselves in an unpaid account management role, because it was their reputation on the line. There are some essential differences between a unified software production house and a pool of freelancers, and Enspiral couldn't be both at once.

At the same time, more people from different professions were getting involved in the network, such as lawyers and accountants, and several startups that had been informally incubated in Enspiral were ready to become ventures in their own right. All of these different companies required different legal and ownership structures, brands, governance, and internal processes.

We were also learning another critical lesson: A community without boundaries is no community at all. A few people abused our high-trust environment, showing us that we needed to draw some lines in the sand. We rallied as a community and agreed a simple but strong Diversity Policy (which remained the only official written policy at Enspiral for some years). Beyond these few extreme cases, there was a growing need to clarify what being "in" or "out" meant, and for different levels of engagement to be defined.

The emergence of these tensions scared me. Looking back, I can see that they were necessary growing pains, but at the time it almost felt like the group was fracturing. Fundamentally, I see creating anything in this world as a fight against entropy; if people floated off in all directions, we'd lose our collective potential. I was torn between holding together and letting go.

Thankfully, we found a way for the network to stay connected, while allowing for a lot more freedom, scale, and diversity.

Building the foundation

Enspiral evolved from one company into an ecosystem of people and companies connected through a co-owned hub, called the Enspiral Foundation.

Enspiral Ltd, the original company, became Enspiral Services Ltd, and continued as a home for freelance contractors, much as it had been. Several other companies were founded by Enspiral people, including a law firm, an accountancy firm, and a more traditional software shop focused on large contracts, where employees got a normal salary and the owners carried the risk. Several product-based tech startups spun out into their own companies, each with a unique culture and structure. The few people who threatened trust were asked to leave altogether.

The Enspiral Foundation was conceived to support the network as a whole, and to further the social mission of more people working on stuff that matters. It served as a home for our collective commons, like the Enspiral brand and website, and for things that applied network-wide, like the Diversity Policy. My job evolved, too, into something like a dual role of Executive Director of the Enspiral Foundation and General Manager of Enspiral Services (although we had no job titles).

Starting the Enspiral Foundation was a critical opportunity to structurally express different levels of commitment and trust in the network. Core participants, called 'members', got one share of the Foundation each, and collectively became its owners.

Newcomers and people who were not as deeply involved were called 'contributors'. Any member could bring in a new contributor, while becoming a new member required a consensus decision by the current members. While contributors were welcome to participate in nearly everything, the members ultimately held responsibility for the core of Enspiral.

To keep these definitions fresh and meaningful, a couple times a year we asked everyone to self-assess their level of engagement and adjust accordingly, creating a gentle current you had to swim against to stay involved.

Shares in the Foundation represented decision-making stakeholding, not financial dividends, and the Foundation was run as a non-profit. Similar to how individual freelancers funded Enspiral Services with a percentage of their income, Enspiral ventures funded the Foundation through sharing a percentage of their revenue. We experimented with contributions of equity, like many incubator programmes, but Enspiral Ventures were optimised for social impact over big exits, and the Foundation needed an operating budget immediately, so revenue sharing made more sense.

The big dream was that some of the ventures would get commercial traction and contribute enough to the Foundation to kickstart future generations of ventures—essentially spreading out some of the risks and rewards of entrepreneurship and multiplying our collective impact.

Levels of Engagement

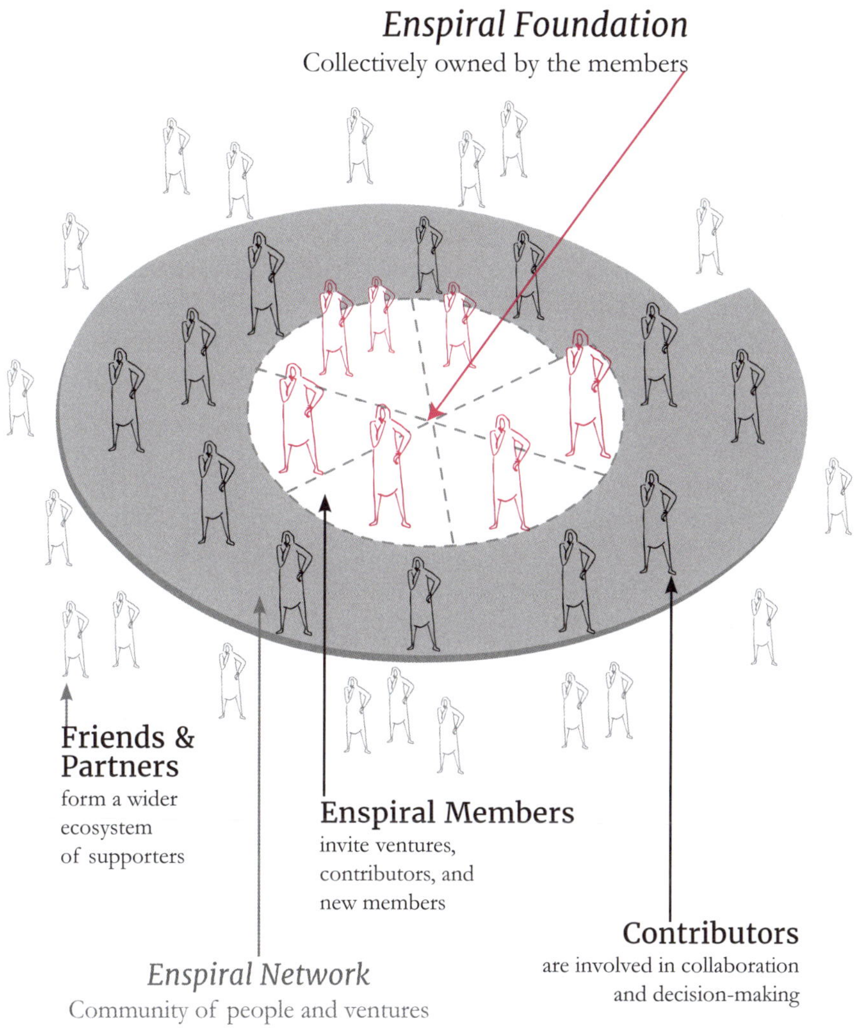

Voluntary Contributions

What we were really building

Reflecting on it now, I think the dream came true to some degree. The network is still going strong, many individuals have been supported to continue as social entrepreneurs through tough times, and many more Enspiral ventures have started up.

But it turns out getting big commercial traction is pretty hard for social enterprises on an island at the bottom of the world. While several ventures have turned into solid businesses, others failed, and none turned into unicorns. We got by, but we never managed to achieve abundance.

Looking back, it's easy to focus on where we came up short. Although Enspiral Services operated for seven years and generated a lot of revenue and opportunities, it never reached its full potential. It was never anyone's main priority, but more of a means to an end. Yet, I still think that, with the right leadership, a freelancer collective using Enspiral Services as an inspiration could be a success story.

That issue—tragedy of the commons, essentially—is the same reason we never excelled at running our coworking office, Enspiral Space. Although good people did a lot of work to keep it going, no one was super passionate about it as their main venture. Enspiral Services and Enspiral Space provided critical functions in the network and benefited a lot of people, but they were no one's baby. There were many other failures along the way too, whether they were someone's baby or not. That's how it is with startups.

What we did achieve, in addition to supporting hundreds of people to earn their livelihoods doing meaningful work, was a web of skills and relationships that enabled profoundly radical socio-technical experimentation. We supported one another, emotionally and financially, to free ourselves from the baggage of hierarchy and capitalism and try out genuinely transformative new ways of working. We can now tell stories of our experiences, which add to the global discourse about new paradigms of business and culture.

The dream lives on, continually emerging. At each stage of Enspiral's evolution, we didn't know exactly what we were becoming. A lot of times it felt like we were a fish with legs. We survived and served the needs of the time as best we could. We didn't have any answers. All we had was a culture of experimentation, a drive to do meaningful work, and each other.

We discover the path by walking it together.

essay.Three

A radically good livelihood

by Susan Basterfield

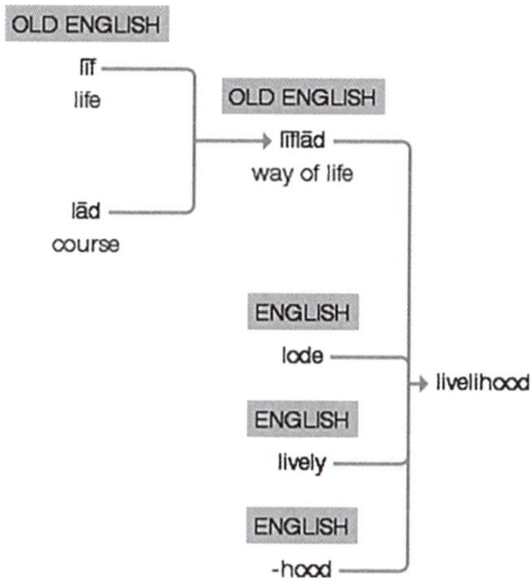

The original meaning of 'livelihood' is 'the way of life'.

How much control do we really have over our way of life? How does our upbringing and privilege (or lack thereof) affect which choices are available to us as adults? If our livelihood is created through our choices, why do some of us choose a path aligned to the predominant stories in our culture, and others choose another way?

We tend to follow that paths we can see.

Momentum carries us along, in the current. For decades, I didn't even consider that there was another option for livelihood - I was in the river, in the flow of traditional expectations of career and financial accumulation. Some of that time I was simply moving too fast, other times I was drowning and fighting for survival. Eventually, I stepped onto dry land, looked around, and decided that the second half of my life was going to be different - and it would be a story I created, not one I inherited.

My Inheritance

I was born in Chicago, USA, and my parents were children of the The Great Depression, the first American-born generation in an immigrant lineage. They were traditional, working class, patriotic, and square—also extremely loving and focused on building the best possible opportunities for me and my brothers. They also hid things. They hid the fact that they lived paycheck to paycheck. I had no idea growing up that our circumstances were so tight—we lived in an archetypal cul-de-sac in an archetypal suburb in sunny Southern California. We kids rode bikes till dark, and lived with a sense of community and safety. Until I was ten, my mom didn't work, and life was a suburban fantasy—of the 30 houses on the street, 25 had kids. The moms and kids were in and out of each others' houses all the time. I thought our family was the same as all the rest, but our 'money story' subconsciously influenced my life significantly.

My family money story reflected the post-war American dream: strongly self-made, anything is possible with hard work, the land of opportunity. My father worked his ass off, he tried so hard, starting a number of businesses, desperate to provide us with everything—the dream. But it didn't always work. I can remember, so vividly, one Thanksgiving someone left a food parcel on our front doorstep—that was my first realisation that our money story was different. Because my parents were holding things together by a shoestring, or maybe in spite of it, there was an expectation, but not a clear message, of what it would take for me to attend university. Neither of them had been, and though my father had won a wrestling scholarship to Purdue, he had to look after his disabled father instead.

So I got my first job at 17 (while still in high school), at what we now call a startup—at the bleeding edge of the brand-new computer industry. PMCP sold computer peripherals, green-screen terminals, printers, etc. I worked there 30 hours a week while I funded my university experience, where I studied Radio, TV, and Film Communications. I thought I wanted to be a sports journalist, but fell in love with business. At PMCP, an IT hardware distributor, I learned everything about business, and did just about every job, from accounts to inventory control to vendor relationships to sales. I loved sales the most—building relationships and solving problems. I also enjoyed making money. I was able to buy my first home at 23. I was on the pathway to the next-generation American dream. I got married and tried to have babies. Neither of those things worked out. My father died two weeks after his 60th birthday, of lung cancer, having worked from the age of ten.

After the breakdown of my marriage, I got on a plane to England. I'd fallen in love from afar with the man of my life, and left everything to be with him. When I say I left everything, I mean I had just one suitcase and a box. I started over at 30, and was completely OK with that.

dot.com BOOM

My years living in the UK radically impacted my money story. It was the time of the first dot.com boom and we were living the high life. There were many great things about that experience that shaped and changed my relationship to power and leadership. The founder and leaders of the organisation were as interested in people development as they were in building innovative technology. I was encouraged and liberated to be myself and see my value as a leader.

The founder also impacted my ideas about building business together on a financial level. He said no to a buyout offer that would have netted him well into eight figures. He said no because it wasn't enough to appropriately compensate those of us who helped build the business. Whether that was selfless or merely pragmatic (he eventually did sell for a sum well into nine figures) is up for question, but the idea that he saw the value of the collective was striking to me. It was a real contrast to my previous experience with monolithic multinationals like IBM and BP who valued shareholders way above employees, and fed my accumulation mindset.

I think my big shift away from an accumulation mindset happened one Saturday during a shopping trip to London. I remember walking down Regent Street and thinking to myself, "What am I doing here? I don't need anything! I don't want anything!".

Emigration and citizenship

In 2003, we emigrated to New Zealand. We had worked diligently and saved up a little nest egg. I was certain that with our skills, we'd easily find work that suited us and things would be rosy. Of course, that was extremely optimistic and naive. But New Zealand felt right. From our first visit in 1998—I literally felt myself sinking into the whenua (the land) - and knew I was home.

Part of the impetus to emigrate was for a more balanced life—I knew that if we'd stayed in the UK things might not change, or slow down enough for us to enjoy the life we wanted: a life connected to the outdoors that wasn't rife with competitive energy. I also knew I wanted work that was both meaningful and engendered a healthy relationship with money. I thought it would be linear: now I knew how to do the 'career thing' I could just keep going. And now that I'd had a great experience with work, I could seek and find that elsewhere, even in New Zealand.

My first three years in NZ I worked with my friend, AJ Hackett, in his international bungy jumping businesses. AJ is a legend in New Zealand—he created an entirely new segment of adventure tourism by commercialising bungy jumping. I was responsible for sites from Bali to Acapulco, Cairns to Macau to Las Vegas. We had interesting projects, new builds and new partnerships. His business was still in startup mode—lots of sunk cost and experimentation. He was (and still is) an enigmatic visionary. People said, "If there is an easy way or a hard way, AJ will always do it the hard way, because it's bound to be more interesting".

Because there was such broad geographic and business model diversity in the bungy business, this experience allowed me to get up close and personal with the money stories of entrepreneurs - and with their capacity for risk-taking. Whether financial risk, or in this case, the physical risk of throwing oneself off a bridge or building attached to an elastic band! This was also my first experience of remote working in a decentralised, distributed team, long before video calling and other virtual work tools. It's hard to believe that this was how the world was only 15 years ago!

After retirement from bungy, over the next few years I tried to initiate the approaches that had brought me business success and personal growth in a number of companies in New Zealand, but it didn't work. In the large organisations, there was a lack of willingness to innovate, in the smaller organisations the founders just weren't into it. I decided to leave the business world and went back to university to do a post-grad degree in education. I became head teacher at an alternative high school for at-risk youth, which was the hardest job I ever had. In 2011, an earthquake decimated Christchurch, the city where we lived, and I suffered significant trauma. I needed a change and that tragedy was the impetus.

Shifting plates

My time away from business changed me. The trauma of living through the destruction of a city, seeing the impact on people I loved and thinking about the people who were lost helped me gain clarity. I was suffering from PTSD, and ironically, the break I needed was to go back to the corporate world, where I knew the ropes and how to play the game. We moved to Wellington and I joined Telstraclear as Head of Enterprise and Government.

I enjoyed the privilege of being 'high up' the ladder because I thrive on system-level challenges, problem solving and context. In most organisations, 'Head of' rank is correlated with being a people manager. Traditional organisations align HR policy, financial controls and professional development with the people-management function. This means giving power over decisions that impact people doing a certain job to others who have proven themselves good at doing that same job. Essentially, being responsible for their livelihood. I've always enjoyed managing activities and making sense of complexity but I've always felt wrong about the command authority and coercion that goes along with being responsible for another person's livelihood.

What gives me authority over another human? How fucked up is it that our system readily gives people that power? I am really, really good at building solutions and relationships. Why should that be conjoined with command authority over the livelihoods of the people who join me on an adventure? That's just the way the game works. Bosses have 'their people', and human resources decides who is worth how much. Most of us willingly go along with this. It's a game that we know the rules of. And of course, our entire society is set up to support and encourage this game, because the interdependencies are inextricably linked. Want a mortgage? Prove you have a stable job and wage. It's rigged and fixed. And we play along.

I played along for another few years. Then I stopped.

Finding Enspiral

I like to say I'm a slow learner. Or maybe I just wasn't paying attention to the potential alternatives. But after over 20 years on the corporate treadmill, I had finally had enough. I was sick of spending so much time on the second job no one was paying me for: the one where I was playing politics and protecting my heart from the bullies. I tried my hand at entrepreneurship and contracting but I did not thrive. What I missed were thinking partners 'at the watercooler'. I appreciated being free from tyranny, but I was bereft of community. A few months after I'd left the corporate world and was trying to find my way, I read this job advertisement:

Enspiral Catalyst

Enspiral – Anywhere

Initiator, Leader, Coordinator, Entrepreneur, Facilitator. What does servant leadership mean in a non-hierarchical, distributed network, where there are no bosses? How could you facilitate and activate the collective potential of an incredible group of 180+ highly skilled professionals brought together by a passion for positive social impact?

Come work with us, and let's find out together.

You're the kind of person who could be on top of a pyramid somewhere else, but you don't like pyramids. There's no such thing here, and that excites you. We are looking for someone with serious skills in strategic thinking, entrepreneurial creativity, process design, and motivating and empowering others, who can bring to life the possibilities of a decentralised organisation.

This is a unique opportunity well suited to someone who can navigate a chaordic environment, build relationships, spot opportunities, and empower people to achieve success. You will be a master of the art of the invitation, and very comfortable leading in environments where influence and inspiration trump authority.

We're organised as a network of interconnected nodes, with the Enspiral Foundation linking it all together. Enspiral Ventures and individual contributors contribute money, time, and skills to the Enspiral Foundation, which become shared resources. Projects to support the network and its vision are funded using a transparent participatory budgeting process. Everyone comes together online and offline to collaborate and make decisions collectively.

After several years of growth and learning, Enspiral is emerging into a new stage of evolution. There is more money, talent, and strong networks here than ever before. The challenge now is to identify insightful next steps to leverage that richness. We're inviting new thinking to find the lever to pull to create maximum impact. As many of Enspiral's core members are heads down on their individual businesses, the purpose of the Enspiral Catalyst is to step into the heart of the network.

When I read this, my heart just about leapt out of my chest. It felt like it had been written specifically for me. But I did nothing. I was so beaten down, so afraid of being rejected. I'm not the typical Enspiral person. I'm in my early 50s - most others are in their 30s and had been involved in the Enspiral community since their 20s. I'd had a couple of entire careers before I arrived in this community. What would these cool kids want with a washed-up, middle-aged corporate hack like me?

However, a year later, I finally took the plunge, connected, and attended a Network Retreat. Around this time the first 'Catalysts' were stepping down and a second iteration of the same experiment was starting. Was this a 'Susan-shaped hole'? I was finally ready to put my hat and heart in the ring and find out. As a Catalyst, I was dependant on Enspiral ventures funding the role through the Enspiral Foundation. It amounted to a basic livelihood, with space to create other income streams and opportunities. I wasn't short of ideas, but building a business takes time. I had never thought of myself as an entrepreneur, but more of a consigliere serving the visionaries with practical doing. I still carried the fear of being self-employed from watching my father struggle for years with one venture after another, never quite reaching sustainability.

Being supported and challenged as an entrepreneur inside a community was a breakthrough for me.

I began to really process my shadows and assumptions about livelihood—the ones that had me believing security was only possible through a corporate job and that there was a correlation between my value and my paycheck. Enspiral's culture involves a real expectation that we will all be processing our 'stuff' together—it's a journey of co-evolution and it's an amazing privilege. As Damian, a fellow Enspiral member, wisely noted: "working in a traditional company didn't work for me; working as a solo freelancer didn't work for me; I tried working in a collective, and it works for me. It works for me because we can manage complexity together, since abundance and diversity are impossible for one person to understand alone'

Enspiral is agnostic about individual purpose, supporting anyone to do meaningful work - or 'stuff that matters' - no matter how they define it. There is no adherence to dogma about specific ways to change the world, other than to help one another. My 'stuff that matters' is helping leaders and organisations co-create and manifest their own version of a place that makes possible what I call a Radically Good Livelihood: a way of life that aligns financial imperatives with meaningful and significant work. Through Enspiral, I can truly express my values and my work comes alive; my purpose aligns with the literal ability to have an impact. In the Enspiral community, each of our very unique livelihood journeys, winding as they have been, are supported in a way not normally seen in startups. We value the person over the product, the flowering and unfolding of the person over profit. And we've created a place where these are not mutually exclusive.

A Radically Good Livelihood - in community

I've made a decision in my life to examine all the stories I've been told about money and worth, and step into a new story that I consciously create. Sometimes this involves painful realisations. Capitalism bombards us with messages of unworthiness and pejorative definitions of success, and advertising manipulates our will. Even if we are aware of this, it's not easy to articulate an alternative story.

Even within a system that's rigged, at some point we all need to make a decision. Whether from exhaustion, inspiration, or an event that shakes our core and changes everything, we can all ask ourselves: How do we want to live? Traditional workplaces built on hierarchy and defined job roles may work well for some people. However, I believe many people would work and live differently if they knew there was an accessible alternative. Stories of alternatives don't reach everyone, and if they do they can seem too radical, too scary or too weird. Risking failure feels unsafe.

I want more people to know how we can live and work differently.

In my twenties, thirties, and forties, momentum carried me - I didn't stop or notice what could be different. Through Enspiral, I've come to believe our greatest opportunity to choose to live and work differently is in community. More than any time in our history, we can choose our communities - no longer predetermined by birthplace, tribe, religion, or caste. More than ever we can explore, convene, and try out new ways of belonging. We can build communities to create livelihoods in the configurations we choose but the onus is on us to make it happen.

I fully acknowledge my privilege. I am a white woman, university educated, a homeowner, and I had the ability to choose the country I wanted to make my home. Aotearoa New Zealand is unique in every dimension: geography, demographics, history, government, and social norms.

Without this privilege, I may not have had the choice, or the chance, to reassess and realign my personal relationship to livelihood—in terms of money, meaningful work, leadership, and community. Creating accessible alternatives is our best chance to give more people a choice. Any organisation focused on the work of reconnecting the evolving capacity of the organisation and its people creates the conditions for Radically Good Livelihood. If we live into the assumptions we have about each other as humans, both hold the space for and intentionally create the conditions for our evolving development, we'll never be static. Nothing ever is. And that's one of the reasons I'm grateful for the 'looseness' of Enspiral—the lack of much written down about purpose or values or mission or vision. That's confronting for many, even for me. I often wish it was easy to describe. But I'm grateful I can't. And I'm grateful it exists.

The development of the self is the development of the organisation.

#

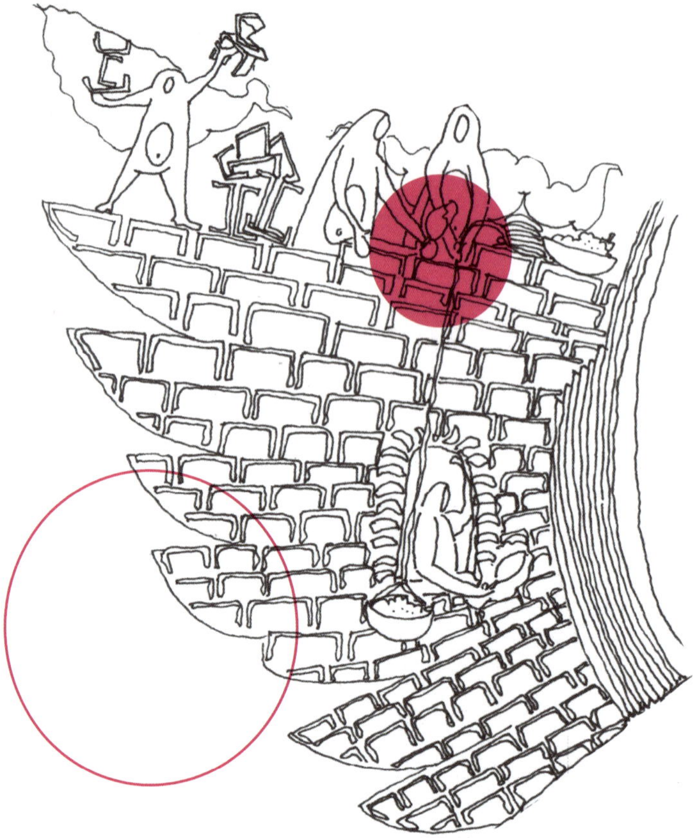

essay.Four

Welcome to the age of participation

by Francesca Pick

A small drop in a big ocean

A small drop in a big ocean—that's how it felt for a while. But drop by drop, it's changing, I can feel it. Drip, drop, drip, drop. Like a wave, slowly gathering energy and speed.

It's February 2017, and I am sitting in a grand geodesic dome, located in a beautiful valley in New Zealand. I'm at the annual Enspiral retreat, sitting in a circle with my fellow members, talking about our work and the future of the organisation. It's the end of the event and one member stands up and says to the group: "Are we the only ones in the world working on this right now? Are we alone in this pursuit?" The question almost sounds rhetorical, which surprises me. There is a loneliness in his voice, a yearning for comrades to work with on this grand endeavour. He wonders whether there are other decentralised communities trying to find more participatory and open ways of operating.

There is a voice inside me, yelling:

No, you're not alone! There are so many others out there, you just don't know they exist!

His conclusion is quite understandable from his perspective of doing "impact work" in New Zealand, a small country in the remote South Pacific. It's easy to feel isolated and disconnected from the rest of the world there. My experience growing up in the heart of Europe was quite the opposite.

I've sat in circles, such as this one, in so many places—Germany, France, Spain, England, Canada, the US, Brazil, Costa Rica—and I helped build a like-minded network in Europe, called Ouishare. It's clear to me that we are not alone. On the contrary, there are more of us than we think.

We just need to open our eyes and see each other.

Barely a year later, we find ourselves in Catalunya, Spain, in yet another circle, the "Network Convergence". This time, not only members of Enspiral, but people from a multitude of networks and communities from around the world are here. We have gathered to connect, collaborate and increase our impact together.

These organisations, communities and networks are shaping an emergent movement together. What are its characteristics? What are the key themes and commonalities? Who is part of it? What could be their impact on the world?

What is this global movement?

After seven years of observing, researching and being part of Enspiral and a number of like-minded organisations, such as the global network Ouishare, I have come to the conclusion that, despite the loneliness one often feels in this work, these are not isolated phenomena. They are part of a global movement that is on the rise, a movement that is leveraging the power of community, networks, and participation to work on systemic challenges. This movement not only exists conceptually, but is a tangible reality with a growing number of projects scattered across the globe. The organisations that are part of it come from a broad range of areas—from environment, to agriculture, to education, to health, to business, to politics. This diversity makes it harder for them to recognise each other. Yet, while their areas of work may differ, their modes of operating are similar. They are aware that their work is a contribution—not a complete solution—to the challenge they aim to solve, and that it is a piece in a much larger puzzle.

Before giving you a detailed picture of the characteristics that make this movement unique, let's look at its origins, influences, and catalysers.

Origins, influences, catalysers

Just as society is always evolving, this movement is so diverse that one cannot name one origin or inciting event. It is more like a series of streams that are now slowly converging. Each has its own influences, ranging from socialism, post-capitalism, and Degrowth[1] to Lean Startup culture[2], the free software movement, and Occupy Wall Street.

Why has this movement taken hold now, and how is it any different from previous movements? Let's consider these frames:

- **Movements** that address societal problems of all sorts are nothing new. From the feminist Suffragettes movement of the early 20th century, to the anti-nuclear movement of the 1980s, to the many student uprisings and sit-ins that have taken place to fight for democracy and human rights around the globe.

- **Communities** have always been essential for providing purpose and structure to humans in society. Although diverse in type (religious, political, cultural, economic), all communities enable people to organise around shared identity, values, and rituals.

- **Participatory** organising and sharing practices are ancient. They started within the natural world, and evolved to tribes and any group sharing time and resources.

However, movements today have one fundamental difference. There's a new dimension that radically changes their potential: connective technology. Thanks to the mainstream adoption of the internet and smartphones, communities now have the tools to self-organise and grow globally at almost zero marginal cost[3].

This new power is leading to the reinvention and amplification of ancient ideas and practices, like sharing resources and producing goods locally. The organisations that are part of this movement have been especially good at embracing and leveraging technology to connect local and global action and form networks to increase their impact. For instance, the Permaculture movement (permacultureglobal.org), started in the 1970s in Australia, has gained new momentum and has, thanks to technology, become a global network. Ouishare (ouishare.net), an international network of changemakers, was literally born online, out of a blog, connections on Twitter, and a Facebook group. By making it easy for like-minded groups to connect despite timezones and distance, technology has helped create and accelerate many movements that were trickling along.

1 The rise and future of the degrowth movement, Federico Demaria, 2018 https://theecologist.org/2018/mar/27/rise-and-future-degrowth-movement
2 Lean Startup principles, http://theleanstartup.com/principles
3 Jeremy Rifkin, The Zero Marginal Cost Society, 2017, https://thezeromarginalcostsociety.com/

Two secondary catalysts are also worth mentioning: the global financial crisis of 2008, and a growing awareness of global problems such as climate change and social inequality. I believe those two factors had an important influence on the professional choices of (Western-world) 'Millennials', my generation, and therefore on the emergence of this movement. Seeing the collapse of the global financial system, having to start your career in a dire-looking job market, and working for organisations that are exacerbating systemic social and environmental problems rather than solving them, have made many young people question the 'business-as-usual' career. As a result, we have seen a wave of professionals choosing alternative career paths or transitioning from traditional employment into freelancing, entrepreneurship, part-time work, or leaving the system all together. Technology has significantly lowered the barrier to making this jump by creating many alternative ways to make a sustainable living other than being employed by a company.

Globally, the percentage of people choosing such paths is significant. According to a study by Metlife in 2018, 40% of millennials intend to leave their full-time employment to work as a freelancer by 2023. Only 23% of Gen-Xers and 13% of Boomers had the same goal[4]. We can't deny the existence of this wave. It is no coincidence that one of the most shared articles in the history of Ouishare's online magazine talked about how young professionals "don't want to board the Titanic they already know is sinking—they want to build the new vessels that will carry us to safety"[5].

Five streams becoming a river

Although the boundaries between the different threads that weave themselves through this movement are blurry, I would like to highlight five that share certain common themes and values.

The sharing and collaborative economy

Coined in 2011, the concept of the 'sharing economy' (also known as 'collaborative consumption'[6]) is essentially the reinvention of the flea-

4 Metlife Annual Report on Employee Beneffts, 2018, https://benefittrends.metlife.com/us-perspectives/ebts2018/

5 Les jeunes talents qui partent en courant, (shared over 10 000 times on social media), Marc-Arthur Gauthey, http://www.socialter.fr/fr/module/99999672/125/ces_jeunes_qui_partent_en_courant

6 What's Mine is Yours: The Rise of Collaborative Consumption, Rachel Botsman & Roo Rogers, Harper Collins, 2011

market and physical pin-boards for things like ridesharing (a concept originally from Germany), through online platforms and smartphone apps. Technology put a critical mass of users at our fingertips, making the collaborative creation, production, distribution, trade, and consumption of goods and services a potentially viable business, and a powerful way to create a more sustainable and socially connected economy. One classic example is borrowing a drill from a neighbor through an app, instead of buying a new one.

The sharing economy is how I got involved in this movement in 2011, by writing a thesis on the topic and joining the nascent Ouishare network. From the beginning, the idea spoke to a variety of actors who don't often mix—from grassroots communities, to startups, to large corporations (commercial carsharing), to government ('Sharing Cities'[7]). This is the soil on which Ouishare grew, dedicated to connecting this rich emerging ecosystem through physical gatherings such as the conference Ouishare Fest.

For many of those involved in its beginnings, the sharing economy has been a big disappointment, as it failed to deliver on the transformational change many had hoped for. As the homesharing platform Airbnb and taxi-app Uber became the posterchildren, it seemed the original values of co-ownership and peer-to-peer sharing were being lost. But many organisations are still working towards what some call 'the real sharing economy'[8]. The P2P Foundation, the Commons Network, and the Platform Cooperative movement, for instance, have been supporting the emergence of peer-to-peer platforms that are owned by the service providers themselves (e.g. Uber owned by drivers, Airbnb owned by hosts).

Circular economy and ecological activism

The circular economy aims to create regenerative systems, in which products and services no longer create waste and have a minimal negative impact on the planet, in comparison to the currently widespread 'take, make, dispose' model of production. Apart from its implications for industrial production and new regulatory standards, the circular economy and a series of related concepts, such as Cradle to Cradle, Blue Economy, Zero Waste and more have given life to a wide range of com-

7 Sharing Cities: Activating the Urban Commons, Shareable, https://www.shareable.net/sharing-cities
8 Sustaining Hierarchy: Uber isn't sharing., Francesca Pick & Julia Dreher, 2015 http://kingsreview.co.uk/articles/beyond-hierarchy-why-uber-isnt-part-of-the-sharing-economy/

munities and organisations aiming to create change by tackling environmental issues from a systemic perspective. This can range from small groups building urban gardens, to beach-clean up initiatives, to regional political activism around the concept of zero waste, to global networks for hyperlocal digital fabrication such as Makerspaces and Fablabs.

Social entrepreneurship and impact

The term 'social entrepreneurship' has been used broadly since the 1980s, but gained in popularity following the publication of Charles Leadbeater's "the Rise of the Social Entrepreneur" in the 2000s. It is founded on the idea that we can use startup companies to implement solutions to social, cultural, and environmental issues. A social entrepreneur focuses on serving people and the planet first, by reinvesting their profits in the causes they seek to address, rather than maximising shareholder value. This concept has inspired the development of a rich ecosystem of communities, accelerators, university programmes, fellowships, impact measurement tools, and membership networks looking to support these businesses. They describe themselves variously as social innovation, social business, impact, and tech for good. The social entrepreneurship sector has grown globally, with various well established actors, such as the fellowship network Ashoka (ashoka.org), the microloan business Grameen Bank, and the entrepreneurship programme Singularity University (su.org).

It isn't these established actors that I am interested in here, but a new generation of organisations moving away from the "Hero Entrepreneur" narrative toward a more nuanced view of impact. Examples such as the distributed coworking network Impact Hub (impacthub.net) or the bottom-up social innovator community MakeSense (makesense.org) show that many of these newer organisations are more participatory, decentralised, and community-driven.

Open source and decentralisation

We cannot overlook that the technologists building the software are themselves a driving factor of this movement. The philosophy of free and open source software—that anyone should have the right to freely use, copy, remix, and distribute software—has been an inspiration to this movement at large. Today, communities of open source software developers are playing an important role in exploring new socio-technological territories, underpinned by strong values of openness, cooperation, and decentralisation. A quick look at Open Collective (opencollective.com), a platform used by many open source projects to transparently collect and spend funds, shows the level of activity and resources in this space. Especially the invention of the decentralised cryptocurrency Bitcoin, blockchain, and other crypto-powered technology has been fertile ground for creating a decentralised, collectively-owned internet. Many of these projects, such as the decentralised social network Scuttlebutt (scuttlebutt.nz), or the web protocol Holochain (holochain.org), seek to use the principles of open source and decentralisation to create a more human internet and transform society as a whole.

Digital nomadism and freelancer collectives

One impact of the modern internet, the increased availability of high speed data connections (and laptops fitting into purses) is the rise of digital nomadism. Fueled by low-cost travel and the ease of working remotely, thousands of professionals are choosing flexible work and living arrangements over traditional employment and a permanent residence. Flocking to places with low living costs and great weather like Chiang Mai (Thailand) or the island of Bali, these freelancers are building internet businesses as coaches, writers, consultants, designers or web developers. A whole ecosystem of products and services has emerged for this audience—so-called 'WorkerTech'[9] from freelance job marketplaces such as Malt (malt.com) and Remotive (remotive.io), to collective buying of health insurance on Wemind (wemind.io).

A generally affluent and white demographic, the sub-culture and lifestyle that digital nomadism promotes is often idealised—think working in bikinis on the beach. But this solo lifestyle comes with many challenges, especially if you want to make it work in the long term. Humans need social and professional support systems. As a response to this need, many freelancers join coworking and co-living communities, or even form collectives to share work and support each other. There are many examples of such collectives[10], from the SMart network (smart-eu.org), a cooperative dedicated to supporting freelancers, to Enspiral itself, which emerged out of the intention to create a place where freelancers

9 How WorkerTech is meeting the need for flexible support for the self-employed, Inline, 2018, https://www.inlinepolicy.com/blog/how-workertech-is-meeting-the-need-for-flexible-support-for-the-self-employed

10 How Freelancers Are Reinventing Work Through New Collective Enterprises, Shareable, 2016, https://www.shareable.net/blog/how-freelancers-are-reinventing-work-through-new-collective-enterprises

and entrepreneurs could support each other.

The common threads: different starting points, same direction?

These organisations and themes may seem quite different. Apart from being driven by technological innovation, how could they be part of the same movement?

Although many of them are not aware of it, the people and organisations I have described above share an ethos, a culture, and many common values. It is a niche—call it a bubble—that has been growing and becoming more clearly defined, developing its own language, memes, references, and ways of doing things. This culture is truly global:

I have often flown thousands of miles only to find myself in the midst of a meeting or encounter that feels more familiar than visiting the company next door to my office in Paris.

In an instant, a way of speaking, referring to concepts or facilitating a meeting, gives me that feeling—"Oh, they are one of us."

What is this culture? We tend to look for differences when we analyse things, and the more similar we are, the more we do it. As diverse as we may seem, I've decided here to focus instead on what we have in common, because I sense that this is what the world needs more of at this moment. I've identified common threads and themes that I believe make this movement one. It's important to keep in mind that each thread is not present equally in each organisation and can vary quite significantly.

These threads are mainly about how we approach challenges, not about the challenges themselves, since the sectors and activities of the organisations I speak of are varied. What unites them is not what they work on, but why they do it and how they work. In my experience, the why has become an implicit consensus: people and planet are more important than profits. This deep sense of purpose is so embedded that it can be assumed. So instead, we'll focus on the how.

Local action, global networks

These organisations are leveraging a powerful duo by connecting local communities through global networks. They have the best of both worlds: tangible local action that is adapted to a specific reality, and access to much broader knowledge, skills, and expertise provided by their network. They build collective brands, which helps with fundraising and increases reach. Take the Zero Waste network, which has dozens of local groups involved in hands-on initiatives, such as campaigning and events, while they are all connected through their shared brand, governance, and annual meetings.

The current socio-political climate has created a strong feeling that now is not the time for sitting around and talking. We can't spend all our energy climbing corporate ladders or wiggling our way through politics before making a difference. Nothing is stopping us from taking action now, we just need to find right people or start our own project to attract them. Goodbye think tanks, hello 'Do Tanks'.

Self-organization and decentralised power

One of the strongest themes of this movement—which has very much been a focus in Enspiral—is experimenting with new ways of governing collectively in a networked, 'emergent', collaborative, and self-organised manner. A key idea is that decision-making power and ownership should be shared among those doing the work. There is the strong belief that the 'wisdom of the crowd' and community-led solutions can be more relevant and create more value in the long term than top-down ones. Great ideas can come from anywhere, and those who implement them should own them. Many communities in this movement started in a bottom-up manner from the beginning.

A concept that accurately explains these new ways of organising is that of New Power, as described by Jeremy Heimans and Henry Timms. As they describe in their book, in our chaotic, connected age, Old Power is controlling, extractive, and held by few. New Power, in contrast, is "made by many. It is open, participatory, and peer-driven. It uploads, and it distributes."[11] While organisations such as Facebook and Uber may leverage what the authors call New Power models, they still represent Old Power Values. They leverage New Power for growth and profit, not to address social or environmental problems. In comparison, the organisations that are part of this new movement aim to align their modes of operating with their values. Their models are contributive rather than

11 New Power: How Power Works in Our Hyperconnected World--and How to Make It Work for You, by Jeremy Heimans & Henry Timms, Doubleday, 2018

Managerialism, institutionalism, representative consolidation	Self-organisation; opt-in decision making; Informal, networked governance
Exclusivity, competition, authority, resource consolidation	Open source collaboration, crowd wisdom, sharing
Discretion, confidentiality, separation between private and public spheres	Radical transparency
Professionalism, specialisation	Do-it-ourselves, 'maker culture'
Long-term affiliation and loyalty, less overall participation	Short-term, conditional affiliation; more overall participation

(Diagram adapted from: https://hbr.org/2014/12/understanding-new-power)

competitive, which means that they only need to capture a fraction of the value they create to survive.

A great example is the Open Food Network (openfoodnetwork.net), an open-source platform for buying local foods, which is run as a self-organised network of producers, distributors, and retailers.

(Eco)systemic thinking

Another characteristic that runs through this movement is the ambition to create change at the systems level, while taking a systemic approach to how the work itself is done. Systems change is both an outcome and a process[12].

In practice, many of these organisations have a broader vision of societal transformation that goes beyond the scope of their own work. They understand that wicked problems are too complex to be solved by one organisation alone and acknowledge the need for collaboration of a diverse ecosystems to achieve the change they are working towards. It is not unusual for these organisations to approach problems with Design Thinking[13], systems design, and ecosystem mapping.

12 The School of Systems Change, https://www.forumforthefuture.org/school-of-system-change
13 A simple overview of Design Thinking: https://www.interaction-design.org/literature/article/what-is-design-thinking-and-why-is-it-so-popular

The ecosystemic approach primes this movement to collaborate with those working in other areas. Key events in the space are interdisciplinary. The digital society conference Republica Berlin (re-publica.com) brings together "artists, activists, scientists, hackers, entrepreneurs, NGOs, journalists, and marketers", Ouishare Fest (ouisharefest.com) connects "tech, society & business", the Impact Hub Network's event Unlikely Allies (unlikelyallies.net) brings together "a great diversity of sectors, geographies and demographics". Events like the NESI Forum (neweconomyforum.org/) connect a broad range of actors from the space of "New Economy and Social Innovation".

Problem-solving inspiration also comes from the natural world. The distributed ledger technology Holochain, for instance, has been designed as a living, evolving system. 'Emergence'[14], which is often used to describe how collective intelligence works, is a concept from biology that explains how bird swarms and ant colonies coordinate without centralised power. Many terms have been borrowed from nature, which has shaped the language of this subculture, making Mycelium (a mushroom network), swarm, nutrients, and compost common metaphors.

Spirituality: balancing doing and being

The systemic approach invokes an understanding that we as individuals are not disconnected from this system, but are part of the whole. "Be the change you want to see in the world" rings truer than ever. Rather than sacrificing ourselves for a cause and perpetuating a 'work harder to save the world faster' mindset, there has been a collective realisation that the path to more impact leads straight through our personal development. If we want to change the world, we need to take good care of ourselves, physically and spiritually.

Communities are important places for those doing change work to receive and give the support they need. Amanitas, for instance, a collective of practitioners, artists and designers of "inner and outer system change"[15], has been experimenting with how to balance being and doing, moving toward a more wholesome entrepreneurship. The project was sparked by a frustration with a culture in the social impact sector that

14 Recommended further reading: Emergence, by Steven Johnson, Scribner, 2001
15 Balancing Being and Doing, the Amanitas Collective, https://www.amanitas.cc/balancing-being-doing/
16 Principles of the Transition Network, https://transitionnetwork.org/about-the-movement/what-is-transition/principles-2/

continuously drove entrepreneurs to burn-out and only valued measurable output.

Making space for our spiritual selves is a theme in almost every project. The Transition Network states that finding a balance between "head, heart and hands"[16] is one of their guiding principles. At Enspiral's coding school, Dev Academy, learning empathy and practising yoga is part of the program. Meditation and mindfulness practices are part of most events and conferences. Vipassana, a Buddhist practice involving ten days of silent meditation, has practically become a right of passage (I continue to be surprised that almost everyone I meet through my work has either participated in or at least heard of Vipassana).

Cooperative entrepreneurship and experimentation

Although the culture of this movement often shows up as very anti-Silicon Valley, we cannot deny its influence. In comparison to some impact-focused organisations, one of the strengths of this movement is an emphasis on pragmatism over ideology. It manifests as a 'get shit done' attitude, along with the popularity of principles from The Lean Startup, such as 'fail often, fail fast'. This culture of experimentation and appetite for crazy projects is often termed "do-ocracy"[17], indicating that power and responsibility accrues to those who execute.

n contrast to mainstream startup culture, rather than exponential 'unicorns' led by masculine hero-entrepreneurs, this space is more collective, feminine, and willing to embrace ambiguity. Faced with the challenge of combining purpose and profit into successful businesses, there is a willingness to hack existing structures. This often means navigating a murky space between nonprofit and for-profit, writing custom bylaws, using accreditations such as BCorp[18], or creating brand new models like Stewardship ownership[19]. Some projects in the Cryptocurrency space are even choosing to go fully beyond the limits of existing legal structures and creating a new type of organization that is not centrally owned, so-called Decentralised Autonomous Organizations (DAOs).

17 Definition of Do-ocracy, https://communitywiki.org/wiki/DoOcracy

18 Bcorp is a certification for social and environmental performance purpose driven businesses, https://bcorporation.net/about-b-corps

19 Stewardship ownership is a set of organisational principles where profits are a means to an end and ownership equals entrepreneurship, http://purpose-economy.org/en/

20 Guiding principles of the P2P foundation, https://p2pfoundation.net/infrastructure/our-guiding-principles

Embracing the new while building on the old

A last characteristic is being able to simultaneously look forwards and backwards. Many of the projects in this space strike an interesting balance between recognising the importance and value of tradition, while embracing the opportunities of new technologies and social structures. The P2P Foundation, for instance, says it is "combining digital culture with older cooperative traditions."[20] The cooperative movement specifically is experiencing a revival, thanks to the advent of digital Platform Coops (platform.coop). The Edmund Hillary Fellowship (ehf.org) in New Zealand, which often selects entrepreneurs working on cutting edge future-focused ventures, has the patronship of local Māori elders and has made connecting with Māori traditions an integral part of their programme.

Who is this movement?

Due to their collective nature, most of the stars of this movement are not famous figureheads, but the organisations and their collective brands.

However, I would like to acknowledge a number of recent thinkers who have deepened my understanding of this movement, such as Elinor Östrom's and David Bollier's research on the Commons, Yochai Benkler and Michel Bauwens' writing on Peer-to-Peer Networks, Charles Eisenstein's Sacred Economics, Frederic Laloux's Reinventing Organizations, and Christian Felber's work on the Economy for the Common Good. I also recognise those who have played an important role in making this thinking accessible to large audiences, such as Chris Anderson, Clay Shirky, Lisa Gansky, Rachel Botsman, Douglas Rushkoff, Zeynep Turfekci, Rick Falkvinge, Cory Doctorow and Jeremy Rifkin.

What follows is a snapshot of the organisations used as examples above. This is not intended to be a comprehensive list and, since this is a very emerging and rapidly changing field, it may already be outdated by the time you read this.

ouishare

Ouishare is a global network that connects people and accelerates projects for systemic change. With 80+ active members in 20 cities, Ouishare has organized over 300 participatory events, connected diverse ecosystems through physical spaces and published research on emerging topics.

P2P Foundation

A non-profit and global network that, since 2005, has been researching, cataloging, and advocating for the potential of P2P and Commons-based approaches to societal and consciousness change.

SHAREABLE

Shareable is a non-profit news, action and connection hub that has been telling stories since 2009 on how grassroots movements including the Sharing Economy are tackling today's biggest challenges.

civicwise

CivicWise is an international distributed and open network that promotes citizen engagement, developing concrete actions and projects based on collective intelligence, civic innovation and open design.

FAB CITY

Fab City is a collective of citizens, researchers, policy makers, teachers, developers, and entrepreneurs working on bringing production back to cities. It is part of the Fab Lab Network, an open, creative community working in Fab Labs around the world.

make sense

An international network of citizens, entrepreneurs, and organisations supporting positive change. 70 active members in eight cities, with 2800 projects supported.

IMPACT HUB

A global network focused on building entrepreneurial communities for impact at scale. They offer workspace, community, and startup programmes for entrepreneurs creating tangible solutions to the world's most pressing issues.

The Edmund Hillary Fellowship is a fellowship programme from New Zealand for purpose-driven entrepreneurs and impact investors, who are working on new paradigm solutions.

The Transition Towns movement started in 2005 and supports communities to address the big challenges they face by starting local and using crowd sourced solutions. Today they have thousands of groups in 50+ countries.

Zero Waste Europe is a network of 29 national and local NGOs promoting the Zero Waste strategy as a way to make Europe more sustainable. It is part of a larger loose network of Zero Waste initatives in other parts of the world, such as Australia and New Zealand.

Holochain is a technology that enables a distributed web with user autonomy built directly into its architecture and protocols. Born out of the Metacurrency project that started in the mid 2000s, its mission is to enable a new generation of decentralised applications that do not abuse user privacy, or destroy the environment.

Scuttlebutt is an open source, decentralised and secure peer-to-peer social network, and its underlying protocol, SecureScuttleButt, works without a connection to the internet. The ecosystem around this protocol is being developed by a self-organizsed community of software developers.

Open Collective enables groups to quickly set up a collective, raise funds and manage them transparently. Many of their users are meetups, open source projects, neighborhood associations, clubs, unions, movements, and more.

Open Food Network develops, accumulates and protects open source knowledge, code, applications, and platforms for fair and sustainable food systems. Its open source platform is collaboratively built by like-minded people around the world.

Malt is a platform that connects +90 000 freelancers with companies and allows for secure collaboration, from initial contact to payment. They are focused on matching high quality talent in close proximity to each other.

Remotive is a platform for remote workers to find jobs, connect with each other and get advice on how to be productive and supported in their work.

Wemind is a platform that offers freelancers and collectives in France home, health, and company insurance through group buying and solidarity that is equivalent to being employed through group buying and solidarity.

Platform cooperativism is an international movement that builds a fairer future of work. Rooted in democratic ownership, co-op members, technologists, unionists, and freelancers create a concrete near-future alternative to the extractive sharing economy.

These examples don't all fulfil the characteristics described to the same extent. Plotting them along the following two dimensions is useful for giving an idea of where they sit: level of openness towards and usage of technology (y-axis), and extent to which they work with traditional businesses (x-axis).

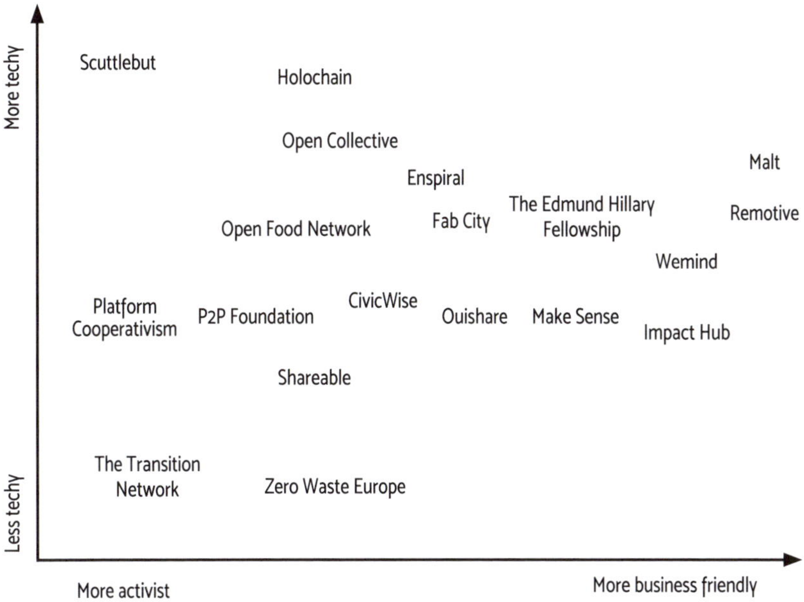

Where to from here? It's time for convergence.

Could this be the onset of a new age, the age of participation? The first important step is already happening: those who want a better world and are forging their own paths to creating it are becoming more aware of each other. They are sharing, copying and remixing each others work.

At the Network Convergence in Catalunya, we saw connections becoming convergence.

The movement has matured a lot since I entered in 2011, and I can see that people are ready to work beyond their own community. In 2016 I ventured to New Zealand to work on Enspiral's conference OS//OS and to share what I had learnt building Ouishare Fest. Small steps like these have taught me that it's not about creating a network of networks, but networking the networks—cross-pollinating, building bridges, and enabling them to blend and flow together.

And 'with great awareness comes great responsibility.' Responsibility to move from connecting to collective action. No matter how many inspirational projects we create, if we can't learn how to collaborate and cooperate more, despite small ideological differences, our impact will always be limited. Convergence is not only about coming together physically, it's about aligning projects, resources, and communications. For this movement to achieve real impact, we need to recognise that we can all be different while united in action.

How? That is the challenge I leave you with. This book is about helping you, no matter who and where you are, to join us—but in your own way and with your own style. It's not going to be easy, but once we truly tap into our collective intelligence it will be worth it. We're greater than the sum of our parts.

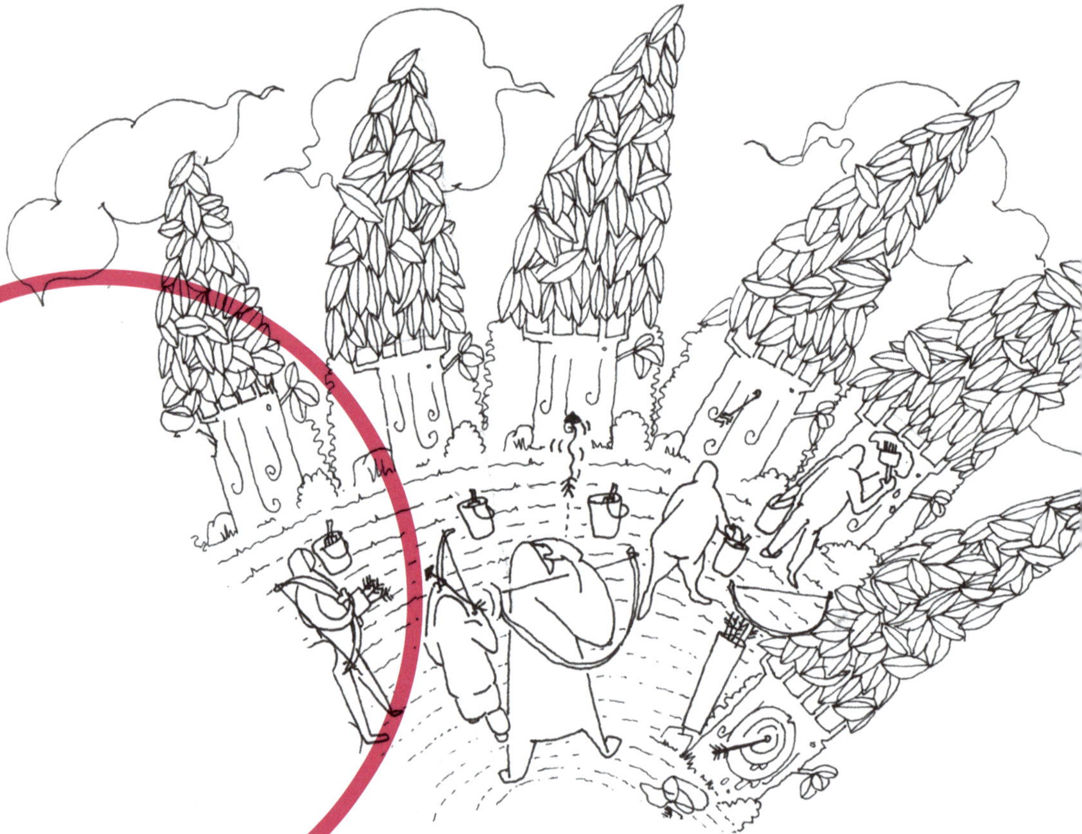

essay.Five

Saying yes to purpose

Vagas: a case study

by Sandra Chemin

Many strings wove me into the Enspiral tapestry. In 2015, I was structuring the international expansion of the innovation startup Mesa&Cadeira in Brazil. A successful design sprint for Auckland Council in New Zealand resulted in an invitation to go to Wellington to attend New Frontiers, a well-curated festival for impact entrepreneurs and change-makers from all over the world.

The day before the trip, I received an email introducing me to Richard Bartlett[1]. "You need to know Enspiral; it has everything to do with your work," said our common friend. Rich invited me for a coffee and the connection was immediate. The idea of a network of activists, entrepreneurs, and companies 'working on stuff that matters' just lit me up.

As I arrived at New Frontiers, Alanna Irving[2] was on stage. "The global economy was not created by the laws of nature. We created it—and because we created it, we can change it." The possibility to codify how economy, society, and organisations work, and then redesign the whole system to attend to a higher purpose was mind-blowing. My journey in Enspiral had started.

Several months later, Joshua Vial and I went to Brazil to host an Open Enspiral tour, a series of workshops and talks to share the learnings of building a participatory network. As we shared our experience with others, we had the opportunity to revisit our personal journeys that led to Enspiral.

Joshua shared the story of his pilgrimage in the Camino de Santiago in Spain, when he questioned the impact he wanted to have in the world:"I came back from that trip and realised that, if everything goes well, I will have 80,000 hours to work in my life. What is the best use of my time? I see there are a lot of people wanting to work on meaningful projects. But they do this in their extra time. What if more people could work full time on stuff that matters? What if I could help them do it? That would be the best use of my time."

1 Richard Bartlett is co-founder of Loomio and the consultancy The Hum
2 Alanna Irving is co-founder of Loomio and was key in structuring Enspiral. Watch her talk at New Frontiers searching in you tube for Alanna Irving, Growing A New Economy.

Our conversations made me reflect:

> *"When did I start to ask the big questions in life?"*
> *I went back fifteen years, to when I was enjoying one of the best moments of my professional career. I had co-founded Hipermídia, one of the first digital agencies in Brazil, at a time when the internet was only accessible in universities. I sold the agency to Ogilvy, a global advertising network, and was responsible for their internet operations in Latin America. I traveled a lot and met amazing people. I was creating the future, and that vision moved me forward.*

But one day, I got news that would change my life forever. I was pregnant with my first daughter, and my partner Lucas was diagnosed with an aggressive type of cancer. The doctors said he would have two years to live. Months later, we found out the diagnosis was wrong: he didn't have cancer. But the transformation inside us had already happened. For the first time we asked ourselves "What would you do if you just have two years to live?" That was the beginning of my purpose journey.

We bought a sailboat and lived on it with our one-year-old daughter, Clara. After two years in the North Atlantic and the Mediterranean, and pregnant with my second daughter Julia, we crossed the Atlantic Ocean. It was an inner journey of discovery as much as an ocean passage. My course was traced by asking"What moves me?"

The questions I asked myself changed over time[3]. When moving to a small village on the coast of Brazil, in search of a better place to raise our daughters and facing the challenge of not having a good education system, I asked: "What are the values we would like to model for our children?" Following that question led us to co-found a Steiner school, designed for social inclusion and owned by the community.

Fast forward to living in New Zealand, far from family. When my father had a serious health problem, it brought on a new set of questions: Where do I want to live my purpose? Where does the world need me most? Where can I make the biggest impact?

Looking back, I realise our purpose journey is a lifelong cycle of Search, Find, Integrate, Search, Find, Integrate in which we continuously chart new territories and leave past ones behind.

As Joshua and I shared our stories, we realised there was a pattern. It seemed to us that the individuals who joined Enspiral had a particular

3 To know more about my purpose journey watch the video in youtube "Sandra Chemin - New Ways of Working, Living and Being" from a talk in New Frontiers in 2017.

experience in their lives, a small opening to the possibility that they could be in service of something bigger than the demands of the day-to-day life. A moment of Awakening, when we start to ask the big questions in life and look for others on the same journey. The Enspiral purpose, "helping more people work on stuff that matters", was attracting individuals that were saying yes to their own purpose journey.

This was happening to people outside Enspiral as well. One of them was the founder of the biggest technology company in e-recruitment in Brazil, Mario Kaphan. His company, Vagas, was a pioneer in horizontal management, working with self-managed teams that made decisions based on consensus. Mario invited Joshua and I to talk at HSM, the biggest management event in Latin America, and we invited him to the Enspiral retreat in New Zealand, our annual network gathering. We developed a deep sense of respect for each others journey.

Vagas wanted to improve its understanding and practice of horizontal management culture and create the conditions for a better decision-making process. The possibility of supporting another company with similar values was the invitation we needed. My partner Lucas and I got excited and accepted the challenge.

So, we began to follow a new question: If we could codify how Enspiral works, could it work in other places?

What we learned at Vagas was that each culture is unique and that what actually happens is a cross-pollination, where Enspiral practices helped Vagas and practices from Vagas inspired us to pursue lines of thought we had not considered before.

Here are some of the design principles we developed together:

1. Collective leadership

As Mario shared the story of Vagas, we understood the reasons behind the decision to be a horizontal management company, with no hierarchy. "We believe in an environment where individuals can live their own values. And values become alive when you make decisions. Because it's one thing to identify yourself with values, and it's another to live them. The only way to live your values in a daily basis is to participate equally in the decision-making process."

They created an unique model, where every decision is made by consensus: when everyone agrees, or no one objects. The idea behind it was simple - anyone can make a decision, the only prerequisite is to make it visible. By doing so, if someone believes there is a better way to solve an issue, they can open a conversation and build a new consensus. The system auto-regulates itself as controversies indicate the need to include others in the process. As a result, a better understanding is reached of the minimal consensus group for each decision.

The model came out of lived experience, but as the company grew, it needed to make the process alive to everyone.

At the start of the Vagas project, we interviewed the team, and noticed the need to move from the vision of the founder to a collective understanding of the organisational model they were pursuing. It can be hard for a founder to let go and let the team co-create their own understanding and sense-making. Joshua faced a similar challenge when he decided to become the ex-founder of Enspiral.

Mario understood the importance of making it a Vagas project and said yes to the challenge. A team of Stewards of Culture and Purpose was formed and together they co-created the plan.

2. Purpose comes first

Purpose aligns us as individuals and can powerfully connect us as groups. Companies 'driven by purpose' are common these days, but there is a difference between having a purpose and having a shared purpose that makes sense for all, drives decisions, and becomes a practice. Vagas already had a purpose, but it was not clearly articulated. The goal the team defined was to improve the understanding, embodying, and practice of the purpose. They recognised the need for strong shared understanding of the bigger reasons why they made the choices they made as a company. Only by understanding **their big why** could they hope to improve their decision-making process.

3. Design for trust and safety

In the report "What makes a team effective at Google?"[4], Google researchers found out that who is on a team matters less than how the team members interact, structure their work, and view their contributions. They identified that the single most important dynamic of

4 You can read the full report here - https://rework.withgoogle.com/guides/understanding-team-effectiveness/steps/introduction/

successful teams is **psychological safety**. *Can I express my opinions and be heard? Can I share the challenges I am facing, both personally and professionally, and be supported? Is there space for vulnerability? Can we take risks in this team without feeling insecure or embarrassed?*

Trust and safety doesn't happen by chance in an organisation. They have to be intentionally designed and embedded with practices such as:

a. Regular check-ins: spaces for sharing how you really are, what you bring to a project, and what inspires you. Verbal sharing, especially a brief story, weaves the interpersonal net and creates trust in a team. It also ensures people are truly present.

b. Check-outs: an opportunity to say how you are leaving a meeting, align expectations, address any frustration, and celebrate what was accomplished.

> *I will never forget one of our remote meetings when the team wanted to cancel the call at the last minute, saying the internet connection was bad. We called them over the phone just to do a quick check-in and found out the real reason behind the change of plans: one of the contributors from another team lost a parent that day and they were very sad. By having space to express their feelings, they could transform the dynamic and find meaningful connection. The check-out was reassuring: "This meeting was the best thing that happened in my day."*

c. Deep listening and facilitated conversations to ensure all voices are heard. In times of polarised opinions, the ability to deeply listen to each other with empathy has a huge effect on a team. Methodologies such as nonviolent communication can help transform conflicts into positive conversations.

4. Purpose is emergent

Purpose is not something you create with a marketing campaign and enforce top-down. I have worked for more than a decade in marketing and branding and know how powerful the right communication can be. There is a huge difference between a purpose created externally and a purpose that emerges from what is already true in the collective. Finding the shared purpose that truly resonates is a process that can take time, and the right conditions, to emerge.

Having purpose conversations is important. As Enspiral formed, Joshua had hundreds of conversations to come up with "Helping more people work on stuff that matters". Mario gave a powerful talk on the 18th anniversary of Vagas, when they celebrated the company's maturity and the ripeness of their purpose *"Purpose is not something you choose. You harvest when it is ripe, like a fruit."*

Because of all the work the team did, Vagas' purpose was already alive in the community when it went onto the walls on a big poster stating: "Contribute to a world where companies can make better choices about the people they work with and individuals can make better choices about the companies they work for. This is what moves us".

5. Purpose has to be embodied and lived

How can you talk about something you haven't experienced? Purpose cannot be created by empty words. It must be alive.

Purpose conversations start by first asking ourselves what moves us, to then see if there is resonance with one another and the collective purpose of the organisation. It is deeply personal.

At Vagas, we carefully designed Purpose Rituals, workshops to allow each person to reflect on their own journey and share what was meaningful for them. For some it was the first time they had questioned their own sense of purpose. A deeper connection was created, even among those who had been working together for a long time. There was also space to have an open conversation about collective purpose: *"What does our purpose mean to me? How does our purpose influence the way we interact with our customers and partners? What is the impact of our purpose in the community?"* This type of conversation requires a safe space and the understanding that the purpose might not resonate with everyone. Purpose Rituals resulted in a significant increase in engagement, retention, and willingness to contribute to other areas of the company. Vagas invested deeply in these rituals, rolling them out to all 150 employees in a series of 18 workshops.

6. Purpose-led teams

"We would like to contribute more to our purpose." That is how the meeting requested by the customer support team started.

"Do you need a bigger team?" we asked. "No, we optimised the way we work and now have more time to contribute to other areas. We thought we could

serve others by offering a customer-centric approach, identifying client needs, and interacting with the product teams."

To my disbelief, this was an actual conversation, led proactively by a team who wanted to champion their own efforts and do more to contribute to overall organisational goals. Throughout this process, we noticed that teams that believed they were working on something meaningful outperformed others.

Here is what we have learned about working with teams:

- **Understand the context:** No two teams start in the same place, so there is no ready recipe. Everything begins with conversations and listening to understand their story and their needs. *"I don't have dedicated staff and share developers with another team. I would like to find what unifies us so we can actually be a team,"* or *"Our problem is that we are very slow in delivering what our clients need"*. Find where the energy is and work with the team members that put their hands up. Co-create rituals together so they can own them.

- **Connect at an inspirational level:** When there is connection with why a team exists and how they can contribute to the collective, there is energy to do whatever needs to be done. It is common to start a meeting with urgent pain points and needs, but trust me. It will make a huge difference to start with *why*.

- **Design for collective intelligence:** Strategic design of conversations and meetings is one of the most important skills of our time. One person just downloading information will kill the potential for productivity. When a team member has something to share with others, design activities to move from an individual perception to shared understanding. Co-create with the team, allowing them to own the purpose of the meeting or conversation. Only then will they be co-responsible for making it happen.

Real stories help me understand what is possible. This was the beginning of Vagas' purpose journey, and I can't wait to see where it goes in the future. Its purpose is alive, so the work continues as it grows.

This aliveness of purpose is also true at Enspiral.

Enspiral is much more than a network of activists, entrepreneurs, and companies. It is a container for individual and collective purpose to unfold, a safe space where we support each other to live and work together with purpose.

essay.Six

All things being equal:

when community is the business

by Anthony Cabraal

You work for a company.
You work at a company.
You work with a company.
Maybe you own the company.

--

Why does that company exist?
How does it serve your life?
What does it do?

What if your company was designed from the ground up to challenge and support you to be the best possible version of yourself?

What if your company gave you the freedom, accountability, and support you need to lead your own work projects in whatever direction you want?

What if your company was also your long-term community, where your co-workers actively supported you to keep moving towards solving the problems you most cared about?

Imagine your company existed to serve your positive impact in the world.

What would you do with your life?

You might...

- Build and launch a product you are truly passionate about, building a livelihood doing what you love—making a positive impact on the world.
- Engage with like-minded peers to deliver amazing, world-changing projects that you could never do alone or within the constraints of a nine-to-five job.
- Access and contribute to common resources that help create opportunities for everyone in your community.
- Develop skills in community governance, leadership, negotiation, and group dynamics that go well beyond your day-to-day work.
- Build lifelong relationships with inspiring people who will challenge and support you to grow.
- Transform how you think about yourself, how you impact the world, and what is possible in your life.

This is not a fictional scenario. This is the ongoing experience and exploration we've been living for more than eight years at Enspiral. What follows is a reflection on the key challenges, benefits and immense potential that sits behind it all. At the heart of this experiment is an intersection of mindsets; it is what happens when community meets business.

Building community is a business strategy.

The strategic challenge.

Building a business means thinking a lot about how to acquire, keep, and grow a customer base. Huge amounts of resource goes into improving our understanding of how we can serve customers and grow our business. For ambitious organisations, who want to thrive over the long term solving big meaningful problems, there is another more fundamental enquiry: how do you attract and support the people you need to get the right work done?

This is important work.

Startups get funding based on the strength of their team. Bad hires and team issues can quickly kill a small business. Growing organisations win market share based on their ability to coordinate and execute together. Large organisations survive disruption and thrive into the future on their ability to innovate, stay competitive, and sometimes entirely reinvent themselves.

This isn't easy work.

For a business, the economics of attracting and engaging amazing human beings are changing. Some cold, hard truths of modern society mean we need to be evolving our thinking about how we build companies and engage highly skilled professionals:

- **The industrialised workplace isn't winning anymore.** More and more leaders, owners, workers, investors, and markets are starting to recognise that many workplaces are failing to serve our best interests. Arbitrary nine-to-five working hours that require long commute times and incremental pay-scale progressions with fixed job descriptions make no sense in dynamic, creative industries.

- **People want purpose in their work.** Corporations with all the money in the world are struggling to engage or retain talented people. Staff are churning through roles and organisations at unprecedented rates. Meaningful work is becoming recognised as a key motivational driver for the millennial generation. These significant shifts in attitude are rising up like a wave ready to wash over our rusting, clunky industrial age economy.

- **More people have more choice.** For many ambitious professionals, the idea of a long-term career has been replaced by a string of projects (and interesting work). The rise of the freelancer and the gig economy means that work choices are becoming more flexible. This leads to new employment models, different structures and everyone to acquires new skills more quickly.

The overall insight and challenge is very clear:

Organisations that best engage and grow talented, caring people that will do the best over time.

In a business context, these challenges might be framed as human resources, innovation management, talent acquisition, or team-culture. The underlying drives they represent point towards more fundamental human truths that have been central in our lives long before the modern workplace existed.

They are about belonging, purpose, and trust. They are about helping people feel safe, connected, and cared for. They are about personal growth and nurturing relationships.

These are the ancient, enduring challenges of community.

The return on investment in community.

To successfully use a community mindset to tackle strategic business challenges, we must think about return on investment. Participating in community is very different to just 'showing up to a job' but it's still 'real work' and takes committed energy. Supporting community to grow is very different to owning or managing a business, but it takes a similar level of drive and focus. So, what's the point in taking on this challenge? What makes the extra work worthwhile? What magic does a community mindset enable?

Reflecting back, as someone drawn to Enspiral for the business opportunity rather than the idea of being in community, I've found three insights to be profound and entirely unexpected from working this way.

Development: Evolution is a team sport.

It is hard to describe the transformative experience where you feel your individual potential radically amplified by a supportive community. Something happens. A conversation, an interaction or a new opportunity emerges. Suddenly, you feel different about yourself and what you can achieve in the world. The growth feels tangible, like you've grown an extra limb or unlocked a new super power.

The community magic bubbles away silently behind the scenes, projects start, companies grow, new people join, and structures evolve and change. The value of strong community becomes clear as we learn to pay attention to it, through the inspiration, motivation, and growth of the people doing the work.

This growth can look like drastic changes in people's physical, mental, and spiritual health. It can look like strong relationships, new friends, or marriages. It can look like awards and recognition, speaking opportunities, and new connections.

As business owners we see the measurable benefits of growing teams, new ideas and innovative initiatives, great people showing up wanting to help, and talented, engaged people deeply committed to the organisation.

The truth under the metrics suddenly jumps out: our professional growth and development is deeply impacted by the people around us. Or, taking it all the way back to the schoolyard; you are who you hang with.

Resilience: When the going gets tough, the community gets going.

In a company built through transactional relationships people move on when the money stops coming in or a better offer comes along. And why shouldn't they? In an industrial economic model we are just rational units of labour, framed by job descriptions, making self-interested decisions. Positioned in a linear model, we make linear decisions about our careers. An organisation built with the social bonds of belonging, relationships, care, and sense of purpose is much more resilient than one stuck together using employment contracts and job descriptions. Decision-making is different when we think as whole humans.

People in community don't stop working when the money stops; often they work harder. Relationships kick in and teams galvanise, align, and work out what to do together because they depend on each other and deeply want each other to flourish. The connection to the mission burns brighter and people dig in and find a way to make things work. In this environment, breakthroughs happen, new projects emerge, and challenges improve the whole system.

This resilience-through-scarcity is critical for long-term endurance.

The challenge for the business is to recognise and develop these immeasurable bonds in a meaningful way. An all-hands meeting, a rousing quarterly speech or poster on the wall won't cut it.

The only real test of an organisation's resilience is hard times. Hard times eventually come to all. Projects will fail. Jobs will disappear. Sectors will be disrupted. That is when people choose how to react based on their social connections and shared commitment to a mission. It won't be perfect, it won't work for everyone (and not always straight away), but in a healthy community when the pressure goes up, things don't break - that's when the diamonds emerge.

Fearlessness: Anything is possible when people have your back.

Turning ambitious, unproven ideas into real action is challenging. It requires an organisation to do something it hasn't done before. It means people doing things they haven't done before. It means operating with uncertainty, accepting risk, and embracing the potential of failure.

Being a 'fearless innovator' is a nice idea that makes inspiring memes. But fearlessness is not (yet) a pill you can swallow. Fearlessness is complex. We can't buy it, and we all have different starting points with different obstacles and privileges. What unites us all is that we all seek safety. To truly put ourselves out there, we need to be confident enough in ourselves and in the support of those around us to push through the barriers, internal and external, real and imagined, that stand in our way. To really extend ourselves we need to feel *genuinely safe to fail.*

For people committed to doing innovative, risky work, a community safety net is priceless and powerful. As an entrepreneur, a safety net buys you leverage and emboldens ambition. When you feel like your community has your back, you feel safer to fail on every level. It's OK to fail financially. You'll survive and more opportunities will come up. It's OK to fail emotionally, you'll be supported to pick up the pieces and work out what to do next. It's OK to fail personally, you'll learn, you'll grow, and you won't be cast into the wilderness and rejected.

Regardless of what you are trying to achieve, a community can amplify your dreams, challenge you to grow, and transform your sense of what is possible. You can try more. You can take more risks. You can reach higher.

Equality is the secret sauce.

If a community mindset provides an advantage, then equality is the secret sauce that drives the mindset. Equality is not an abstract notion or 'core company value' to talk about in the induction of new team members. It is a constant practice that is improved over time. It only exists when it is put into action. If we take the invitation, community can be the literal, great equaliser of us all. It provides us with one of the greatest gifts we can receive.

It is in the places where we can practice being equals that the most important work to develop ourselves can happen.

Not all equality practice is equal. We need to consider how our organisations are designed and operated to enable (and disable) equality in different ways.

Structural equality.

The governance, power and operational control dynamics of most businesses are rooted in structural decisions that are not designed to be equal. Business structures generally centralise ownership (and financial return) with a small group of owners and maximise efficiency by implementing a command and control hierarchy. Equality can be a confronting idea to raise in these spaces, specifically designed to be more powerful than others.

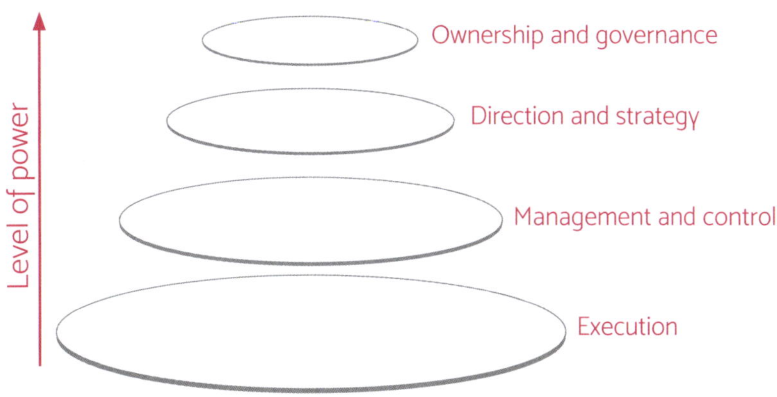

Who sits in the power rooms to decide how things are? Which voices dominate these rooms? Which ideas get listened to? Which ones ignored? Who makes the decisions at the end?

These questions strike right to the heart of where power is held in the organisation.

Redesigning a business structure for equality is not always possible inside inherited systems, especially where existing funding or legal relationships are entrenched. However, recognising where power really sits can illuminate the opportunity to change decision-making and cultural dynamics at any level of an organisation.

How can owners engage as equals with employees? How can executive teams engage as equals with investors, financiers and governance? How can working teams engage as equals with their leaders and managers? How can juniors been seen as equals to seniors?

As an overall system, Enspiral was structurally designed around principles of equality. The central entity in the middle of the community, Enspiral Foundation, serves as a vehicle where all members are treated as equal shareholders with equal voice. No Enspiral member comes to a conversation with more structural power than anyone else.

This structure has been central in helping us reinforce a culture of recognising and sharing power. This continues to ripple out to influence all the ventures and initiatives in the wider ecosystem.

Cultural equality

Cultural equality can transcend structural limitations, as long as everyone is willing to engage as equals and listen to each other.

Regardless of how entrenched or hierarchical the structure of an organisation, at some level people can always decide to engage informally as equal people—not as job titles, managers, CEOs or board members.

However, building a culture of equality is not a decision that is signed off by a leadership team and then magically happens. Making it actually feel OK to act as cultural equals, regardless of position, payscale, or experience takes real work and commitment to ongoing practice.

A simple, profound and ongoing practice within the Enspiral community is the check-in. Before a significant meeting or gathering starts, regardless of the internal or external stakeholders in the room, time is assigned for everyone in the room to speak, uninterrupted, to 'check in' to the meeting.

The process is not intended to be a formal introduction and reinforcement of status and job title. It is used as a chance to be human, vulnerable, and open and becomes a profound reminder of equality.

It is a practice that brings relationships back to the human level. It often has a radical effect on the outcome of the meeting and subsequent work. It surfaces context that would never normally have been seen, it creates openings for empathy and stronger relationships to form, it gives everyone more understanding of the breadth of talent, passion and humanity in the room.

With one person in the room speaking, uninterrupted and uncontested, everyone else gets a chance to build their active listening skills, clear their own minds and be present in the room. It is a recognised investment in time, sometimes 15 minutes of a one-hour meeting may go into a full round of checking in. This may seem like a challenge, but it invariably creates more long-term alignment to get the 'rest of the work' done together.

This practice builds self awareness in both the speaker and the listeners, and becomes a cornerstone in a culture of honesty and support for people to be their full and whole self in the workplace. Like any other learned skill, the more practice and commitment, the stronger the results.

Making it personal

Working in spaces of structural or cultural equality can have profound effects on how you operate professionally and make decisions (not to mention how you treat people and see the world).

However, for this to happen significant personal experiences need the space to land. These are the personal 'aha' moments where something deeper shifts. These are the visible lightning strikes that come after the slow build up of pressure inside the thundercloud.

They will arrive differently for each person and it is by paying attention in a culture of equality that they are made possible.

- By learning to listen more closely to how others are feeling, or understanding what is going on for someone in their personal life, you might realise how the weight of your voice lands in a way you hadn't intended.

- Recognising how you react and behave when your ideas are challenged, ignored, or disregarded, might change how you give feedback and value the ideas and efforts of others.

- Your understanding of group intelligence might shift while waiting for your chance to speak in the closing circle of an event when someone says the exact words you have in your mind.

- Disregarding positional hierarchy and authority to confront people far older, more senior or high ranking might enable you to have more influence than you expect, in circles that might have seemed inaccessible before.

A culture of self development arises through these personal experiences of feeling equal, challenged, and supported. In these experiences we recognise and smooth our rough edges, we learn to listen, empathise, and grow in confidence. Slowly we can begin to change our own expectations of ourselves.

These types of realisations are deeply personal and difficult to engineer, yet have lasting impact when a community can create the conditions for them to happen.

A healthy balance creates a culture of mutual service between individual growth and collective co-evolution. Community bonds prove strong and resilient when the community is stressed by external challenges and lack of resources.

People make breakthroughs on ambitious, daunting projects. The community enables people to operate at their top of their game. They are not just fluffy, feel-good spaces, they are competitive structures that will perform well in the marketplace.

This is where, as business owners, we all harvest and share the abundant rewards of doing community well.

Pointing towards a world that *works better.*

By supporting one community of entrepreneurs to build successful, impact focused companies, Enspiral is adding a tiny sliver of capacity to the global effort to help make the world a better place. But a couple hundred people supporting each other to have a nice time together is not going to make any meaningful impact on our global issues. So, what are we actually doing?

Is Enspiral just creating a self-serving bubble of privilege for a few people to grow up and create a livelihood together? What's the point when we need to fix climate change, structural inequality, systemic racism, and plastic in the ocean? How is this going to help? What's the hard problem we are trying to solve here?

The answer is in the underlying structures that govern our individual potential to make decisions and shift systems.

Systems change work isn't about one tangible output. It's not just about solving plastic waste, or food miles, or government corruption, or fast fashion. It's about changing the underlying structures that enable and disable how the world can work.

What would the world look like if...

- It was normal and expected that businesses in any industry were run with equitable ownership, transparent control, and governing decisions made accessible at all levels of the organisation?
- It was normal to engage equally and practice vulnerable, honest self development alongside co-workers in our workplaces?
- It wasn't an unusual privilege to earn your livelihood working on problems you care about, where you could grow to be your best self, surrounded by people who care for you?

Our exploration at the intersection of business and community moves forward in the direction of these questions. It is through these questions that we continue to envisage, test and improve the structures that enable impact driven entrepreneurs to do their best work. When you keep pulling the thread, it ultimately leads back to people.

All things being equal, every world-changing initiative, company, project or institution achieves greatness with the same core inputs: beating hearts and inspired minds.

With this view, a central question of this whole community / business experiment emerges: can these structures and processes help support enough people to build the solutions we need to transform the world?

There is a version of the world where people engage as equals in the workplace, developing themselves and growing their resilience, ambition, and capacity for success alongside community.

There is a version of the world where people find the connection and support they need to take the risks they have always wanted to take, to do the things they have always wanted to do, to build their livelihoods in line with their values.

There is a version of the world where all the people wanting to change the world are enabled to spend more of their lives doing just that - and we are all better off for it.

Our work continues, in service of that world.

#ChangingTheFuture

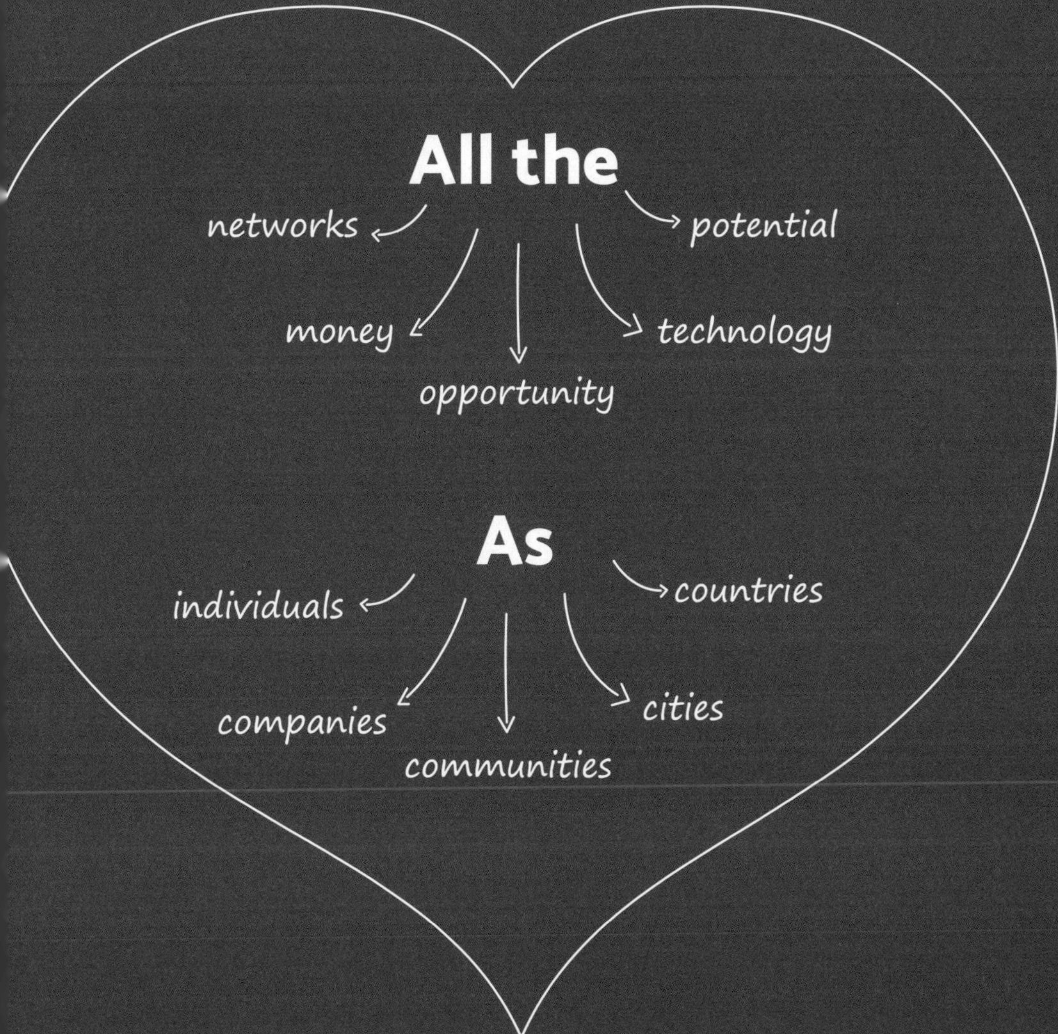

If we don't have love,
we don't have anything.

The Open Startup:

Copy / Improve / Share

By Anthony Cabraal

Enspiral is not a business that builds, protects, and sells intellectual property. It is not a startup trying to disrupt and claim a market for the benefit of shareholders or investors.

Enspiral is a way of organising and working together. It succeeds when we all make the world work better for everyone. It is not designed to be competitive, playing a zero-sum game against other organisations trying to do the same thing.

The pages of this book tell our stories of dreaming, experimenting, and iterating, and the ongoing development of enabling structures and patterns that support a community of people to earn their livelihood. These structures are now supporting some ambitious companies to launch products and people to do work to drive a social mission.

How can a small group of people doing this kind of work have meaningful impact on the world?

There is a chance that the companies we build impact markets, change behaviour, and influence how we solve specific problems in our society.

There is a chance that the people we support and connect with might have some notable influence in the work they choose to do.

However, as a community, the more progress we make, the more we recognise that our most powerful, impactful work is the processes, systems, and culture we are developing as we go.

This is what this book is all about.

If Enspiral continues developing innovative, entrepreneurial methods of organising together to deliver impactful work, then perhaps we can influence how other people choose to build their livelihoods, design their companies, and invest their resources.

We want to make the most useful parts of our culture as replicable as possible. By codifying replicable chunks of organisational DNA, we can seed more participatory, collaborative, impactful organisational culture to grow in many forms, in any sector, in any market, all around the world.

Building new pathways for how society can work isn't easy. Challenging and replacing existing dominant paradigms doesn't come cheap, or quickly. There aren't many direct precedents to copy, which means we bear the cost (and risk) of pioneering and invention. It requires entrepreneurship and persistent, focused effort.

We know a new, different, and radically better world of work is needed. We're making slow and steady progress, and we know we aren't the only ones doing the work. It is being built every day, by many people, invisible brick by invisible brick.

If more people, more organisations, and more communities recognise and contribute to this work, we will build our better future faster.

Our invitation is to ***copy*** *the patterns, processes and ideas that make sense to you.*

We want to support you to test them and ***improve*** *them within your own context.*

We encourage you to continue to ***share*** *learnings and improvements openly.*

We all know we need some
new solutions in our world.
We know no one has
all the answers when they start.
We have made plenty of mistakes.
We've made some good progress.
We have a much longer journey ahead of us.

Let's work out the future of working together, together.

Where did 'The Open Startup' idea come from?

Two strands of culture that have greatly influenced the development of Enspiral have been The Lean Startup and the Open Source movements.

Eric Ries' book The Lean Startup (http://theleanstartup.com/) gave an identity to a new way of thinking about building companies. The work borrowed best practice processes from waste reduction in manufacturing and applied it to how founders could think when they start a business. One of the fundamental lessons from 'lean startup' is to focus on building measurable experiments that are as small (and cheap) as possible in order to be effective. Working this way means ideas grow and iterate with constant feedback from customers, minimising wasted effort and resources. This helps founders to avoid architecting a grand system or spending a long time developing an expensive product that may not be needed by the market.

The process suggests the primary challenge of any startup business is to run experiments to build something, measure the results, and integrate the learning before repeating the process. Executed successfully, the result will be faster, cheaper, more effective ways of developing the right product for the right people at the right price.

It could be argued that the Open Source movement does not have one founder or specific origin point. It is a broad set of ideas and principles that encompasses commercial licences for software code, ethical frameworks, communities of practice, and advocacy groups. Underlying the movement is a mindset that encourages transparency of work, making collaboration and participation accessible to anyone, and encouraging people to innovate with existing resources as much as possible. Open Source culture and tools are responsible for shaping much of the early growth and infrastructure of the modern internet. The principles are also beginning to be applied outside of software in government, data, hardware, art, and business practices.

Using an Open Source mindset encourages thinking beyond your own project and business to recognise the wider ecosystem of partners and collaborators who might gain value from your work. It is a reminder that to solve complex problems (like how to build the internet) leveraging many minds is better than only using a few.

Blueprints for a community that works together

By Anthony Cabraal

Unbundling a complex, dynamic organisation into 'clean theory' requires some creative licence. This breakdown outlines different layers of Enspiral as a cohesive total system that is simple, clear and replicable.

It starts with a mission

As members and shareholders of a central legal entity

Members

are equal shareholders of Enspiral Foundation. Constitution dictates no personal financial return from shareholding.

MVB

A 'minimal viable board' of directors for the Foundation is elected by the membership. The board takes responsibility for the legal compliance of the entity.

Enspiral Foundation Ltd is a registered company (New Zealand) with a non-profit constitution.

This entity exists to serve the community as a vehicle for the shared social mission.

- Runs core financial operations
- Legally owns Enspiral brand

Members engage as active citizens of the community, with a relationship predicated on participation rather than profit extraction.

As members and contributors of a community

Members invite trusted **contributors** to the community and act as cultural stewards.

All members and contributors choose their own financial contributions toward the community commons.

Everyone in the community engages each other as equal human beings.

As active participants of a community

Members and **contributors** choose to opt in and participate in community working groups. **Sponsored catalysts** act as sense-makers, facilitators and coordinators of action.

Community enables new experiments, testing ideas, and building connections.

Working groups act as organs that maintain critical functions to ensure a healthy community.

As collaborative ventures

Members and contributors in the community own and run ventures. Ventures define their own value exchange with the community.

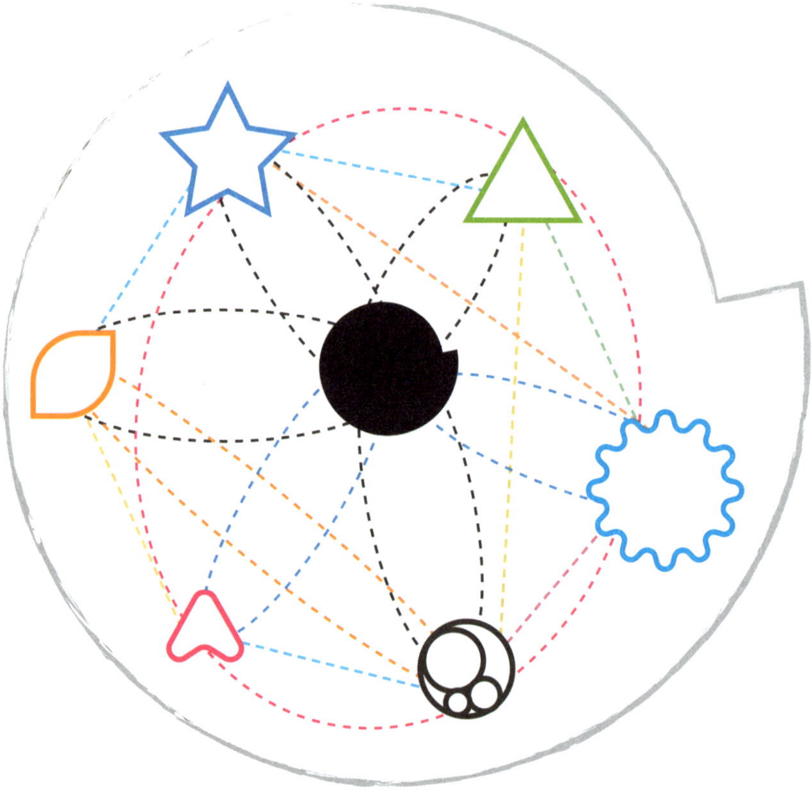

- Creating opportunities for each other.
- Providing operational infrastructure and services to each other.
- Sharing resources and learning together.

An ecosystem of companies with distributed ownership and control, representing a diversity of methods and tactics.

As an interconnected system

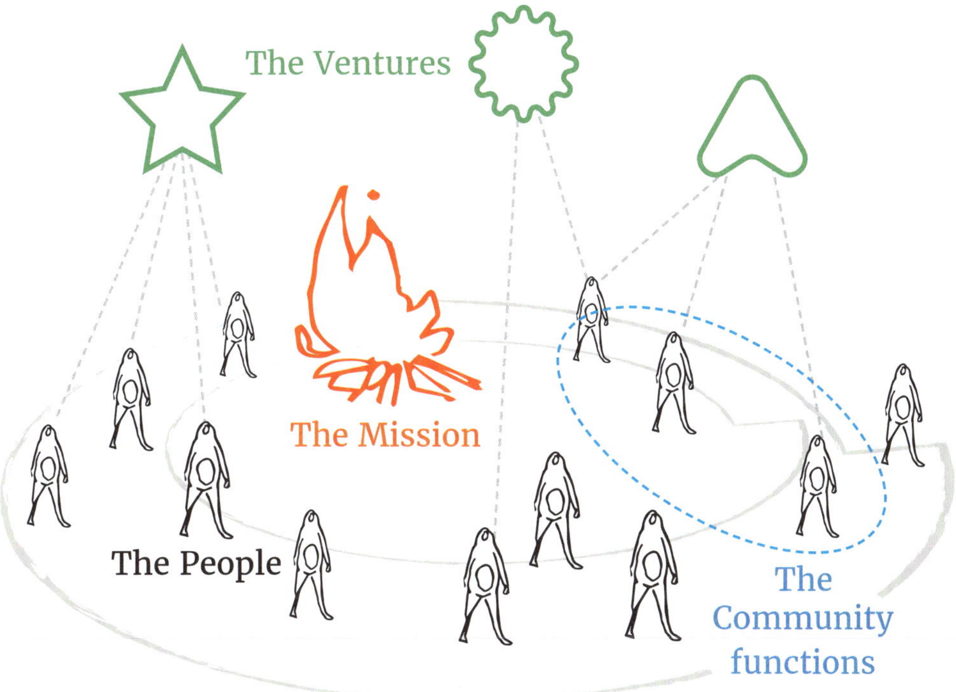

It's not one company. There isn't one person in charge.
It's is a changing, growing system.
The future is unwritten...

handbook.enspiral.com

By Anthony Cabraal

How do you develop structure, rules and agreements in a community founded on principles of radical autonomy and non-hierarchy?

How do you build cultural coherence in a vibrant community system that encourages innovation and trying new things?

How do new people and outsiders joining the community make sense of things without years of context and relationships?

For Enspiral, part of the answer to these questions comes through our open, public handbook.

A single source of impermanent truth

handbook.enspiral.com is publicly available online for anyone to read, download, fork, or translate. It is open for anyone in the community to update or contribute towards.

It was written to help the community align around our core agreements and share practices and processes for getting things done together.

It is a living document. It grows and changes.

Hold the truth tightly or lightly?

Written documents, policies and guides will always, at best, be one or two steps behind the truth of the day. This is especially true in a fast moving, dynamic organisation without centralised control.

The goal is to create a resource that reflects the current processes without enslaving you to them when they no longer serve.

Different voices in the community will recognise and respect written policies in different ways. It is important to recognise the spectrum of opinion in your community:

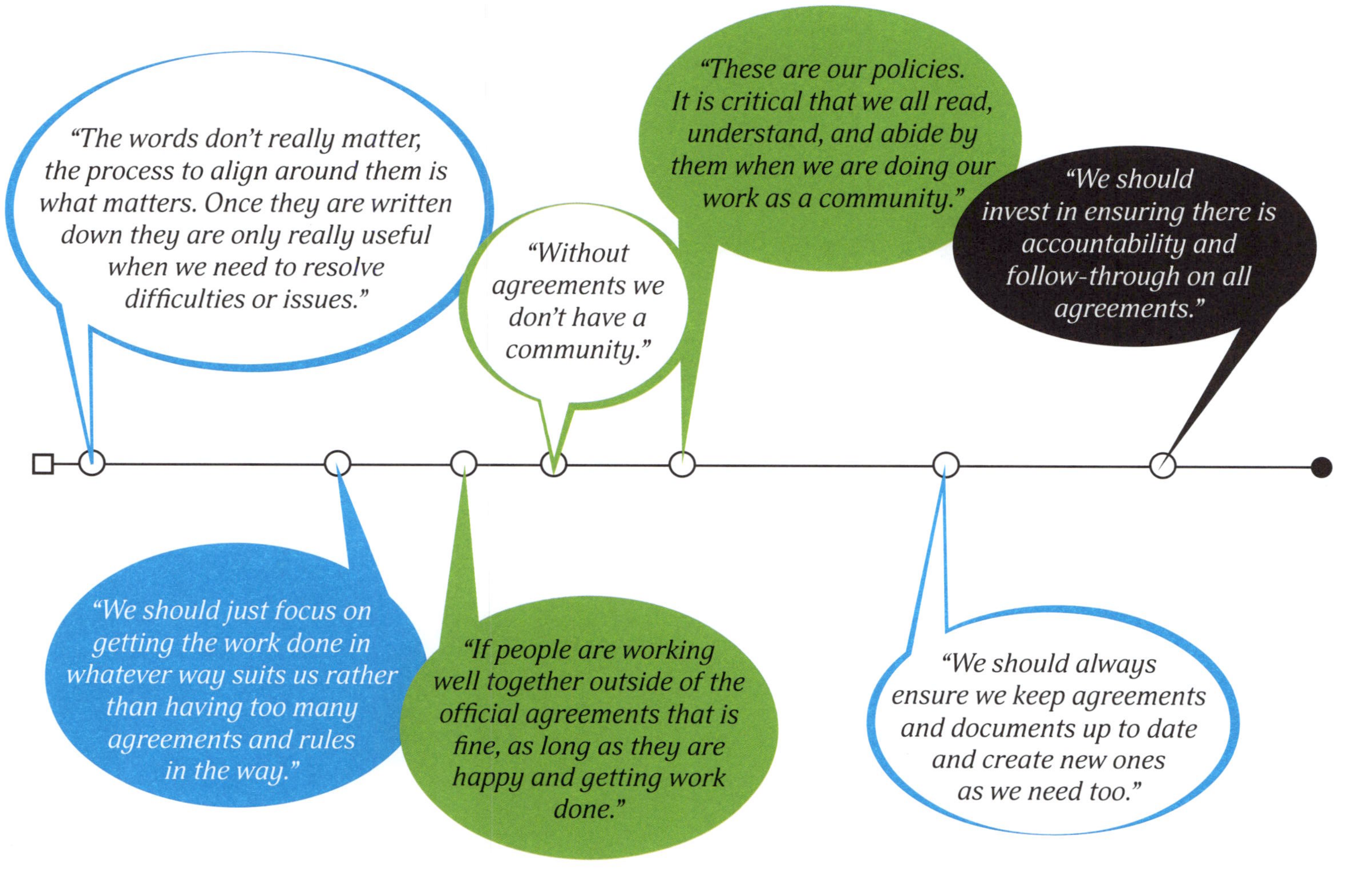

"The words don't really matter, the process to align around them is what matters. Once they are written down they are only really useful when we need to resolve difficulties or issues."
"We should just focus on getting the work done in whatever way suits us rather than having too many agreements and rules in the way."
"If people are working well together outside of the official agreements that is fine, as long as they are happy and getting work done."
"Without agreements we don't have a community."
"These are our policies. It is critical that we all read, understand, and abide by them when we are doing our work as a community."
"We should always ensure we keep agreements and documents up to date and create new ones as we need too."
"We should invest in ensuring there is accountability and follow-through on all agreements."

Sometimes the work isn't easy.
So much is invisible or unknown.
Things don't go to plan.
Not everyone agrees.
Things fail.
People get hurt.

We hosted several group conversations to reflect on the harder, hidden parts of this work.

This is a harvest of insights, reflections and ideas on the topics of power, control, privilege, and the social complexities that arise when ambitious ideas are put into action.

These insights are paraphrased and condensed from the thinking of many hearts and minds.

Collated by Gina Rembe-Stevens

Contributing voices:
Nati Lombardo, Sarah Houseman, Anake Goodall, Charmaine Meyers, Richard Bartlett, Francesca Pick, Damian Sligo-Green, Teddy Taptiklis, Susan Basterfield, Anthony Cabraal, Silvia Zuur, Nanz Nair.

Hierarchy and capitalism

Hierarchy means someone higher up tells you what to do. Fewer people are in control at the top of the pyramid, and more people are doing what they are told further down. Challenging the dynamics of hierarchy goes hand in hand with challenging capitalism. Capitalism keeps people small. It is designed to have winners and losers. Not everyone will have enough; this power disparity is maintained using hierarchy. We end up with billionaires extracting profit from companies while workers struggle to live on the wages they earn.

Respecting different voices

I am interested in the manifestation of extroverted power as authority: the deep voice, speaking with confidence, answering quickly, speaking authoritatively and categorically. I see a lot of it, from communities like Enspiral right through to corporate boards I'm on. Early movers have the power in conversations.

What interests me more is the quiet person who's deeply introverted, who processes more slowly with less confidence, and who is perceived as being quiet or disengaged. What's not being said and who's not speaking? How do we invite those people and create space for them? How do we recognise this need and practise getting better at it?

Power and privilege are linked

In largely volunteer-run organisations like Enspiral, you need high context to do the work. If you are privileged with income and spare time, you have more capacity to engage, which is crucial to gaining power and influence in the network.

The ones closer to the middle of the circle, who have more capacity to be engaged whether it's mental, physical, or energetic capacity are the ones who earn more influence and social capital.

Privilege of place

A lot of us are based in New Zealand. It's a place with a social security system, where you can feel safe to fail. We can experiment, and if it doesn't work, you're still safe, because you won't be homeless or starve. This is less common in other parts of the world.

This privilege is even stronger in Wellington. Government, which is based here, is a client of some of our products commercially. Wellington provides a noticeable intimacy of place and relationship. Enspiral grew here for a reason.

Just keeping up is real work

Sometimes it's hard to keep up, let alone find time to contribute to the ever-changing context and deep and thoughtful conversations about the future of the community.

There is always a temptation to do more, and it's easy to burn out. To be sustainable, communities need to be aware of this and provide care. Every community of purpose has grappled with the capacity and burnout question. Burned out people can't do their best work in the world.

What is non-hierarchy actually about?

We often talk about non-hierarchy, but that's saying what we're not, not what we are. Hierarchy is the distance between the people making decisions and the people affected by those decisions. We're talking about reducing that distance. Ideally, there would be no distance at all.

If hierarchy is the model, then power relationships are the practice. Power is manifest through practices. What we are is healthy power relationships and practices.

Exclusivity

Enspiral originated as group of IT contractors. Some of our language is IT-based, which can be a stumbling block. It felt exclusive. I almost dropped out because it seemed too hard to understand what people were talking about.

We are a really computer-literate group, relatively speaking. What does this require from people who don't have that background to find a way to really embed themselves in the community?

Learning the weight of your words

Three or four years ago I didn't have the power in the community that I have now. When I spoke in a circle, the weight of my words was not the same as it is now.

Even if I was as fierce about what I was trying to get across or it was just as important, it didn't land the same. That feeling is very hard to describe. You can learn to be conscious of the weight of your words, and how they are landing with other people.

That's a skill that directly relates to understanding your individual power.

Leadership without hierarchy

In the work of dismantling hierarchy, it's important to consider experience, influence, expertise, and capacity. It's romantic to think that everyone in a group situation has the same power; that's a confronting conversation. It becomes easier when we start to acknowledge that soft power comes in different forms.

We should redefine the role of power and talk more about leadership. We should be talking about stewarding, facilitating, and coordinating. Instead of empowering others, it's about holding space for them to step into power.

It's all about supporting people

The best model we've come up with to support this work is to offer support to each other. It may be social, emotional or financial support, and it differs for every person. Rather than a blueprint of non-hierarchy, perhaps we've created a blueprint of supporting a whole lot of amazing, well-rounded, effective, passionate, and caring humans to do great work in the world.

We need management, not managers

Even though the role of manager may be redundant, the function of management—of tasks, work, and people— is still needed. This function can take the form of coaching, guiding, and supporting, rather than coercion or direct power from a job title. It comes down to how people can be supported to manage themselves and develop the skills they need, rather than relying on someone to tell them what to do.

Its about people

In hierarchy, we can blame the structure for any wrongdoings, and deflect responsibility to others. But can we blame a structure when it is just the sum part of the behaviour of individuals? On a fundamental level, it is just about how we as humans behave, and relate to each other.

Whether or not we work in hierarchical ways—clarity is key. When power and responsibility are clearly assigned, so that we can consciously opt into power and responsibility, working in a hierarchy can be empowering. A clear dictatorship is better than a murky, faux non-hierarchical situation.

Confronting power leads to self awareness

Acknowledging your own power, and recognising how you wield it is a secret piece of work that changes how you think. Just saying, 'I have more power or influence,' doesn't happen much in our society. Maybe that's one of the biggest wake-up calls people get at Enspiral. Everyone has had some sort of journey of personal development and self-awareness in this community. That sort of journey itself is a privilege, and really valuable for everyone involved.

Influence and responsibility are earned

Over time at Enspiral, we've learnt to distinguish between the coercive power that someone holds over another person, and the social power that someone has earned from their contributions to a group over time. They don't just happen, they have to be earned. The balance is between respecting someone who has earned influence while not putting them on a pedestal or creating a fixed power dynamic.

The power of meeting offline

I have witnessed online conversations where I've, seen a change of tack and wondered what happened—only to realise that an offline conversation had happened to help resolve a conflict. The importance of being physically present, face-to-face, is hard to overstate. There are very few people who've only connected with us only online and managed to understand large amounts of context and stick around for very long. For most of us, it all depends on starting and building relationships in the real world.

How to grow distributed leadership

by Alanna Irving

In a pyramidal structure, leadership is concentrated at the top. But what if your organisation is more like a network, community, or ecosystem?

How does leadership without bosses grow? How can I grow as a leader if there's no ladder to climb?

4. Flowering: Growing Leadership

The ultimate success is growing so much leadership that you make yourself obsolete.

You see that long-term success depends on constantly nurturing more leadership. You craft opportunities for people to step up, even when you think you could do it better or faster yourself. People feel safer practising leadership skills with your support.

3. Sprouts: Leading Others

Coordination without hierarchy is the art of facilitation.

You design and implement effective systems and processes to distribute power. You have a knack for unblocking people. You're a mentor to people learning about self-leadership.

You can see how a project fits into the big picture. You help groups delegate, communicate, and collaborate, without coercion.

2. The Seed: Self-Leadership

Distributed leadership begins with leading yourself.

You can identify and execute work on your own. You set good boundaries. Both your 'yes' and your 'no' are powerful, because you only make commitments you can keep. You adapt and collaborate. You know and communicate your preferred ways of working. You can weave yourself into a project usefully.

1. The Soil: Shared Power

You can't just declare 'There are no bosses,' and expect everyone to 'self organise'. Hidden hierarchies will emerge and distributed leadership will die on the vine.

Power doesn't just come from positional authority, like a job title. It accrues to people for a lot of reasons, like founder status, communication style, gender, age, and skills. Power dynamics will always exist. What's important is how a group deals with power.

5. Pollination: Ecosystem Leadership

Ecosystem leaders work across all these modes of leadership, and think about impact beyond their own community.

How can we create catalysts who seed new collaborative communities? How can we support network-to-network collaboration?

How can we restructure our communities, cities, and companies so everyone can lead? How can we change societal power structures? How can we give more people access to shared power? How do we coordinate collective action without flattening diversity? What are processes, structures, and ideas that create whole new levels of collective agency?

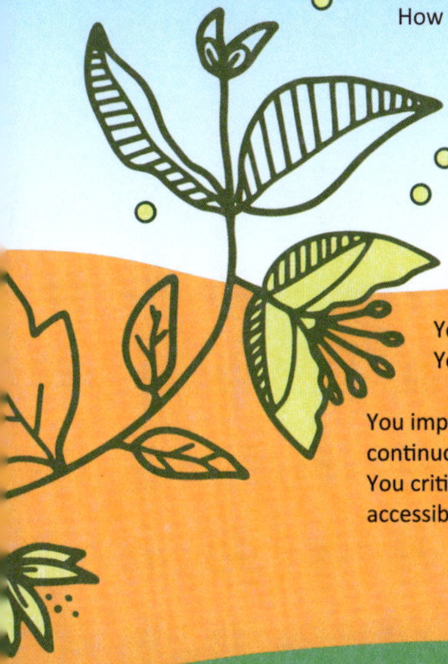

You are a mentor to others working to distribute power. Your track record of gaining consent engenders trust.

You implement systems for support, accountability, transparency, and continuous improvement that can operate without your direct involvement. You critique power on a systemic level: if the pathway to leadership isn't accessible to everyone, it means there are seeds left unsprouted.

You're good at building and nurturing teams, appreciating people's differences and preferences. You synthesise diverse perspectives into continuous improvement.

You facilitate ongoing critical engagement about power, and use any that accrues to you to create ways for distributing it.

Experts at self-leadership know when to follow.

You can take instructions and communicate when you need help. You contribute to continuous improvement and share ownership of outcomes. You've developed a critical level of self-awareness and practice self-directed, continuous personal and professional development. Skillful self-leadership builds credibility, creating possibilities for engaging in other modes of leadership in the future.

If the culture is hostile to questioning power, co-leadership can't flourish. To have an effective critique of power, everyone needs a voice.
In the absence of an explicit hierarchy, those with power have a responsibility to recognise that and proactively distribute it.

Harvest: Growing Understanding

In a collaborative environment, we're moving around each other constantly—giving and taking, leading and following.

- If someone tried to step into leadership here, is there room for them to grow?
- What power am I holding? Can I distribute it?
- Am I taking care of myself? Do I have self-awareness? What do I need to learn?
- In a given situation, do I want to work on my own, collaborate, follow, or lead? Can I see how to make my most valuable contribution?
- Am I creating opportunities for other to do their best work?
- Who is showing leadership around me? Am I noticing it and learning from it?
- Do I know when to step in, and when to step back?
- Am I building systems that don't depend on me directly?
- Am I thinking long term about growing leadership in my environment?
- Am I contributing to the wider discourse about leadership evolution?

Breaking bread

At the table
There sits between us
A wild ferment

And as we fill our bellies
We may also fill our hearts

As our conversation simmers
It may reveal a savoury broth

And this can be the basis
For a life that's steeped in love

Connecting together over food is a fundamental building block of community. Taking the time to ferment sourdough culture and make bread is a powerful reminder of ancient processes that teach us the wisdom of patience.

After all, good things take time.

Rye sourdough bread.
For two loaves, takes 24 hours

Recipe and Reflection by Doris Zuur

Find a starting culture.

Sourdough bread is baked from a live yeast culture.
If you do not have a starting culture, instructions for making one are outlined below. A much better way, however, is to make a call out into your community to find a starter. Use it as an excuse for a coffee - meet up and chat when you go to pick it up. Starter cultures often spread throughout the community and can stay alive for years. Discover its origin story, and make a new friend.

We have one circulating around Paekakariki, New Zealand with a reputation of being over a hundred years old!

Mine is five years old. This year, I dehydrated it, spread it out on baking paper and let it dry for 24 hours. I travelled around the world with these dehydrated starter crumbs and left a bit of my starter culture wherever I went. It only takes one tablespoon of the starter into a new mixture and the original culture carries on.

Think of your personal life, your story, your mission, your legacy. What will live on beyond you? A story, a song, a poem, a start-up (or is it 'starting-culture'?), a nature sanctuary, a policy, a family tradition, a recipe… it only needs a spoonful and your legacy will live on.

Ingredients

1 tablespoon of sourdough starter culture
4 cups of rye flour
2 tablespoons molasses (or treacle)
3 tablespoons of oil
(rice bran, grape seed or sunflower oil)
2 level teaspoons of salt
5 cups mixed flour

Optional
Mixed seeds: Linseeds, sunflower seeds, sesame seeds.

Step 1: Preparing the dough

In the morning (or evening), mix
4 cups of warm water
4 cups of rye flour
1 tablespoon of starter culture.
Mix well and let stand at room temperature for 12 hours. Should be 'alive' after 12 hours. Now you have a bowl full of renewed starter!

Save some of this mixture away as renewed starter culture. Store it in the fridge and discard the old starter.

This culture will stay well for around 4 weeks. Each time you make a loaf you can renew/replace your starter culture.

Step 2: Making the bread

Add the following to the dough you have prepared:

- 2 tablespoons of molasses (or treacle)
- 3 tablespoons of oil (rice bran, grape seed or sunflower oil etc., not olive oil as the flavour of olive oil is too strong; olive oil is used for pizza dough)
- 2 flat teaspoons of salt

Mix well with a sturdy wooden spoon, and only then, when above ingredients are mixed in well, add the remaining flour:

About 4 ½ - 4 ¾ cups of flour in whatever ratio and combination you like (eg. half white/half wholemeal, or more rye, or include ¼ cup of rolled oats), adding the flour gradually until it just starts to come 'off the bowl',clumping together into a ball, but still too sticky to knead. You could also add some sunflower seeds, sesame or linseed seeds. Hold the spoon at the bottom of the handle to get better leverage, or you might otherwise break the spoon!

Step 3: Baking the bread

Put the sticky mixture into two oiled tins and leave for another 12 hours and bake in the morning (or evening), in preheated oven on fan bake, 200ºC, for 20 minutes, and then turn down to 180º for another 30 - 40 min.

The actual time will strongly depend on your type of oven. Put an ovenproof dish full of water in the oven at the same time, to provide extra moisture. Remove loaves promptlyfrom the tins so they remain crusty.

If they stick to the tins, let them sit in their tins sideways for five minutes, and then try again. If you like it extra crusty, you can put them back in the oven for five minutes, after you have taken them out of their tins.

Starting a starter culture

If you don't have a starter culture, you can make one.
Mix ½ cup of rye flour with ½ cup of warm water and let sit it for two days at room temperature. Then make a new mixture of ½ cup of rye flour with ½ cup of warm water and add one tablespoon of the first mixture to this second mixture and discard the first mixture. Repeat this process every two days until the mixture looks and feels 'alive' (10 – 14 days) and then proceed to bread baking using this as your starter culture.

When we eat
May we be nourished
In our bodies
In our beings
In our actions

And may that sustenance
Flow into the lives
Of all those that we meet

So everyone may be sated
So everyone may break bread

Poems by Lucy Carver

We Can't Get 'There' From 'Here'

We have always done this - you and I.

This might be your first time here, but your
bones know what to do,
And although we've just met, no one is
really a stranger in this place.

For as long as human memory we have
gathered around fire in the evening
Deep into the night we have talked, stayed
warm, told our stories, and looking up we
have tried to understand the heavens.

So, here we are once again - you and I,
Looking at each other across a circle
wondering who will speak first.

It's this tension that does the work.
This is the lighting of the fire.
Don't slip back into the shadows.
Stand, and speak your truth.

By Billy Matheson

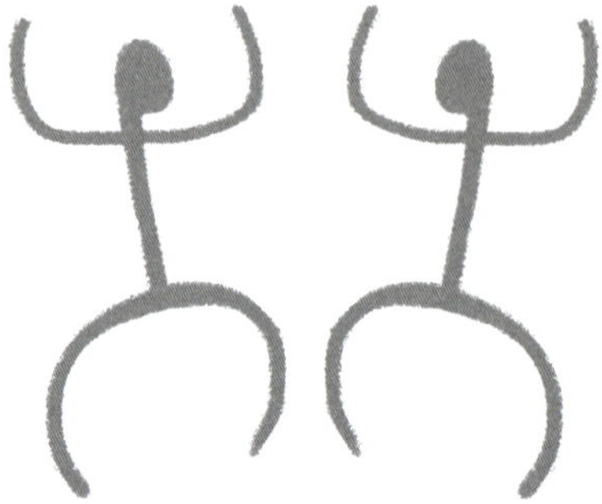

The Ceremony of Meeting

As we all spend more and more time 'in the virtual', this strange form of relating with our fellow human beings online, I suspect that the power of meeting 'in person' will grow and grow.

Perhaps we will rediscover the art of connecting face to face, in community, as a sacred act. Maybe it takes a crisis to bring us together. Or it might be something we do when we recognise some new potential, or when we know that we have important work to do together. Perhaps it is when we notice love is present.

As our technology continues to evolve and our behaviour changes along with it, how might we honour the deeper intention of meeting? How can we make the time we have together in physical space truly exceptional?

This is not an abstract question. If we are travelling hundreds of miles, spending thousands of dollars, and burning tonnes of carbon in order to be together for a few days, we need the experience to be exceptional, important and purposeful. Our world needs remarkable outcomes from our meetings like never before.

Perhaps to envisage this new future we must look backwards, and remember the power of ceremony.

The power of simplicity

Over time, ceremony can become elaborate - costumes, incantations, songs and dances, smoke and mirrors, obscure rites and rituals, priests and priestesses. Traditional ceremonies can be very beautiful and powerful, but they can also seem arcane, superstitious, and foreign, especially when you are not familiar with them.

Ceremony can also be very simple, and perhaps in that simplicity there exists another kind of power. According to Joseph Campbell, ceremony is composed of three elements:

1 Severance

We have to be willing to leave the known world behind. This is the price of entry. If you are not willing to pay this price and step out of your comfort zone, ceremony is not for you. If you are willing, we can begin our journey.

2 Threshold

Having left the known world behind, the task is always to find our own threshold. We can make the journey together, but each one of us has to find our own unique purpose for the journey. What is the line that you are nearly ready to cross? What is the risk that you have not yet taken?

3 Return

Your personal adventure might have been a success, or a failure, simply confusing, or perhaps even incomplete. Whatever it was, at some point you have to come home, back to the familiar world you know, and back to your people. What did you learn? Who are you now? Who are we as a result?

The gift of ceremony is so simple that it is easy to miss, so I will try to be very clear about it here.

As we grow up and get further into our lives, we will want to get to places that are not accessible to our present self, or in our current identity. We (hopefully) have aspirational goals that we simply cannot reach from our everyday 'normal' state of consciousness. In other words, when it comes to achieving some the things we most want or need in life, oftentimes we can't get there from here.

Sometimes we need to let go of where and who we are now. We need to cross a line, to come back a 'different person', and to a 'different place'. We need trusted community to witness and share our new identity so we can recognise our new selves and know how to bring these new gifts to the world. Then we find ourselves in a new reality where our goals and visions are suddenly within reach, or at least within sight.

To reach these exceptional destinations of transformation, revelation, connection to deep purpose, and insight, we may need to rediscover the art of creating ceremony.

There are a thousand ways to kneel and kiss the ground

There are so many ways to create and incorporate ceremony into our social process.

- The journey can be elaborate or simple. It can be dressed up or dressed down. It might take the shape of a multi-day corporate retreat. It might be a hiking trip into the mountains. It might be a two-hour strategic planning meeting. Let the people and context help create the form that will best serve the groups needs at the time.

- There are no rules, or right or wrong concepts. It might be a 'deep dive', or 'four quadrants' exercise, or a 'hero's journey' or 'six stage design-thinking'. There are many great books to read, methods to follow, and maps to guide you. Try to avoid process fundamentalism and don't be afraid to experiment.

- It is useful to consider the role of the participants and the role of the hosts or guides. Having some trusted friends who are willing not to participate and can hold the space, manage logistics, and support people in their individual and collective processes are invaluable. They might be from in your tribe, or people you bring in 'from outside'. Trust is the key, and usually is earned as you go along.

Whatever spaces you chose to create together, the challenge of using ceremony is the challenge of embracing a paradox. The process of gathering as a group is deeply rational - there needs to be a purpose, and a design, and people need to be organised to get there and back again. When we get there, we need to be open to the non-rational. Our rational minds keep us trapped in what we think we already know, often arguing with other people who think they already know something different.

Ceremony is the key to this door. It is the timeless way out of the 'prison of the known' world. It is an invitation to 'get lost'.

Only when we are lost can we find ourselves again, find new ideas and possibilities, and perhaps most importantly can we find the other people who we need to work with on this great adventure called life.

Doing what we can only do together

By Susan Basterfield

"....there is something about building up a comradeship — that I still believe is the greatest of all feats — and sharing in the dangers with your company of peers...."
~ Sir Edmund Hillary

Sharing in the dangers of building a business, or working together to achieve a specific goal is fairly commonplace. Although most stories of outrageous success focus on one person's dream or vision or leadership, we recognise that there are always others supporting or contributing. But to truly do something together, as a collective of peers, is much rarer. How do we nurture and develop our individual gifts for better work together?

What does it take to build a comradeship?

How do we develop as individuals so that we can engage as true peers?

As individuals, our ego and velocity propel us through life. However, it is in community that we really learn how to be. For most of us, this happens primarily in two places: first at school and later, at work. A common assumption is that school is for learning things and practising relationships beyond our immediate family unit. We learn how to play together, to build together. We feel what it's like to be laughed at or bullied, and, if we are honest, often what it feels like to laugh at and bully others. We share ideas and have our first experiences of groupthink; we learn what it's like to be on a team and what it's like to win and lose. We fall in love and have our hearts broken. We work hard and learn that's sometimes not enough. All of this happens in the classroom and in the schoolyard. It's expected that developing as humans is part of the deal - it's acknowledged and usually encouraged.

What changes when we enter the workplace? One theory is that the workplace is just for working - a place for solving problems and extracting value from each other. It is a place of mechanical optimisation - not a place for ongoing psychosocial development. Even in organisations that espouse purpose beyond profit, there is no assumption or requirement that they will nurture the human needs of the people who work there. And yet there is an increasing understanding of how critical it is to maintain ourselves in supportive, developmental environments. We are discovering that our brains have the capacity to continually evolve:

> *Scientists used to think that brain connections developed at a rapid pace in the first few years of life, until you reached your mental peak in your early 20s. Your cognitive abilities would level off at around middle age, and then start to gradually decline. We now know this is not true. Instead, scientists now see the brain as continuously changing and developing across the entire life span*[1].

What would happen if we designed our workplaces to support our individual and collective evolution?

Leaders we admire strive to lead from a place of service to the whole - creating opportunities for those they lead to flourish. However, there are far fewer stories of organisations focused on doing this work together. Fewer yet are stories about organisations where it is encouraged and expected that work should be a place where we can process our shadows, recognise our neuroses, and gently support one another to keep on developing.

1 https://www.health.harvard.edu/mind-and-mood/how-memory-and-thinking-ability-change-with-age

When we do the work collectively, we change ourselves.

At Enspiral we can tell one of those stories. Maybe because it all began with a group of twenty-somethings. Maybe because it grew up in a small, connected university city. Maybe because it was both those things and the lines between educational and work environments got blurred somehow. Maybe it was the radical ambition to shift the whole world. Or maybe it was just the overt expressions of compassion and doing 'stuff that matters' that left those edges raw. Something about Enspiral has always honoured and nurtured the 'inside work'. Enspiral has never been simply about earning money, it's also always been about our hearts.

"Those who build the house are built by the house"
~Founding Proverb - Tapu Te Ranga Marae

When we move beyond our concept of leadership being one benevolent person doing good for the rest, and into a true comradeship of peers, we move into the realm of danger and discovery. Sir Ed didn't climb Mt. Everest on his own - and he didn't do it in one go. The team comes together, toils together, goes up, comes back down, acclimatises, waits out storms, humbles itself in deference to what it can only do together. This isn't the work of the individual, but the individual must do their work to be prepared for the work of the team.

Together, through the challenge, we gain strength. Together we support each other to learn, to dig in and to expand the realm of what's possible. Together teams scale mountains.

What are the mountains we can only climb together?

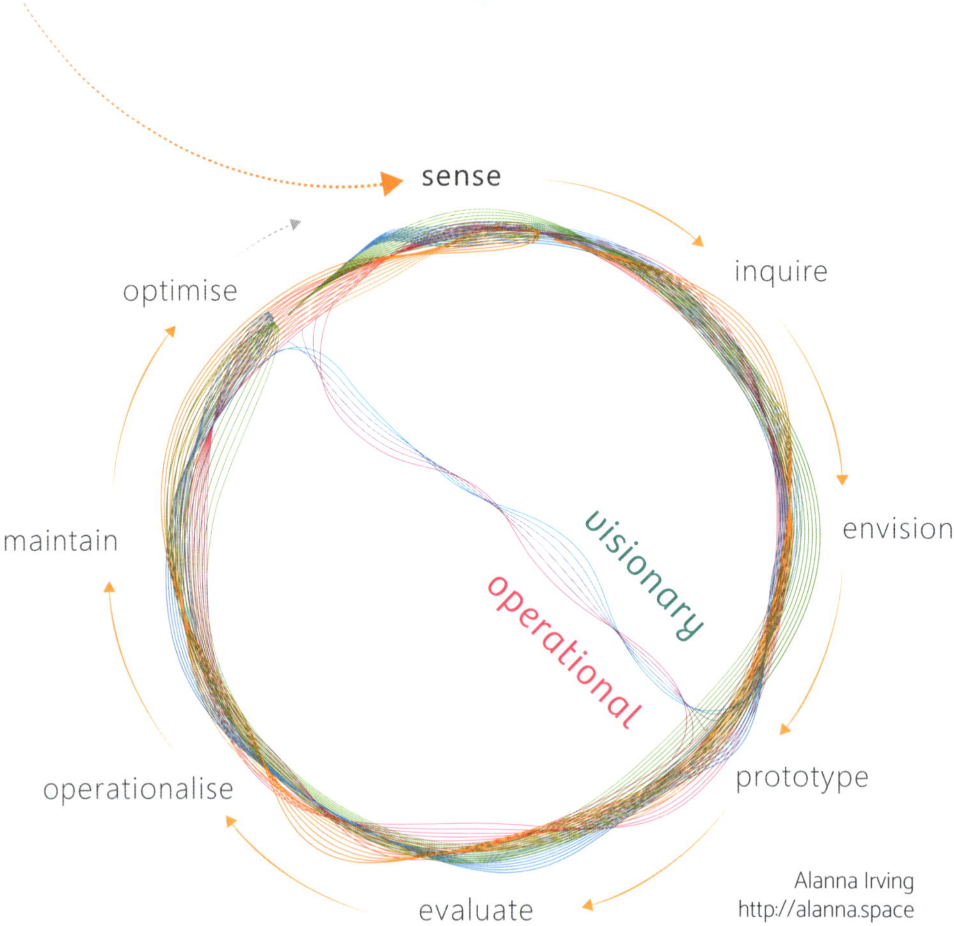

Full Circle Leadership

Leadership takes many different forms, particularly in dynamic, participatory environments where it's decoupled from positional authority and job titles. Our challenge is to recognise all the different forms of leadership needed for new projects to progress and communities to grow.

Full Circle Leadership is a model that helps us recognise and celebrate different forms of leadership, and understand the different phases of executing work together.

The Full Circle Leadership model works on two levels:

- *a way to understand and visualise diverse kinds of leadership*
- *a way to map the innovation and execution lifecycle of projects*

Full Circle Leadership is a recognition that aspects of leadership are found across a range of people with diverse strengths. Groups that can recognise and balance leadership across the circle will more successfully engage their full leadership potential.

Work can proceed through the eight stages in different ways, but the process of going all the way around enables the engine of innovation and execution to turn over successfully. The last stage of the circle leads naturally back to the first, opening up the possibility of an upward spiral of increasing collective capacity.

For each type of leadership, there is a persona, an archetype we might recognise in those who excel at it; a measure, indicating whether an environment is conducive to that type; and a shadow, representing the flip-side or risks.

Sense

The leadership of empathy

Persona: the nurturer
Measure: vulnerability
Shadow: overwhelm

You are a spider. Something small touches the far side of your web. The vibration tingles your leg.

You've been reading the online discussion. You went to the event and heard people talking. You brought someone a cup of tea and they shared their thinking. You've got feelers out. You are practising the skills of noticing and listening.

This same topic has come up in several conversations. Interesting.

You gossip. Gossip in your culture is about how to help people and build them up, not about cutting them down. You help create a community that is a safe space for sensitivity, your own and others.

Where you thrive:

The work of listening and the skill of noticing are acknowledged, valued, and selected for. People aren't stuck in silos—they can sense across the whole. Sensitivity, vulnerability, and openness are seen as strengths.

Inquire

The leadership of contextualisation

Persona: the facilitator
Measure: inclusion
Shadow: permission-seeking

You've got an intuition and you want to explore it. You put it out there: Has anyone else noticed this?

You're seeing it from different angles. Who has experience here? Have people worked on this before? You know how to identify stakeholders and go talk to them. You are a relationship builder. Your questioning is a kind of support, not an accusation or overstep.

You had some assumptions, but you've let them go. What you first thought to be the problem turned out to be a symptom of a larger issue. You're seeing connections. When you pull this thread here, that knot tightens there. Interesting.

You understand the attention economy. You hold this issue up next to others. Is it a priority right now? Do people want change? You move forward when you feel that mandate from the group.

Where you thrive:

Questioning is not taken as criticism, and past failures are shared as valuable lessons instead of being hidden away. Changing one's mind and letting go of assumptions is seen as a sign of strength. Skilled facilitators are recognised and recruited.

Envision

The leadership of aspiration

Persona: the dreamer
Measure: creativity
Shadow: distraction

Something is forming in your imagination. It's new and exciting. You're inspired. Your creativity is flowing. You're ideating in the shower. You're furiously drawing maps of unknown territories.

You've got the courage to imagine a future that's different—better. You are fueled by the pain of the problem, but your act of creation is deeply optimistic. In your mind, you're already living in the new reality.

Unfamiliarity and risk enlivens you. You are courageous in the face of change, even giddy. With a broad brush, you paint castles in the sky.

The hugeness of the possibility is calling to you. The gravity of the opportunity is pulling you in, and spreading beyond just you. You're a storyteller. Your passion starts to bring others with you.

Where you thrive:

Innovation encouraged, and dynamic change is welcomed as the essence of living systems. No one will shut you down just because your thinking is unfamiliar. There space for exploration. Past failures are accepted, even celebrated, so you want to go again. You aren't hemmed in by artificial boundaries.

Prototype

The leadership of experimentation

Persona: the hacker
Measure: efficacy
Shadow: obsession

You've drawn some architectural plans for your castle in the sky. You've created a scale model to interact with.

You hone in on the fastest, cheapest, most achievable way to test your key assumptions. It's a hacked version of that off-the-shelf tool, or a hand drawn simulation—ugly, but functional.

You're lean and mean, knowing what not to care about yet. You're watching the local attention economy. Are people feeling the pain this idea solves, or will it just be a distraction? A critical mass has to be willing to engage.

You've shoulder-tapped some willing guinea pigs, who represent key stakeholders and personas. You've prepared the context, the READ-ME, the instructions. You've imbued the invitations with your genuine enthusiasm.

Where you thrive:

Your community is open-minded, and used to trying out new things, even if they're held together by bubblegum. If it doesn't work at first, people cheer you on instead of punishing you. There's enough patience and long-term thinking to invest in testing and feedback before jumping straight to implementation.

Evaluate

The leadership of measurement

Persona: the scientist
Measure: integrity-
Shadow: cynicism

You show care through critical analysis. This is the moment right before things start to get expensive. Before the build begins is the time to make sure you've got it right. You are compelled to get beyond your feelings, intuitions, biases, and blind spots. It has to be rigorous.

It's a survey, or a series of interviews, or quantitative data. You do the legwork. You're constantly tracking to the original purpose, the key questions, and the assumptions that needed testing.

You understand how to get people to respond usefully. Your approach inspires honesty in others. You take feedback gratefully, as a sign people care. You take honesty as a sign of respect.

You have a sense for what's signal and what's noise in what you're hearing. You process the feedback and make changes in response. Maybe what's needed is a whole new prototype, or maybe just some small tweaks. You build trust with your stakeholders, by showing that their feedback has an impact.

Where you thrive:

In your culture, the process is emphasised more than the result. The value of iteration is well understood. Diversity is a deeply held principle, because without it, testing can be misleading. You inhabit a safe space for honesty.

Operationalise

The leadership of implementation

Persona: the negotiator
Measure: accessibility
Shadow: ruthlessness

This is the moment when something goes from concept to reality. When it's time to do the work of making it happen, and making it stick, you roll up your sleeves.

You have systemic awareness combined with operational knowledge. You know how the software functions, what the law is, and how the machine works. There is a map in your mind of people, resources, regulations, culture, and strategy.

You ask: How does this fit into existing processes, habits, tools, and policies? Will changing this thing over here impact that thing over there? Who will need to be trained or onboarded?

You are not a purist. Elegant implementation is knowing how to compromise, and this is where your creativity shines. You problem-solve as you go.

How can this be implemented to leverage what's already here? How are we going to resource this on an ongoing basis? How should it be documented, so the next person will know how to keep it going?

Judgement calls are required. You sense what can bend without breaking the kernel of original purpose.

Where you thrive:

The cost of high-quality implementation is recognised and resourced as an investment. There's no illusion that people will magically 'self-organise'. Admins, coordinators, and the back office are empowered and respected. Decisions are made close where they are put in practice. You're given mandate in the face of complexity, compromise, or resistance.

Maintain

The leadership of sustaining

Persona: the captain
Measure: reliability
Shadow: bureaucracy

Staying the course means keeping focused, saying no to distractions, and following through on commitments. In non-hierarchical networks, steering happens from the rear.

Holding steady is far from an inert state. It's dynamic, like sailing a ship on course in a changing sea. When the storm comes, you are in a state of mindful focus.

It's your soothing voice saying, "I know it's unfamiliar. But let's just give it a chance and see how it goes." It's your grounded voice saying, "We said we'd do this, so please follow through."

You watch the clock and the calendar. When the time comes, you send the reminder, push the button, run the process. The link is not broken. The email has been responded to. The room has been booked. You imbue the experience with a sense of trust, patience, and reliability. You hold stable the foundation upon which all participation can occur.

Where you thrive:

Skilled maintenance and operational reliability is acknowledged as active leadership. Visionary innovators around you understand that it is your work that makes their next exciting idea possible. There is discipline about following through on the last change before rushing into the next. Commitments are taken seriously.

Optimise

The leadership of improvement

Persona: the perfectionist
Measure: commitment
Shadow: meddling

The status quo makes you itch. You notice when a new tool or practice isn't so new anymore. Being comfortable is not quite good enough. You see the slack that could be tightened. You've identified some blocks for removal. You want to tweak things.

Yours is a gesture of iterative looping. Perhaps it's a small change that goes right back to maintaining. Maybe it's circling all the way back to prototyping.

With the courage to let go of the old and welcome new possibilities, you are listening, empathising, sensing. Having journeyed all the way around the circle, you're coming right back to the beginning—it's your moment to start the cycle again.

Where you thrive:

Everything is up for questioning and improvement. Systems are modular, not gridlocked. Inertia is not destiny. Agitating for proactive change is understood as a sign of loyalty, not undermining. Ego can make space for change.

Seeing the whole circle.

Having come all the way around the circle, you find that the final step, optimisation, is quite close to the first step, sensing. In fact, it leads right into it. A full cycle makes organisational collective memory possible. If you don't go full circle, it's very difficult to build on what's come before—like trying to construct on quicksand.

When there is an operational foundation on which to build, visionary innovation can flourish. Distributed leadership happens when different people with new ideas can pick up where others left off. This is the engine of innovation and execution, of evolution and growth.

Balancing the whole circle.

Diversity and balance are the keys to a healthy leadership culture. Different people are strong in different areas, and regard different parts of the cycle as important. Often, it's these very differences that create the power of the engine, with complementary forces causing it to spin.

If a certain kind of leadership is unseen and undervalued, people who excel in that area will not be able to work to their strengths, and others will miss being balanced out and complemented by them. Ultimately, the whole will suffer. Developing Full Circle Leadership means helping people and teams grow competency all around.

Going Full Circle, together.

Team Workshop (60 minutes)

The Full Circle Leadership model can be used in a workshop format that allows groups to quickly recognise and visualise their leadership profile.

This workshop can be facilitated for small groups of six-ten, or larger groups who can then discuss and share learning in smaller break-out groups.

Introduction: 20 mins

Introduce the Full Circle model to the whole group and explain each step. Point out how it can be applied to an individual or team (where different strengths lie) or a project lifecycle (taking it around the circle).

Self reflection: 10 mins

Have each participant consider their own leadership skills using the provided spider graph template. Ask them to give themselves a score 0–5 for each one, making a dot on each radial axis. Connect the dots to reveal the shape of their leadership.

Prompting questions:

- Where do you see yourself as strong and weak around the circle?
- Does rating yourself in this way reveal where you might do your best work, or how you might like to develop as a leader?
- Our vision of leadership is often skewed by our own lens. Think about the aspects of leadership that are most challenging or unattractive to you. Are you truly seeing those areas as leadership, and people who excel at them as leaders?

- Do you tend to get stuck in one step or a loop? For example, the entrepreneur with a 'great idea' who spends years oscillating between sense, inquire, and envision, never building anything.

Small group discussion: 20 mins

Combine the individual shapes in small groups to form a picture of the team's overall leadership shape.

Prompting questions:

- Is the team skewed toward part of the circle? How is that reflected in your working style and output as a team?
- Consider the individuals. Is one person alone in being strong or weak in a certain area? How has this affected collaboration?
- Are you balanced as a whole? What might that say about your culture or recruitment practices?
- Is there a place in the circle where initiatives tend to fall over? For some it will be the courage to innovate, for others the discipline to implement. What kind of leadership might you need to develop in your team to address that?
- Is the whole organisation stuck at a particular stage? Are we enabling or constraining some forms of leaders globally?
- If your work gets stuck, what might help you push through to the next stage?

Moving ahead: 10 mins

Bring the whole group back together to share insights.

Prompting questions:

- What are the big insights and learnings for the group?
- How might the team better support diversity of leadership?
- Are there processes or activities that might enable new leadership to emerge?

Full Circle Leadership

Thinking & Learning Tools

Project lifecycle map

Think about how your work tends to go around the circle....

- → Are there steps that you skip?
- → Are there steps where your projects often fall over?
- → Do you get stuck at a step, or in a loop? (Ex: oscillating *sense*, *inquire*, *envision*, but never building anything; or getting stuck at *maintain, maintain, maintain*).

Leadership profile graph

- → Score yourself 0-5 on each type of leadership, and make a dot.
- → Join the dots to reveal the shape of your leadership style.

For teams: superimpose everyone's individual leadership profiles to discover the profile of the group overall.

More info
Alanna Irving
https://alanna.space
hello@alanna.space

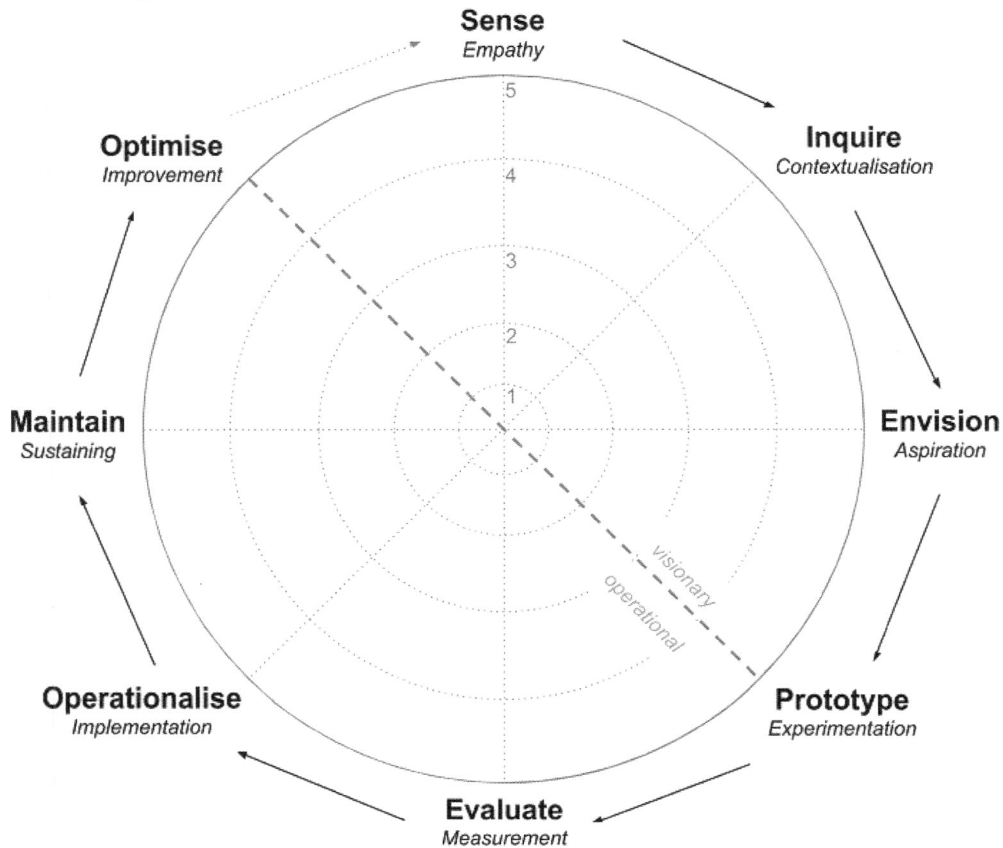

8 Patterns for Decentralised Organising

By Richard D. Bartlett

Thriving teams

Teams are the organs of your organisation. The only way to have a truly thriving organisation, at any scale, is to develop thriving, committed, collaborative teams.

As a cofounder and coordinator at Loomio and Enspiral, I have worked closely with dozens of teams experimenting with decentralised organising. In my past two years on the road, I've worked with hundreds more. All of these folks are prototyping organisational structures for distributed leadership, high autonomy, and shared ownership.

It takes a constant effort to build our personal and collective capacity for shared power, robust relationships, and autonomous work. The team scale (say, five to eight people) is the perfect place to exercise these muscles, learn some difficult lessons, and develop the readiness for larger scale collaboration.

Painful challenges

In all my work with teams all over the world, I noticed many of them faced similar, painful challenges:

How do we deal with power imbalances? How do we prioritise what to work on? How do we undo our cultural programming and develop an open, collaborative environment? How can we be inclusive without spending all our time in meetings? How do we balance autonomy with alignment? And where does accountability come from if there is no boss!?

I believe the right organisational structure is unique to its context, people, objectives, and history. So I wouldn't recommend building an organisation from a predetermined blueprint. However, we don't need to start from a blank slate either. Somewhere between the fixed blueprint and the empty canvas are these 'patterns'. Each pattern is a module, designed to be remixed and adapted to your local environment. This resource names some of the common challenges of working without a management hierarchy, and shares practical responses you apply immediately.

This segment is a sample of a larger project. See thehum.org/book for more

8 patterns

Intentionally produce counter culture

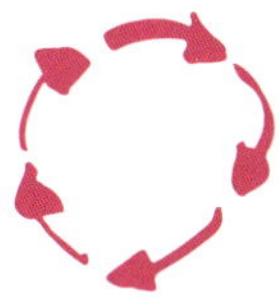

Systemically distribute care labour

Make explicit norms and boundaries

Keep talking about power

Agree how you're using your tech

Make decisions asynchronously

Use rhythm to balance flexibility and focus

Generate new patterns together

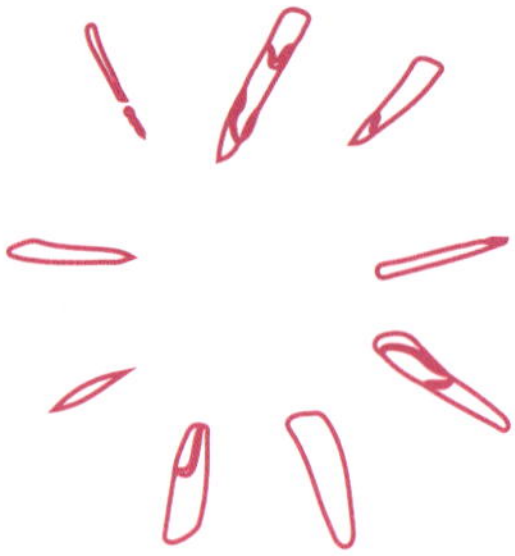

Intentionally produce counter culture

Challenge

You want to be non-hierarchical but you have **hierarchical habits,** e.g. telling people what to do, or looking to others for answers. We are **conditioned by culture:** if sexism and racism exist in your environment, it can be imprinted into your habits.

Response

We can **unlearn hierarchies** together. We can **co-design a culture** that encourages each of us to develop our best qualities, making us all more generous, respectful, trusting, courageous, etc.

How do you produce culture? **Fermentation!** To make sourdough bread, you have a **'starter dough',** mixed with **fresh ingredients,** and put it somewhere dark and safe for some time. To ferment a new group culture, your "starter dough" is a person or people who **embody some of the qualities** you want to develop. The "fresh ingredients" are **new people** who have a **desire** to grow in a specific way. We combine these ingredients in a **retreat:** safe, quiet, isolated from the outside world for a few days.

Results

We learn about each other's dreams and fears, building deep relationships of trust and belonging: the most important resource for all your upcoming challenges.

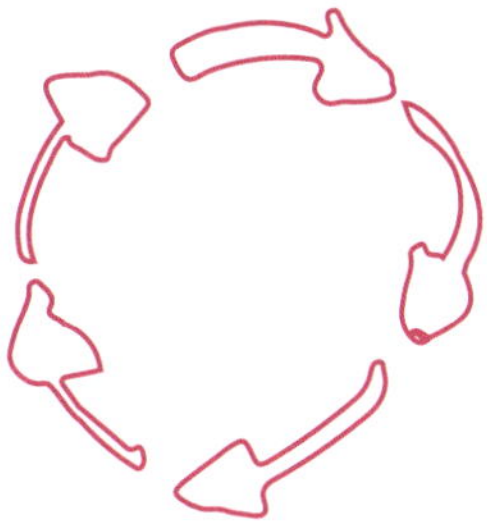

Systemically distribute care labour

Challenge

Hierarchical culture trains us to not **share the care labour fairly.** Most groups have one or two people, usually women, doing most of the care work. If they get overwhelmed or frustrated, they'll stop, and the group loses its gravity.

Care includes the practical stuff of **hospitality:** preparing a comfortable room with food, lighting, decoration, refreshments, collaboration tools, and tidying up after. It also includes **emotional work,** like noticing tension between colleagues and supporting them to resolve it.

Response

Make all work visible, so you can share it fairly. E.g. the Loomio team uses **'stewardship'**, a peer-to-peer support system. Everyone supports one person, and is supported by someone else. Each pair meets once per month, the steward asks "how can I support you?" and they figure out the answer together. More info: loomio.coop/stewarding.html

Results

Builds deep **trusting relationships;** dissolves **conflicts;** continuously **improving emotional intelligence** of everyone in the group; more distribution = **more resilience.**

Make explicit norms and boundaries

Challenge

Norms = **how we do things** around here. Boundaries = **what we don't do** around here. Many groups leave these things unsaid, relying on "common sense".

Conflicts grow when people have different unspoken assumptions (everyone has different 'common sense'). When you cross an invisible boundary, it takes huge energy to make the boundary explicit, before you can get to the behaviour.

Response

Talk about your norms: **how do we want to be together?** e.g. open, honest, authentic, gentle, inquisitive...

Talk about your boundaries: **what behaviour do we want to exclude?** e.g. no mean feedback, no sexist jokes.

Results

Buy-in — clarity helps people evaluate whether or not they want to be here. Expectations are clear. There is a process for challenging destructive behaviour, and a process for updating our agreements. E.g. see roles + responsibilities described in Enspiral's People Agreement: handbook.enspiral.com/agreements/people.html

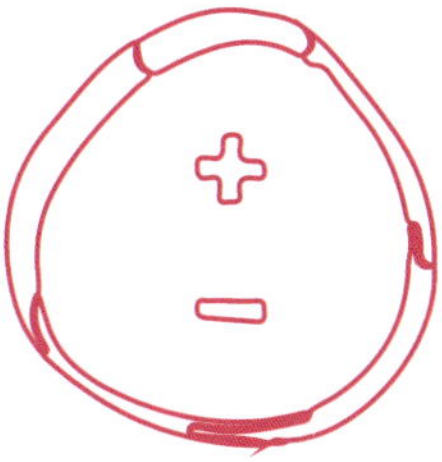

Keep talking about power

Challenge

Power, influence, status, rank, social capital, volume, access... whatever you call it, I've never met a group where it was equally distributed between all members. Equality is a compass point to navigate towards, not a destination I've ever arrived at.

Response

Groups thrive when anyone can safely talk about power differentials. Imbalance can be bad, e.g. inherited privilege, coercion, manipulation, the 'old boys club'. Some imbalance can be good: earned trust, reputation, eldership. Transparency reduces toxicity.

Discuss together: **"How's the power?** Who has it? How do you earn it?" Some roles attract power (e.g. manager, facilitator, spokesperson, coordinator, director).

Rotation increases access: take turns, step out, encourage others to step in. E.g. Loomio team coordinators are elected by the team for a limited term; we intentionally support less experienced people to try the role. See loomio.coop/coordination.html

Results

The best 'elders' use their status to praise, acknowledge, and encourage people with less.

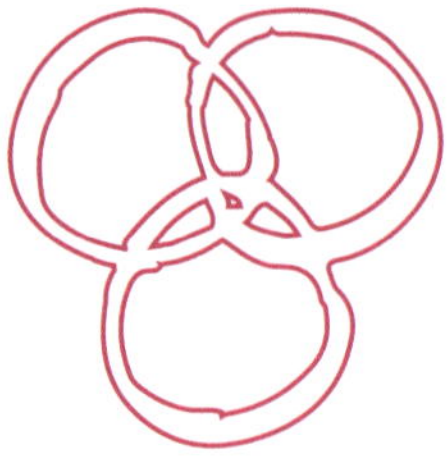

Agree how you're using your tech

Challenge

Many groups are dissatisfied with their communication technology. Information overload: too much data but can never find the thing you want. Half the team uses this tool, the other half uses another one.

Too many tools, don't know how to get everyone's attention, can never find the document I need.

Response

Agree together what tools are for what job. E.g. the 'trinity of digital comms':

- **1. Realtime,** like chat, messenger, or Slack. Informal, quick, organised around time: it's about right now.
- **2. Asynchronous**, like email, forum or Loomio. More formal, organised around topic. Has a subject + context + invitation. Can take days or weeks. Makes a useful archive, considered comments rather than random messy chatter.
- **3. Static**, like a wiki, Google Docs, handbook, or FAQ. Very formal, usually with an explicit process for updating content.

Results

Depending on your work, you will need different tools. The important thing is that you have an agreement together about what tools are for what job. With a shared understanding of the tools, they all fit together beautifully. When people have different ideas, it gets messy.

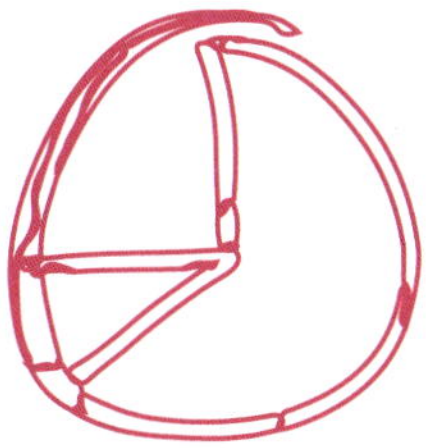

Make decisions asynchronously

Challenge

Most collaborative groups make decisions in meetings or conference calls. Meetings are a kind of **synchronised** or **realtime** communication: you have to synchronise people's calendars to find a time that works, then when they arrive, everyone has to pay attention to everything at the same time. It's very **expensive, excluding** the input of people who can't attend, and often results in **hurried** decisions.

Response

With a little effort, you can develop a habit of **asynchronous decision-making.** People can participate in their own time, contributing only to the issues relevant to them. This is what **Loomio** is for: more inclusion and collective intelligence, less time in meetings.

E.g. I'm on a Board of Directors. We meet monthly. We co-create the agenda in a Loomio thread ahead of time. A few days before the meeting, a Loomio poll confirms everyone is happy with the agenda and we've all read the reports. We all arrive at the meeting prepared and focused. We'll make some decisions face to face. For decisions that require input from more people, or more time to consider options, one of the directors will take the decision to Loomio. We also use the software to sign off the minutes, and find another meeting time.

Results

Over time you learn the unique qualities of realtime and asynchronous communication. Meetings are good for bonding, brainstorming, and dealing with complex or sensitive topics. Loomio creates more space for deliberation: you can take more time, consider more options, hear from more people, and keep a record.

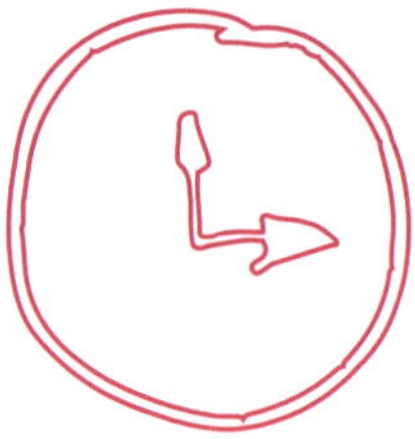

Use rhythm to balance flexibility and focus

Challenge

Hierarchies are designed to manage flows of communication and decision making. When you remove the hierarchy, you need to replace it with something. If there is no agreed structure, your group can suffer from information overload (everyone asked about everything all the time) and exclusion (decisions made without appropriate input).

Response

Rhythm helps balance speed with participation. People can trust each other to seek input at the right time, so they don't need to be involved in every decision. *For example:*

Here's a set of working rhythms we have used in the Loomio team. You can adapt to your context, e.g. maybe it makes sense to align with seasons or moon cycles:

- Daily 'standup' meeting. Everyone answers, "What did you do yesterday? What are you doing today? Are there any obstacles we can help you with?" Quick info exchange, accountability and support.
- Weekly 'sprints', a regular working period. E.g. on Monday we agree what work we're going to do this week. On Friday we share progress and have a 'retrospective' looking for improvements to try next week.
- Quarterly objectives. Every three months we have a planning day, looking for agreement on three or four measurable targets to align all of the work in the cooperative. After we finalise the decision on Loomio, everyone has freedom to do whatever work they feel is most relevant to achieve those outcomes.

- Bi-annual retreats. Every six months we go away together for three or four days. This deepens our relationships, and creates a space for the kind of conversations that can't happen in the office, e.g. dreaming together about our shared vision, or dealing with a complex tension.

Results

We create distinct communication spaces for different time frames, e.g. today's work is discussed **every morning;** if you want to discuss the long term strategic direction, we have a dedicated space for that **every three months.**

Generate new patterns together

Challenge

There is no such thing as an organisational structure that suits every team. Processes that worked for you last year are made obsolete by changing environmental conditions and team makeup. You need a reliable way to notice what's not working and make improvements without losing people along the way.

Response

Retrospectives turn frustrations into improvements. You can choose a frequency that suits you, but let's say weekly. At the end of each week, stop working. Have a **retrospective** meeting. Review the week just been. **What was good?** Notice it and do more. **What was bad?** Discuss. **Agree a change** that you're going to try next week to make it more good and less bad.

Results

Over time you learn the unique qualities of realtime and asynchronous communication. Meetings are good for bonding, brainstorming, and dealing with complex or sensitive topics. Loomio creates more space for deliberation: you can take more time, consider more options, hear from more people, and keep a record.

5 threads that weave strong community fabric

By Anthony Cabraal

Building a strong, participatory community can't be dictated by force, or decided by a few on behalf of many. It requires the collective weaving of hearts, minds and intent, like the creation of a vibrant fabric from many different threads.

Weaving this strong fabric requires the community to invest time to understand the work they need to do together. When it begins, everything might look a bunch of bright coloured, tangled threads, so before we even recognise the 'cloth' that's emerging we need to create shared understanding of the challenges for the group. When more people understand what the group needs to succeed, and where the skills are, more people can step into effective co-leadership, and the overall organisation strengthens and moves forward. This powerful group consciousness is what enables the weaving of collective identity, intent, and action.

This complex community fabric will be woven differently in every organisation, but we can simplify things by considering five fundamental threads that run through all. Consider these five threads open conversations with no permanent answers.

To weave community, the collective job is to recognise these threads and define the right answers for your unique group. They each need to be considered in their own way. The critical work is to have the conversations, identify where the group stands and build towards collective understanding, together. There are no universal truths define success in this work. All stakeholders: leaders, founders, participants, advisors, clients, and supporters will have different intent, needs, and ambitions. Surfacing and recognising dissonance, conflict, and difference of opinion is part of the job. Strong community fabric holds tension and weaves coherence, so everyone knows where they stand and how best to be in service, especially when there is disagreement.

Doing this work of weaving together is what brings the community alive; makes it fun, meaningful, and worthwhile. Participation in this journey is where the pattern of the community fabric emerges. The strength of this fabric will get you through hard times, attracting and engaging amazing people. The time invested together will create ongoing returns, well beyond the expectations and imagination of any one person.

Making Decisions

Deciding who decides and how this happens means addressing governance, power, control, and the limits of personal agency within the community. Making the decision-making processes explicit is critical to healthy participatory culture. It sets out the guidelines for how power and control will flow. Creating the decision making protocol is like writing the rules of the game.

You might worry that making your decision protocol explicit feels 'too formal'. But keep in mind that all groups, regardless of size, have a decision-making process - it's just a question of whether everyone is aware of and agrees with it. Creating formal decision-making rules doesn't need to be heavy or formally structured. If a lightweight process works best for your group, just agree to that proactively. It is still immensely beneficial to think it through together.

When starting out, it is difficult to know what kind of decisions are going to come up, and where the balance between bureaucracy and 'structurelessness' lies. As the community fabric grows, surfacing tensions and dealing with power dynamics requires vigilance and communication. The needs will change so expect this thread to evolve over time. Expect to find knots, unpick them, re-weave and re-weave until a strong, clear decision-making culture emerges.

Questions to consider

- Where might we learn about different decision-making protocols to find out what's right for us?
- How many people do we want engaged in the day-to-day running of the organisation?
- Do we want all our voices to be considered equally? Should some people's voices have more power than others? How do we choose this?
- Who do we want to hold the ultimate, emergency powers to veto decisions or make interventions? How do we want to govern the use of these controls?
- Where do we want to delegate decisions to people with specific skills and experience, and where do we want to ensure the collective intelligence of the group shines through?
- What formats and tools do we want to use to make formal decisions as a group?
- How much engagement in decisions is expected from everyone? What are people expected to contribute to decision making?

The Enspiral approach

Enspiral has a well developed decision agreement in the Handbook (find it here: https://handbook.enspiral.com/agreements/decisions.html).

We seek open, transparent decision-making, and strive to enable the people who are affected by a decision to participate fully. Anyone can propose a formal decision at any time.

This agreement has been improved slowly, over many years of community discussion. Hundreds of decisions have been made, including changing the decision-making process itself.

- We use Loomio (loomio.org) for formal discussion and decision-making.
- We use our Handbook (handbook.enspiral.com) to document our formal processes.
- We try to be clear about what kinds of decisions don't need to go through a formal process, and encourage people to take individual action whenever possible. Resources like the Teal wiki are helpful: http://www.reinventingorganizationswiki.com/Decision_Making

Building connections

Strong, mutually supportive peer relationships are critical to the health of any community fabric. Peer-to-peer connections are the first and last defence for keeping people healthy and aligned. These stitches that hold people together are often invisible or exist outside of formal community process. Without them the entire fabric can fray or fall apart.

Without clear structure, the value and benefits of strong connections can be spread unevenly in groups. Some people are able to attract the relationships and connections they need, or are naturally more independent, so they have less need for formal structure. Others feel an isolating vacuum without structure and suffer silently, falling into the gaps or feeling unable to voice their needs.

Taking time to recognise individual requirements in the group is important work. Everyone is cut from different cloth and one size will not fit all. Offering only what works for the majority will miss critical minority needs. A community should develop a diversity of tactics to support different people in different ways to feel connected and supported.

Questions to consider

- What levels of support do people in the community need to feel connected to each other?
- How much do we want to foster self-reliance and informal connection, and how much do we want to formally offer support services?
- How can we create support structures that build relationships across the community, to strengthen bonds as evenly as possible?
- How can we encourage people to grow the capacity and learn the skills they need to better support others?
- Are we understanding and meeting the diverse needs in our community?

The Enspiral approach

For some, Enspiral is a series of relationships more than anything else. We aspire to operate from a place of empathy, generosity, and deep care for each other. Over time we've tried many different approaches to support these relationships.

- Buddy systems (everyone gets connected to someone when they join).
- Informal support pods (small groups of people informally creating a check-in rhythm to support each other).
- Formal pods (small teams that have strong, formalised interdependent connections or co-own a company together).

Stewardship is our most developed collective method of relationship support. Everyone who joins the community has a steward, as at least one strong point of contact. Stewarding pairs decide the rhythms and dynamics of their own relationships together.

More information on our experiments and resources can be found in our handbook guides: https://handbook.enspiral.com/guides/stewarding.html

Allocating resources

Although money isn't the only important resource, because of its power in our society and psyches 'the money thread' has a special role to play and requires specific attention. Allocating resources and spending money are powerful dynamic in how a community operates. Deciding how precious, shared financial resources are spent defines key patterns. Should it be decided by just a few people? How can the group engage? How can everyone have some influence? How can people engage with resource allocation?

Building strong financial literacy in the community takes time and effort, but its impact is powerful. Developing the strength of this thread can help support other threads, especially decision-making and coordinating action.

Questions to consider

- How much money will be flowing through the system? Where is it coming from?
- Is financial transparency important to us, and how could we achieve it effectively? Do we want to be transparent only internally, or externally as well?
- How much resource should be invested in the community commons? How much should be held by individuals?
- Who is legally liable for compliance? How is their legal risk being managed? Is our legal structure conducive to how we want to function?
- How should we manage accounting and financial reporting? Does our record-keeping enable us to follow tax laws, or respond to due diligence requests?
- If we have financial surplus, how do we decide what to spend it on?
- Do we have processes to help us align our financial decision-making with our larger strategy and goals?

The Enspiral approach

Although this thread has evolved significantly as Enspiral grew from one company to a community of autonomous companies, the overall intent stayed constant - we stayed committed to working out how to distribute money, information and power.

Building strong financial literacy in the community is made possible by investing in:

- **Clear transparent financial reporting.** Details of all income and expenses of the Enspiral Foundation community entity are published and kept updated in our Handbook: https://handbook.enspiral.com/financial_transparency.html
- **Collaborative spending experiments.** We have built software (co-budget.co) to help us spend money together and we continue to test methods to facilitate group spending of shared resources. https://handbook.enspiral.com/collabfunding.html
- **Starting an interconnected ecology of companies.** When Enspiral evolved beyond one company, we distributed ownership throughout the community. Earning and allocating resources to the commons as individuals became the distributed process.

Gathering together

Gathering is where a community comes to life. Face to face, we take off our masks and see each other's vulnerability. We share our gifts and talents, sing, dance, play, and celebrate together. We remember that we are equal as humans on this journey together. It is where we build deep connection and really invest in our relationships.

Facilitation of gatherings is an art. Whatever the form that gathering takes, paying conscious attention to the design and facilitation of this time is critical. When we spend time together, we learn about each other, recognise each other, and amplify our potential to achieve together.

Questions to consider

- What kind of connection do we want to foster and grow in the community through gathering?
- How much time can we as a community invest in multi-day gatherings together?
- Who can design and lead a culture of gathering? Who can teach and share gathering practices? Where can we learn the art of gathering together?
- If we can't all get together in person, or cannot meet as much as we would like, how can we introduce aspects of this thread in other ways?

Even with technology and our globally connected modern society, we remain biological creatures who yearn to connect in person, breathing the same air, and sharing physical space.

The Enspiral approach

Enspiral grew under the guidance of several skilled social process designers and facilitators. Bi-annual, multi-day community retreats quickly became the heartbeat of our community. This rhythm built early momentum for the reflection, connection and aspiration we needed to commit and grow our livelihoods together.

There is no formal dogma or structure to our retreats. They normally include a healthy mix of productive working time, connection around new projects and opportunities, alignment and inspiration around vision and direction, time for quiet reflection, and space for wild celebrations that take on a life of their own!

Over the years we have borrowed heavily from many gathering traditions and methods including:

- Open Space Technology. This facilitated process allows groups to 'self organise' an emergent agenda, distributing leadership and control over 'the content of a gathering. Resources for running open space technology are widely avaliable online: https://en.wikipedia.org/wiki/Open_Space_Technology

- The Art of Hosting Conversations the Matter. The Art of Hosting is a series of tools, practices and methods designed to harness collective wisdom and the self-organising capacity of groups. Enspiral has used many dialogue practices, facilitation and the principles of co-creation to design and evolve our group experiences over the years. http://www.artofhosting.org/
- Sharing Circles. Sharing Circles are based on ancient practices to create sacred spaces for groups to reflect, witness and align. Well facilitated sharing circles are powerful experiences, where individuals are liberated and transformed. They become a wellspring for empathy, trust, and deep connection between people. https://en.wikipedia.org/wiki/Council_circle

Coordinating action

How a participatory community 'gets things done' raises questions of leadership, direction, accountability, commitment, and follow-through. This is where we address who does what, what needs to happen, how and who gets it done, and what is needed to support them to do it.

Healthy community fabric must ensure that critical functions are coordinated and actioned, ensuring space and openness for people to participate and lead their own work in the directions that call them.

The right balance encourages action without waiting for resources or heavy permission seeking. It lets people see (or create) opportunity and then lead the action that feels most important to them, learning and growing along the way.

The community needs to find the patterns that allow it to achieve and progress without stalling action, wasting resources, and wallowing in frustration. The knit of the fabric must be tight enough to hold together and loose enough to breathe. As the community grows, the right way to coordinate this action can change radically. Be prepared to unstitch threads and weave new designs.

Questions to consider

- What is the core work that needs to be done to keep the whole community healthy?
- What skills are needed to do that work?
- Who are the people ready and willing to do the work and what support do they need to do it?
- How open do we want the scope of action to be? How tightly do we want to control what can happen and what can't happen in the community?
- How can we sense and scan across the community to understand the most important work and brightest opportunities?
- How will we prioritise the work to do? How will we approve work to be done?
- When work is approved to be executed, how will we support the people to do the work and hold accountability for outcomes?

The Enspiral approach

"No one leads all of the time, everyone leads some of the time" is a principle Enspiral adopted very early on.

There are no 'mandated leaders' that do the work on behalf of everyone else. Leadership or leading pieces of work is open to everyone in the community to step into. Over time we have tested and evolved many structures to hold the leadership and execution of community work including:

Centralised support crew.

A few people with delegated authority and budget to execute specific tasks and held to account by the whole community. This worked well until we grew beyond 30 people. Eventually too much responsibility and control was centralised, which disabled wider participation, so the Support Crew was dissolved.

Catalysts.

The catalyst role is an ongoing experiment that evolves with the people who step into it. It has morphed through:

- a 'distributed executive' group,
- scanning, naming and coordinating tasks using public improvement boards (improvements.enspiral.com),
- facilitators holding spaces and creating connections that help others make sense of things, organise work and coordinate action.

Servant leadership, working in service of the collective rather than one's own opinions is the fundamental mindset. This allows the group to trust catalysts to bring their own perspectives and gifts to the role without mandating a specific actions.

Working groups.

Working groups hold defined areas of work in the community and take responsibility for coordinating and delivering specific functions or projects.

Pulling the threads together

Because the threads are woven together by many hands, strong patterns emerge in the fabric. The vision, leadership and overall direction of the community shows up in the fabric as the work is being done - it is not decided or delegated beforehand.

There will be confrontation and uncomfortableness in this process. When there isn't a black and white way to do things, being in-between, in the grey, is difficult for many people. Is it unhelpful controlling, dominating traits being triggered? Or is the group just being too messy?

Are the threads too loose?
Are people falling through the cracks?
Is the weave too tight?
Is it too stifling, with no room to breathe or try things?
How much messiness is too much?
How much shared risk can we tolerate?
Are some patterns OK even if some people don't agree?
Can we use clashing colours?
If no one is getting what they want, is everyone wasting their time?
Is the fabric holding us together?

Long term success for this work looks like 'leaderful' fabric, full of active participants who are capable and ready to lead all kinds of work in many directions. If people are truly engaged in the community their leadership will be expressed through their participation in the group. The result will be a unique, collective signature - it is the feeling, the vibe, the spirit, the pattern. This signature is what it feels like to be at a gathering, it is how uncomfortable moments in meetings get addressed, how challenges are solved and how people are supported in hard times.

What is your organisational fabric?

The only way is to find the edge of a thread and pull on it. Ask questions. See what it unravels, see where it snags. Keep following what works, start to recognise the key threads in your organisation and begin to notice the unconscious patterns woven anew into the fabric everyday.

Checking in

A simple process where a meeting or gathering starts with everyone having a chance to speak...

Without
- → interruption
- → judgement
- → constraint

Space
- → to be heard
- → to be safe
- → to actively listen

Where
- → connection happens
- → empathy forms
- → self awareness grows

It is a practice where everyone gets to see everyone else differently, and it changes how everything gets done.

Unfolding Purpose: A five-step journey

by Sandra Chemin and Sandra Otto

What are your big questions in life? What does Purpose mean to you? How are you making sense of Purpose for yourself and for the teams, organisations, and communities you belong to? What gives your life meaning?

This guide describes five steps extrapolated from multiple purpose journeys to help you to consciously experience and unfold your own journey to purpose.

Cycle: Purpose Unfolding Patterns

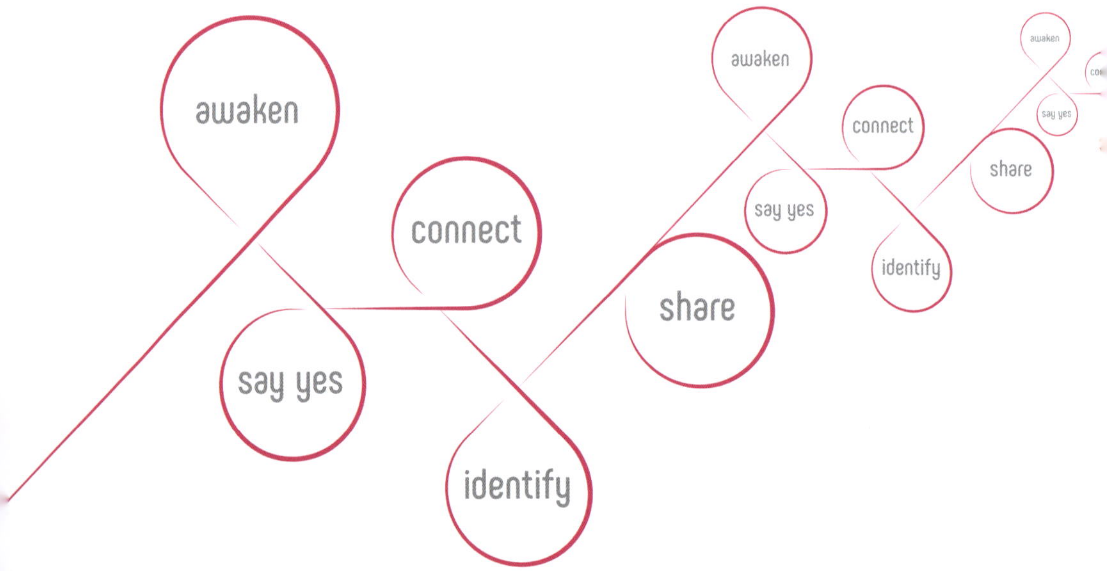

This frame has been structured to offer guidance for people on their personal search for purpose through:

- Questions that can guide reflection and sense-making.
- Experiments you can try.

A Purpose journey does not necessarily follow a logical linear sequence, but like other natural phenomena, it unfolds as a cyclical and iterating evolution. Some people might experience steps 1, 2 and 3 at the same time or go from one step back to an earlier stage.

The same patterns can also be relevant for teams and organisations, but with more complexity to consider. An example of this is illustrated in Essay 5: Saying yes to purpose.

1 Awaken / Asking new, bigger questions

Awakenings are the moments where we ask ourselves deeper questions of life. They arrive when we can sense life beyond ordinary pleasures and duties. Often the questions arise when we have a chance to find peace from everyday overload - on holidays, in new environments, or travelling. These moments may also be triggered by a significant experience or crisis. They might arise and then go dormant again, until one day we really step out to find an answer. An awakening cannot be forced, it emerges and can be consciously recognised and supported by reflection.

Questions

Am I ready and committed to change my life?
Am I ready to let go of the past?
Am I ready to potentially let go of a certain lifestyle and financial security in order to pursue my purpose?
Am I ready to tell everyone that I am changing my life?
Am I ready to say YES?

Experiments

Take yourself somewhere new, or out of the ordinary compared to your normal routines. Gift yourself some quality time to reflect and write in a journal:

What are the big questions I am asking myself?

How fulfilled do I feel with my life?

What is alive in me right now?

Is something coming to an end?

2 Say Yes / Conscious decision and commitment

Once we start asking the big questions, the moment comes when we commit to a new purposeful way of living. We have an opportunity to choose *life by design rather than life by default.* This takes courage as it can have profound consequences on our decisions so far. It might throw us into a state of uncertainty when we do not yet know what exactly we are going to pursue and we are scared of letting go of the old ways.

At this stage, you might not be aware of your purpose, but you are probably getting more clarity about your passions: what makes you smile, the things that make you lose track of time. You need to trust the path of passion until the purpose becomes clear.

Questions

Am I ready and committed to change my life?
Am I ready to let go of the past?
Am I ready to potentially let go of a certain lifestyle and financial security in order to pursue my purpose?
Am I ready to tell everyone that I am changing my life?
Am I ready to say YES?

Experiments

Intention setting for life by design rather than life by default:

- Seek advice from someone that has already taken a similar path - choose a mentor.
- Create a vision board: a collection of images that represent what you want to manifest in your life. The difference from a written plan is that a vision board can represent what you want to feel - not just the practical things you would like to manifest in your life.
- Create space in your life for purpose to unfold. It could be reducing the hours you spend at your day job, studying something new, or participating in community projects in your areas of passion.

3 Connect / Connecting with others

More and more people are transitioning to new ways of working, living and being where they follow a higher calling. Connecting with others is one of the main mechanisms of support and learning as the unknown emerges. Connecting with like-minded people helps to hold the uncertainty so you can feel supported in your exploration into new territory.

Questions

Are my experiences normal?
How have you experienced this journey?
What were your experiences?
How can I stay on track?
When you witness me, does it sound authentic?
Does it resonate?
How can we support each other?

Experiments

- Find others who have made a transition to a new lifestyle or new ways of working and invite them for a coffee. Have an honest conversation about their journey:

  What was the life event that precipitated that decision? How did you plan this move? How long did it take? What resources did you bring with you and which resources did you discover, that you didn't know you would need?

- Join a group of like-minded individuals. Think about your interests and passions and find a group of people who may have walked along this path before.

4 Identify / Naming your purpose

Naming your purpose in life can be daunting. You might think it is like waking up one morning to discover the ONE thing you were meant to be in life. It doesn't need to be like that. As we change, what is meaningful for us can change as well. What if instead of searching for the big answer you just focus on what moves you now?

Looking backwards at your life can help you identify what brought you joy and satisfaction. From here, you can better understand your authentic interests and passions, and possibly the next meaningful calling that is emerging.

Questions

What were my favourite activities in the past? What about now?
What brings me joy and fulfilment? Where do my energy and my willingness naturally flow to?
What are the things I do or am so passionate about that I don't notice time passing?
What is the ONE thing that I can't even stop myself from doing?
What are my natural talents, what is my superpower?
What do others say about my talents and superpowers?
What would I get up for at 5 am on a Sunday?

Experiments

Create quality time for yourself and use a journal to answer the questions. Consider your responses.

- Are there common elements in the answers, can you identify patterns?
- Do they reveal something about the things that you find fulfilling?
- Can you identify any internal resistance?
- How could you overcome these to name a purpose that you could bring to life?

5 Share / Making it visible

Making our purpose visible increases the understanding of why we do what we do, bringing our community onto the same page. The more clarity about our purpose, the more conscious we get. As our awareness increases, and we begin to communicate our purpose, we begin to attract others that resonate with it. This is when the work begins to grow.

Questions

How can we share our purpose with others?
Who do we want to tell about our purpose?
Who would be interested in our purpose and why?
What are good ways of engaging others with our purpose?

Experiments

Print a poster and put it on your wall to help you focus on what really matters, reminding you why you are doing this work. Include these words publicly on your website or social media channels.

Invite others for a conversation about the impact your work had in their lives.

- Take a moment to reflect on what you heard from them. Does it resonate with your original purpose? What could be improved to make it alive?
- With their consent, share their reflections on your work and purpose to create more visibility.

We hope this guide contributes to your journey. If you made it to this point and have clarity about what moves you, celebrate!

You have taken a clear and concrete step toward a better future. Keep in mind that life will keep changing and it is good to check from time to time if this purpose still resonates with you, or if the future calls you towards slightly different paths.

To continue this conversation and find other ways of developing your purpose journey go to www.futureyou.be

Sharing power, money, and information

by Alanna Irving

Sharing power, money, and information has been a theme of Enspiral since day one, but what does that actually mean in practice? As a network, we figured it out for ourselves, and then out of what we learned, created tools that could transmit this cultural technology to others. There are as many ways to tell the larger Enspiral story as there are people in it. I can only speak to how my own work contributed to that bigger story - building open source tools to enable highly collaborative, transparent social processes, facilitated by technology.

Making decisions together

As Enspiral became larger and more geographically distributed, inclusive decision-making became more challenging. We wanted to distribute power, but power doesn't just disappear because no one has the job title of 'boss'. It accrues like water runs downhill, following paths of least resistance and ruts of habit. It takes time and effort to know what decisions are being made, and to provide the context needed to participate. If including more people in decisions is too hard, power will centralise. I was acutely aware of this, as a person often trying to understand and act in accordance with the collective will of the network.

As I was grappling with these issues at Enspiral, only a few blocks away Occupy was camped out on the lawn of Wellington City Hall. Fate was about to bring us together. A couple of Occupy organisers came to see me at Enspiral, looking to talk to people who were good with technology. They described the challenges of consensus decision-making in general assemblies: meetings were getting longer and longer, people who didn't have a lot of time or lived far away were being left out, and it was very hard to hear all voices.

Everything they were saying sounded familiar. These activists had the same problem with decision-making that we had as a business network. I knew that if we could develop a solution that worked for both communities, we'd really have something. They asked me if Enspiral could develop a software tool for collaborative decision-making online. I told them I couldn't do it for them, but I could do it with them. After supporting many others in the network with their startups, I was being called to found a startup of my own. Enspiral provided a desk in the office, those Occupy activists became my co-founders, and we got to work.

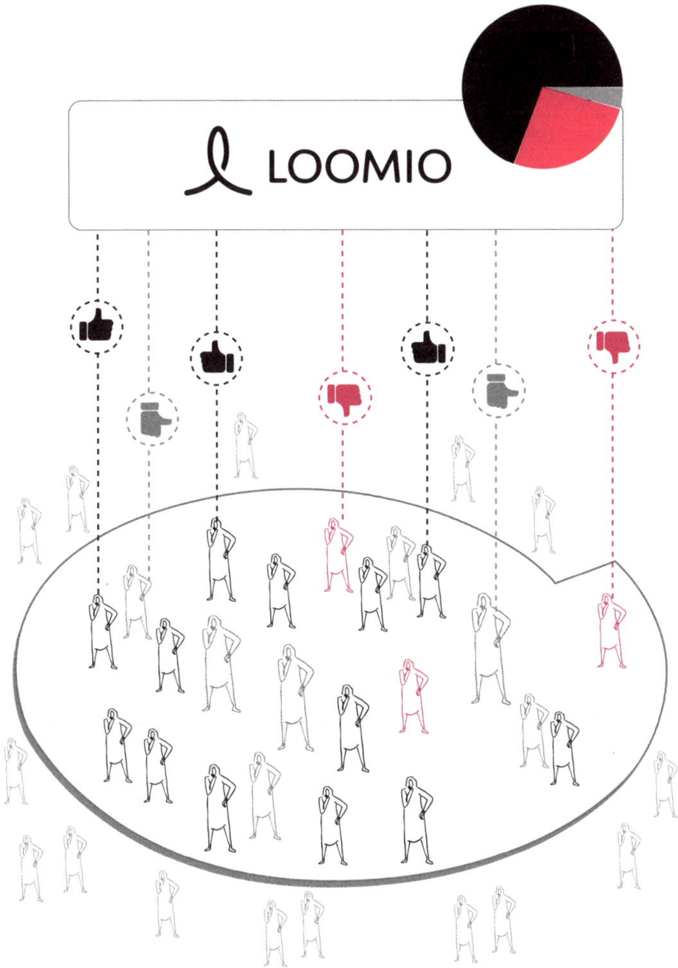

Collaborative Decision-Making

Diverse perspectives come together to make decisions online, enabling shared understanding and collective action

Together, we built a software tool called Loomio. No complex functionality magically makes collaboration happen; it's deceptively simple. You create a group and bring in your collaborators. Anyone can start a discussion with a clear topic and context. As potential solutions arise, you can make a proposal. Everyone can state their positions and explain their reasoning.

As this process plays out, a visual summary of where the group stands on the issue emerges. It's clear if some people disagree, and the whole group is motivated to swarm and address their concerns. It's not about your solution versus mine; it's about coming together and synthesising something even better. Unlike a typical voting or polling app, Loomio is not a conflict-based, majority-rules system. People are encouraged to change their minds as they hear from one another. By the end of the process, everyone has shared understanding and is ready to take collective action.

The first decision made on Loomio was agreeing the language of the Enspiral Services employment contracts. The very concept of workers crafting their own employment contracts and agreeing them by consensus online was the essence of Enspiral in action. Loomio allowed us to significantly scale up participation and transparency at Enspiral. It didn't matter where someone was located or whether they could make the meeting time. People participated in the decisions they cared about, and let others decide the rest. Loomio automatically generated an archive of decisions, so new people could see what had been decided previously, and why.

Soon, others started to use Loomio in their own groups, like businesses, government agencies, community groups, schools, and political movements. Loomio spun off into an independent worker-owned cooperative to forge its own path as an Enspiral venture. Although enabled by technology, the true impact Loomio had on Enspiral was cultural. In order to effectively contribute to a decision, people needed context. This meant more transparency, reporting, and effective information flows. We developed a practice of working in the open and giving and receiving constructive feedback. That's not to say the online space superseded the offline space. Conversely, by moving some discussions online, precious face-to-face time could be freed up. As we used Loomio more effectively, network retreats became less about working intensively and more about decompressing, having fun together, and deepening relationships.

Take it apart and put it back together again

Loomio allowed us to transform roles and powers held by a person into distributed processes everyone could engage with. I began to see a lot of our work at Enspiral as deconstructing core organisational concepts and reconstructing them for a collaborative paradigm. As a bunch of anarchists, activists, hackers, and disruptors, we saw the inefficiencies and negative impacts of legacy patterns, and we wanted to do things differently.

The saying goes, "Don't ever take a fence down until you know the reason why it was put up." Our motto was more like: "Rip down the fence, get lost in a muddy field, question the underlying morality of fences, try and fail to build a car out of fencing materials, hold hands to make a human fence, then, while having a picnic, enthusiastically reinvent the concept of fences under a new name and resolve to build a better one where the original fence was." Sometimes this was a waste of time. But sometimes we built a much improved fence 2.0, or proved we really didn't need a fence there at all, or replaced the fence with a waterslide that was much faster and more fun. Through this process, we went back to first principles and thought about what we were really trying to achieve, instead of unquestioningly using off-the-shelf solutions.

Some of the best learning opportunities of my career have come from tearing down 'fences' like governance, employment, company structures, and investment models. I talked to lawyers and HR professionals, and delved into employment regulations, to figure out how to align the experimental ways we wanted to work with the law. Through exploring alternative funding models, I came to understand how risk, control, and ownership actually function. I figured out why tax regulations are the way they are by asking our accountant a lot of crazy sounding questions. I discovered why it's important to separate governance and executive functions, and what each really means. I gained an appreciation for how the form of the corporation has evolved over time, and what makes it powerful.

Along the way, we invented some genuinely new ways of working, and built tools to facilitate them. The most exciting were when we took something normally centralised and transformed it into a distributed, transparent, participatory process. Many times, we took the long way around right back to the standard way of doing things. But by doing so, we gained a level of understanding that only comes from taking something apart and putting it back together again to see how it works.

Sharing money

As Enspiral grew beyond 100 people, there were still only a few of us who interacted with the bank account and budget directly. This had worked for a while thanks to high trust, and because busy entrepreneurs are generally happy not to have to delve into balance sheets and profit and loss statements. At this stage, posing financial decisions to the network as a whole usually resulted in responses like, "Uh, sure, sounds good.... Wait, how much money do we have, anyway?"

Our collective money came from all of us, and belonged to all of us, as did the responsibility to spend it well. We needed an accessible way to engage with the larger strategic and financial context. We were inspired by a community we read about that hosted an event where participants were given play money to put in buckets corresponding to the projects they wanted fund. Out of all those individual decisions, a collective budget emerged. Getting 100+ people together every time we needed to make financial decisions wasn't feasible. But I thought we could run a digital version of the process using a shared spreadsheet. I called it Collaborative Funding.

Down the first column of the spreadsheet, I listed all the contributions to collective funds that month. Then I listed the fixed overhead costs (previously agreed on Loomio) and subtracted that amount, leaving the discretionary budget. Across the top row, I listed buckets, i.e. funding requests, which anyone in the community could make. Each person or company allocated funds in proportion to what they had contributed financially, either into buckets or into savings. Everyone, even those without money to spend, was invited to observe and ask questions. Despite being a spreadsheet, the collaborative funding process was actually pretty fun. It was gamified and engaging. People could directly see and influence the impact of the funds they contributed, and those with more money than time could fund those with more time than money to get important work done. Crucially, collaborative funding helped us consider budget priorities cohesively. It made it clear that saying yes to one thing meant saying no to something else.

This was the beginning of collective strategy setting at Enspiral. We began to do more experiments with strategic thinking, trying various combinations of surveys, online discussions, in-person workshops, and working groups. Once a year for several years, we all (300+ people at times) agreed a few strategic pillars for the network as a whole, and made collaborative funding decisions with them in mind. While we never fully perfected this process, we sparked many rich conversations. The combination of co-created strategy and collaborative funding led to a mindset of cooperation over competition. People would willingly set aside their pet projects to fund the most important work overall. If we decided to take a financial risk and it didn't pan out, we all owned the outcome together, instead of blaming. Replacing centralisation with a participatory process breaks down the 'us and them' dynamic, inviting people to step into collective responsibility.

Real transparency isn't just about making the information available; it's about accessible information that people can engage with meaningfully.

Being able to understand the budget was a major boost to trust and empowerment. People could get their heads around the numbers, and thought in terms of how they could support collective goals with their individual choices. Bucket proposers didn't have to convince everyone of their idea, only enough people to get it funded. Collaborative Funding is an example of emergent decision-making, where lots of individual choices add up to the collective will, in contrast to Loomio's convergent decision-making, where a common outcome is negotiated among participants. We started developing a sense for which type of decision-making to deploy in different contexts.

After several years and many incremental improvements, we decided to build a piece of software based on the collaborative funding process, called Cobudget. A purpose-built app made the whole process simpler, more visual, and more conducive to feedback and accountability. It also made it possible for other groups to try collaborative funding for themselves.

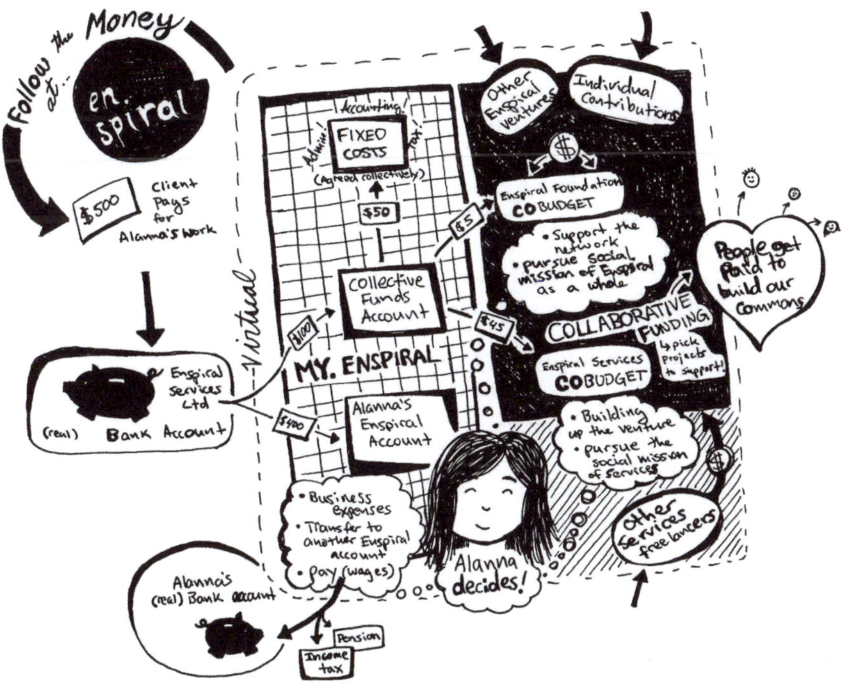

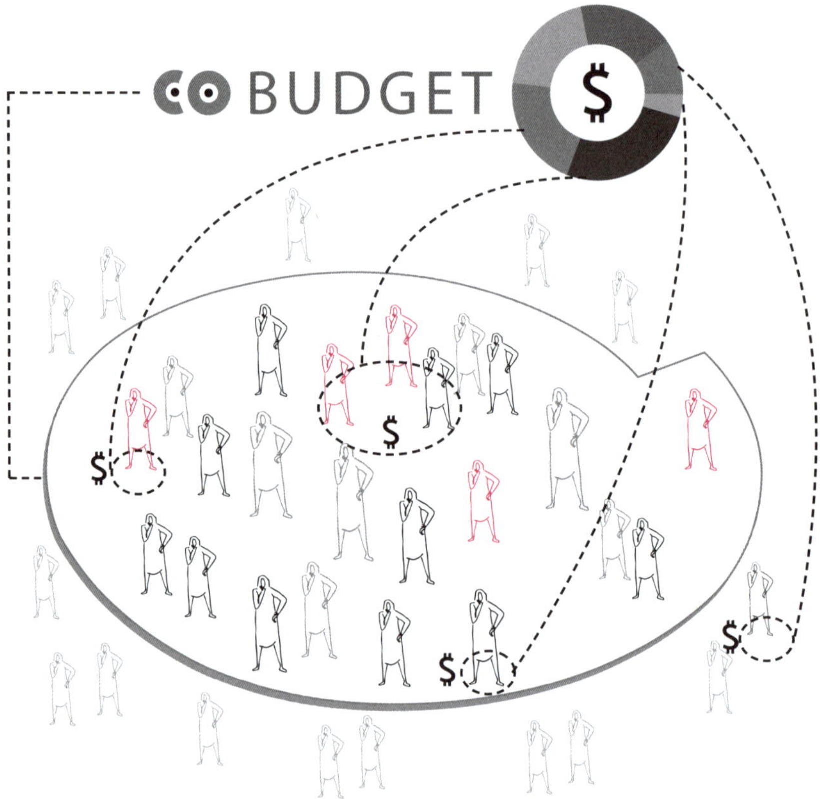

Collaborative Funding
Projects to support the network and its vision are funded using a transparent participatory budgeting process

Living documentation

The Cobudget app allowed us to share the collaborative funding process beyond Enspiral, as Loomio had done for decision-making. I began to see a pattern emerging in our work: deconstruct and reconstruct an organisational process, prototype and improve it internally, and then transmit it to others through a useful tool.

Software is one form that transmissible cultural technology can take, but there are many others, such as documentation. Like a budget spreadsheet, documentation sounds incredibly boring. But also like a budget, it holds a lot of inherent power. For years, we had very little documentation at Enspiral. There was a one-pager we'd send to new people with practical stuff about the office and a list of software they'd need logins for. The only written policy we had for a long time was the Diversity Policy. Our website was ironically unimpressive for a company who made websites.

Strangely enough, this was mostly intentional. Many more people were interested in joining than we were ready for in the early years. We needed strong natural filters, so that only those who were really aligned and committed would find their way in. For a long time, I answered the question, "What is Enspiral?" with "We're not sure. Come join us and we'll find out together." Enspiral was in constant flux. In a bossless, non-coercive environment, policy is about discovering how people are doing things, not dictating. If reality gets out of phase with documentation, the documentation is rendered useless, and people will simply move on. Trying to pin things down too soon can choke emerging evolution, and leads to a bunch of reports no one reads.

It's also disingenuous, or even dangerous, to spread cultural technology before you've lived with it enough to understand its true impact.

It's possible to wait too long, hoarding stories that could be of service to others and denying yourself data for internal reflection. Timing is key. A few years in, the time for documentation arrived. You can feel it when it comes. Your heart beats faster when it's your turn to speak. You keep getting annoyed that people don't know what everyone should know. The outline of the yet-unwritten document crystallizes in your mind. You mentally prepare answers to questions you know you'll be asked. That's when it's time to write things down.

It started slowly, with internal documents to set the context for Loomio decisions, and some updates to the website. I wrote six-monthly reports on collaborative funding, showing how we'd spent money and what the outcomes were, and worked on an in-depth timeline of the history of Loomio. Creatives in the network made videos and infographics attempting to explain what we were to the outside world (and our parents). We began saying yes to some media interviews.

I wrote up our experiences developing Loomio and Cobudget for a contest seeking new approaches to management, and won, which meant I was invited to give a talk at a conference in New York. This snowballed into a steady flow of speaking invitations for myself and others in the network, and some of these talks turned into videos we could share online. Getting people to write blog posts had long been an uphill battle, because it was too hard to come up with 'the Enspiral story'. But once we funded a Cobudget bucket for the "Fairy Blog Mother" to support people to write their own stories, called Enspiral Tales, our collective story began to emerge through many voices.

I started the Loomio Co-op Handbook and the whole team contributed to detailing our internal processes and practices. Surprisingly, it went viral online (among a certain kind of cooperative organisational development geek). I gave a talk about it at an open source conference, where I repeated a refrain that had been sounding in my head since I first heard it:

"If it's not documented, it's not open source."

Being a transparent organisation without great documentation is like saying the finances are transparent because, technically, you'd share the financial reports if anyone asked. If it's not accessible and usable, it's not really transparent. I wanted Enspiral to live up to its ideal of transparency more authentically. With this in mind, I began writing down some Enspiral policies that were embedded in our culture. Some were explicit decisions from the Loomio archives, while others were implicit practices. For example, what exactly it meant to be a member or a contributor, how the finances worked, and how we made collective decisions. For a while, these documents just floated around our shared drive as unofficial guidelines.

The power of documentation only became fully clear to me during the Enspiral Refactor of 2015. Refactoring software is when programmers go back and clean up code, taking care of 'technical debt', accrued by moving quickly and not knowing exactly how things should work at first. The Enspiral Refactor was a major project to clean up our 'organisational debt' in a similar way. I created the Enspiral Handbook to pull various documents together in one place. At first, I thought it was just an admin task, to make things easier to find. But I discovered that what I was doing was actually a type of documentation-driven leadership. Once I created the structure of the handbook, I could finally see what all the headings should be, whether we already had content to go under them or not. Blank spaces represented questions to be answered. The handbook could be edited by everyone at Enspiral, like a wiki, and was visible publicly. We ran a process of seeking affirmation on Loomio for various policies and agreements, and the pages started to fill out.

Reflecting on it now, I see the handbook as perhaps my most important intervention to distribute information and power at Enspiral. Unwritten rules cannot be challenged, and unexplored areas are hard to identify without a map. Far from writing things in stone, documentation created a point around which people could gather to constructively discuss changes. For all of that to work, documentation has to be alive, to serve as a resource to its users and be co-created by them on an ongoing basis.

Practitioners beyond Enspiral who are really getting down to the brass tacks of collaboration in their own communities have told me that the Loomio and Enspiral handbooks have been important resources for them. Because every community is unique, when I hear this I wonder if perhaps we've hit on some deeper truths, and that makes the challenges we went through to learn those lessons seem worthwhile. The work of sharing power, money, and information doesn't end, because communities are living, dynamic systems. It is the constant process of understanding and meeting emergent challenges that binds a community together. There is no endpoint or final answer, only ever-deepening relationships, ever-braver experiments, and ever-broadening possibilities.

#ChangingTheFuture

with
profit,

not for
profit.

#

Coffee, beer, and pizza

A stable community financial model where everyone gets to choose and no one is in charge.

by Anthony Cabraal

The Enspiral community financial model didn't emerge fully formed - it has evolved over many years. Enspiral is not what it was three years ago, five years ago, or even six months ago, when this book project began. Who knows how different it will be by the time you read these words!

So, how does the Enspiral financial model actually work!?

Over the years we've experimented with many financial models. We have moved from the original 20% revenue contribution when Enspiral was a freelancers' collective, to revenue shares from ventures, to self-set annual individual contributions. There were times when we tried to maximise the resources going toward the collective and times we tried to minimise them. Each experiment taught us a lot, each solution was right at its own time, and the learnings always folded forward into the next evolution.

For many years Enspiral grew without reliable funding for people working to support the critical core functions of the community. No matter how hard we tried, it was easier for a few passionate, creative people to just to get on with it, than it was for everyone to work together to recognise, label, and understand what they were doing With people continuing to stretch themselves to cover 'the invisible work in the middle' we were not recognising the costs of supporting ourselves.

In 2017 we reached a critical juncture that began a process of changing the core financial model that held the community together. This is the story of that iteration. In some ways, this evolutionary step for the community is nothing special - it's just another iteration in a long line of experiments, executed by hundreds of people over many years. In other ways, it was a huge leap. We changed the core financial model for the whole community. We moved from relying on the love and adrenaline of a few passionate, talented people volunteering their time, to a model where our critical core functions are recognised, costed, and financially supported. The model we chose was the right model for us. As for many start-up projects around the world, in the end, the critical ingredients were coffee, beer, and pizza...

6 collective steps towards a stable community model

This is a reflection of how Enspiral found a financial model that worked for us, and the questions we answered along the way. Consider these steps as signposts for any group embarking on a similar adventure.

1	2	3
Defining the work and how to do it.	**Aligning a shared view.**	**Defining the core functions together.**
4	5	6
Deciding the core costs together.	**Building a shared story.**	**Giving people the best opportunity to choose.**

1) Define the work and how to do it

Collective work doesn't 'just happen' and people don't just 'self-organise' to solve problems. The work needs boundaries and clarity before anything useful can happen. It begins with broad core questions to diagnose starting points:

- What's the problem?
- Why is it a problem?
- What is the opportunity we have to fix it?
- How many people need to contribute their thinking?
- How fast does the project need to move to be successful?
- How do we work inclusively with divergent opinions?
- Who is going to do the work and what power do they have?
- How many people need to agree with the formal decision for us to all feel OK to move forward?
- What happens when people completely disagree about what to do?

There is no one model or right answer to any of these questions. Every community has different needs and ambitions that they have to navigate. When considering inclusive, participatory processes, acknowledge these trade-offs:

- Sitting down with a few people in a small room and creating a model on paper is relatively easy. However, relying on input from only a few people means a model may not get buy-in and may result in the community disengaging.
- Trying to involve too many people at every step can stall the work, resulting in consensus paralysis, increased frustration and stifled motivation.

The elusive 'Goldilocks zone' is a process that reflects a culture of inclusivity, and values the initiative and time of people executing the work. Regardless of the outcome, openly confronting these questions is critical because it is here that the issues of power, governance, control and mandate to execute come to the surface.

Reflections from Enspiral

After several years of evolving ideas about what Enspiral was, how it was structured, what it did, what it didn't do, who did what, and how much it all cost, keeping everyone on the same page became almost impossible. As a result of this we did not have shared clarity across the community. Only a few people really understood what our core costs were, what we were collectively paying for and what we were supporting with volunteer energy.

Enspiral was a startup community being bootstrapped by entrepreneurs building startup ventures - fortunes were changing all the time. Ventures and contracts were up and down, and as a result our community revenue was not reliable. In March 2017 this dynamic surfaced three critical challenges:

1. The legal business entity (Enspiral Foundation) in the centre of the community was losing money every week and would have been bankrupt within months without an intervention.
2. The current board members (legally responsible for Enspiral Foundation) had provided years of service, were tired and wanted to step down.

3. A few critical community members had moved on to other work outside the community and others wanted to step back - leaving a vacuum to fill.

We were lucky to have a strong engaged group of members who were ready and willing to step into this work - the luck was no accident either. It took years of work to build the distributed leadership in the community where an intervention like this was possible at all.

Following a significant piece of work to 'refactor' the community in 2015/16 we also had a clear decision making process in place (find it at handbook.enspiral.com). The community membership used this process and made a collective decision to mandate a small group of volunteers to lead a piece of work to 'balance the books'.

So, at this stage we had the fundamentals of a "self-organised" immune response to a threat:

- We had a clear challenge with known parameters.
- We had a small group of people - a 'working group' - with a mandate to operate on behalf of the community.

We were ready to start.

2) Aligning a shared view

A distributed organisation will not have one shared mental model of what the community looks like or how it works. There will be a mixture of tight coherence, dissent, and alternative thinking on everything, from defining what the community does to what the most important and urgent problems are. This vibrancy is important, but it sets up a big challenge.

When everyone holds a different view of the community (It's like a forest! It's like a computer system! It's like a campfire! It's an elephant! It's a really complicated! It's really simple!), deciding what is central to its existence can be a challenge.

Regardless of the starting point, taking the first step towards a stable core model requires wide consultation with the community in a variety of ways. The goal is to understand what people currently understand and expect from the community, as well as what they think the critical challenges are.

Reflections from Enspiral

The first step of the working group was to consult widely, gain an understanding of the different mental models in the community and surface a model we could all agree on as a starting point. The working group formed a picture of the entire Enspiral system so people could easily understand their place within the system and how they related to the critical core: the Enspiral Foundation. (See the chapter 'Blueprints' for the example of this).

We shared this view with the community to ensure people could ask questions and raise concerns before we continued.

So, at this stage:

- We had a clear challenge.
- We had 'enough' of a mental model of the different puzzle pieces in the community.
- We had 'enough' understanding of how most people understood the financial model and where the big gaps were.

What did we do next?

3) Defining the core functions together

This is a critical step that has important implications. Any community requires huge amounts of work, effort, skill, and attention given to different functions that are all valued differently by different people. How do you collectively decide what work lies within the 'critical core' and what is outside it?

- One person's description of what the core does might be a long list of important functions that hold the community together and desperately need funding.
- Another person might believe that the core doesn't need to do anything at all, so no funding is needed.

A key concept in this discussion is centralisation. How much should the core be given a mandate to do in relation to what the community allows to emerge organically?

Reflections from Enspiral

As a general cultural principle, Enspiral has always tried to be as open to participation and collaboration as possible. We have always designed our structure and processes around maximising individual autonomy over centralised control. As a result people are always doing experiments, testing patterns for organising and working on projects they believe in without needing permission. Centrally coordinating all the things that happen at Enspiral would be very expensive, and perhaps impossible, given our culture of open participation and autonomy.

Our challenge was to work out the minimal set of core functions Enspiral Foundation should be responsible for in order to support our decentralised, participatory environment. Through wide community engagement and surveying, the working group surfaced a broad view of the current 'common' work being done and its benefits to the collective. With this data and some further discussion, the working group began to distinguish between core enabling functions, and everything else.

It was proposed that these core enabling functions include:

- Fiduciary management of financial contributions to the community
- Maintaining onboarding and offboarding processes for people joining and leaving
- Legal compliance, reporting, and records maintenance of the Enspiral Foundation
- Administrating software systems for core communication tools

These (also important) functions were excluded, amongst others:

- Newsletters
- Leadership coordination and reporting on work in progress across the community
- Organising gatherings and retreats
- Managing peer support processes

- Managing our participatory budgeting and spending process
- The list goes on...

The focus was to ensure that the absolutely critical operational functions could be covered with paid hours, so everyone could trust these operations to continue. From this stable base, it would become the responsibility of the community to self-organise and pick up whatever other pieces of work they felt were important or needed. It was decided our financial model would cover the absolute baseline but our community would continue to rely on active participation and collaboration to thrive.

We had enough shared clarity to move forwards.

4) Deciding the core costs together

The rubber hits the road when you start to define the costs. When abstract discussions about what is valuable and critical turn into numbers on a spreadsheet, everything starts to feel different: objections get raised, trade-offs become visible, and real progress starts to be made.

Not all work is valued the same.

An easy-to-read financial budget and discussion where people are actively encouraged to raise concerns and questions are also vital at this stage. Time spent making clear spreadsheets with detailed breakdowns is time well spent.

Reflections from Enspiral

Enspiral was lucky. We had a dedicated, skilled operations team with high community context.

This made it relatively simple for us to gain a view (with granular detail) of how much time (and therefore cost) would go into supporting our core functions. The result was a clear cost model that could be developed on spreadsheet and shared with the community. You can see the full model spreadsheet linked from handbook.enspiral.com

We facilitated a two-step online proposal process using Loomio - first asking advice, then seeking agreement. As a result of this process we gained approval on a spreadsheet as a 'single source of truth' of our core costs, and how we would aim to cover them. This ensured the community had time and space to raise objectives, ask questions and point out holes in the model, before agreeing together.

So, now we had:

- General agreement about the shape and structure of the community
- General agreement about what the core functions were
- A spreadsheet outlining costs

We were ready to move ahead.

5) Building a shared story

In a normal business with a linear value proposition, customers pay X and get Y. The business can then work out how much it needs to sell at what price to cover its costs. In a decentralised community, people receive and contribute value in totally different ways, and no one is in the middle ensuring they are all happy and their needs met. This is a critical function in ensuring an environment of indirect reciprocity, where people understand the need to be active participants, creating value for themselves and others in the community. How can a community ensure enough value is generated for enough people to retain its identity and ensure the core is funded?

The most powerful tool is a story: a collective story of value in the community.

Because communities generate different value for each person, those in the centre, who are most convinced of the value (founders, leaders, highly invested people) often do not see the whole story and need help to articulate it. It is critical to build a story that represents the diversity of value exchange in the community, including for people right at the edges. This story needs to be aspirational and something people can take pride in. People have to see themselves in the story and feel part of co-creating it. Investing in quality design, video and art to create beautiful artifacts is resource well spent.

Reflections from Enspiral

For some people, Enspiral is their core livelihood vehicle, their social group, and a huge part of their personal and professional identity. For others, it might be a group of friends they interact with occasionally, an office they visit for Friday drinks, or an event they like to go to once or twice a year. Our challenge was to clarify a value story we could all feel good enough about to opt in to together, and ensure that the baseline costs (outlined in Step 3) were met.

The working group started a rough draft of a story using a slide deck and consulted the community. Our goal was to surface enough of a shared story that enough people could agree to. The words changed, the narrative was questioned, the order of sentences moved around, the overall structure dismantled and rebuilt. However, the important hook in our story was clear: Different for everyone, defined by you.

Enspiral was not going to tell you what made it worth joining. The value you recieved was up to you. Critically, there is no central command group to complain to if you aren't getting the value you thought you would. This is not a customer-vendor relationship, it's a community where the work of generating value is in the hands of everyone.

The working group engaged creative professionals in the community to turn the story into a video and slide deck that framed the mission of the community, gave some examples of how people have interacted with it, and listed shared tools and different ways people could participate. The work to surface the collective story was invaluable in creating cohesion and connecting people at the edges who were still trying to understand what Enspiral is and how it works. As in previous steps, the process was more important than the outcome.

At this point in the process we had:

- General agreement about the shape and structure of the community
- General agreement about what the core functions were
- A spreadsheet outlining costs
- A story we could all say yes to

It was time to put the model to the test.

6) Give people the best opportunity to choose

This final step is about trusting people to make their own decisions. The work is to make one clear, strong signal so it is as easy as possible for people to understand their options (and hopefully say yes). In a decentralised community, total engagement is a rare occurrence. The attention economy is tough. People are busy and will engage in the process in different ways. This is challenging because the people doing the work have the highest context and are the most likely to misjudge how engaged others, are and what they do and do not understand. Designing for the lower end of engagement means carefully thinking through the minimum information required from the entire process to bring people quickly up to speed. The work is less about leadership and facilitation and more about good user experience design so people can easily access the information they need to decide and act.

Reflections from Enspiral

Enspiral is a busy community of working professionals. Everyone is out there in the world building companies, raising families, and delivering projects, so it takes real effort to turn inwards and reflect. Dancing between group engagement and pushing forward with whomever has the most energy is always a balance. It is a mixture of art and science, emotional intelligence, facilitation, and guesswork.

After nearly six months of working through this process, some people were completely up to speed and ready to act and some had not engaged at all. The final step was to give everyone the information they needed to quickly understand the initial challenge, get up to speed with the decisions made, and take quick simple action. The result was a semi-public one page website and an internal engagement campaign we called 'Coffee, Beer and Pizza.'

The offer was clear:

- To support Enspiral, you could contribute the monetary equivalent of a coffee, beer or pizza every week, depending on the value you felt you received. Those facing financial barriers could ask for a 12 month bursary.

We made the interaction simple:

- On welcome.enspiral.com, we outlined the video story, the slides, access to the cost spreadsheets, and space for questions. With one interaction, anyone in the community could choose an option and sign up to say 'yes' to the next phase of Enspiral.

It worked! We 'balanced the books' of Enspiral Foundation with a clear financial model supported by individual members of the community recognising the diversity of value they received. At a fundamental level, the model gave the whole community confidence that the core was safe and we could focus on the next challenges.

Sort of.

After any piece of decisive action that changes something, new complexity arises with questions to solve. For us that looked like:

- What happened to people who didn't engage?
- What happened to all the other functions we didn't cover in the core expenses?
- How does this change the community roles and responsibilities?

This work to surface answers to these questions continues and the answers will no doubt create more questions.

Stability achieved. Now what?

Recognise the value is in the process

The key word in each of the steps outlined is 'together'. That is where the deepest challenge and value exists. Going through the process together is how collective muscles get built. There are no universal answers. Every group has to go through a process of working out their own coherence to gain a clear sense of their reality. The process to engage the community and instigate discussion is as vital as the answers that are surfaced at the end. The model Enspiral landed on for this next phase is a simple 'pick your own value' subscription that ensures that core collective costs are met. Proposing this solution at the start of the process would not have created the necessary alignment built by working through the six stages together.

Recognise the model will change again

The model will never be finished because the needs of the community will change again (indeed, they probably already have). Our goal is not to 'solve' the question of the model forever or propose this as the right solution for other groups. By reflecting and sharing these milestones we hope to provide useful tools and maps, both for ourselves and others interested in building and growing these types of structures in the world.

Recognise the benefits of a stable core

At a tangible level this is can be seen in a community financial model that covers base costs, enabling people to focus on other, more pressing challenges. In our case, how to build livelihoods that change the world.

It is like the underlying skeleton that gives shape, strength, and flexibility to the whole system. It should be strong enough to hold its shape with the challenges of diverse opinion, but loose enough to evolve and grow. Together with the governing agreements, this skeleton creates the structure that underpins everything. The ventures and humans being the organs, flesh and muscle that bring it all to life.

As a community member, the stable core model should not feel like a mechanism of control that determines what you can and can't do. It should feel more like an enabling platform that you can leverage to extend what you can do in the world.

This thing called Enspiral:
holding a collective story

by Nick Laurence

Across a dinner table the other night, my sister remarked: "it's never simple to describe what you're doing is it?" I was telling my cousin about the New Frontiers, (affiliated with the Edmund Hillary Fellowship), a community gathering I was working on with many others from Enspiral. My family are interested in what I'm doing and ask good questions, but it can be difficult for them to keep up. They're used to conversations about a regular nine-to-five job or starting a business that has a specific, easily defined purpose.

In one pithy comment, my sister captured much of what had changed for me since becoming involved with the 'Enspiral world' (as I refer to it in my head). For me, it's a world of paradigm-shifting conversations and working in the gaps between sectors, connecting disparate groups or ideas and asking "how about this way?" There are lots of incredibly smart, socially aware, and active people working in different sectors and in different ways. There are some common threads; innovative uses of technology, horizontal or non-hierarchical organising, high-quality facilitation, co-operative business structures, open source, collective decision-making and budgeting, systemic thinking, to name a few. But how to describe this to others? It's not as easy as saying "I'm a nurse, I work at Wellington Hospital". It's more like "I'm a… generalist? I work at... no, with... um, in collaboration with Enspiral."

What's Enspiral?

Good question! In true Enspiral fashion, to gain more perspective on this question we put together a survey and asked the community... Below are some responses we got to the following questions:

How would you describe Enspiral? What is your connection to Enspiral? How would you describe the value that Enspiral contributes to your life and work?

"I've been a member for more than 7 years earning a living with Enspiral for most of that time. Enspiral is like family and friends with a professional intent and shared values. Part personal development experience, part purposeful opportunity generator, part weird/wonderful friends dating service."

"I'm hanging in as a member by my fingertips."

"I'm a contributor, have been on the fringes for three years or so. I find it helpful to see Enspiral as a network of human relationships, rather than as a solid, unified organisation."

"It's a 'community in the cloud' for me. A group of people who I can bounce ideas off and check in with. It is a North Star and an example of how things can be done differently with strong leadership, shared resources, and a rebellious attitude. I've learned a lot in Enspiral and practised a lot. It's also the hat I wear when I show up in my work with other networks, and ambassador the Enspiral spirit and story."

"I've been in the swim for a few years, going to retreats, and starting to do projects with Enspiral folks. I dip in and out, but I own an Enspiral t-shirt."

"I heard about this Enspiral group when in Melbourne but it seemed too hard to grasp, so when I moved to New Zealand, I had the opportunity to dive all in and go to a summer retreat – it was one of the best things I ever did. It introduced me to concepts that blew my mind and has put me on the incredible learning journey I've been on since. You feel held in such a safe, intense, magical space, listening to and sharing your deepest truths in a story circle or short but deep intimate connections with strangers."

These snippets show that there is not one way of relating to Enspiral. It's described as a "spirit", "retreats and projects", as both "a whole" and as separate Enspiral "people", a "safe, intense, magical space", "family and friends with professional intent and shared values", and as a "network of human relationships".

One of the things that struck me about Enspiral is the resistance to homogenisation. Members value "being a fruit salad, not a smoothie" and this creates resistance to a homogenised story. Descriptions like "more people working on stuff that matters", while useful, don't quite get at the magic of Enspiral or what makes it unique. For me, it's more to do with the depth and quality of thinking about social issues as well as the practical things that could be done in the world to address them. And then not just thinking about problems but actively pursuing solutions in the world, together, in one big bold, interconnected experiment.

There's a multidimensional meta-story that exists because of all the connected parts. What's more, this meta-story is always in flux, always emerging and the stories that fuel it live in interbeing with each other. One useful visual metaphor for this is the 'Buckyball' (the carbon-based geometric structure named after Buckminster Fuller, shown below) where every surface represents a slightly different story of the same overarching metastructure.

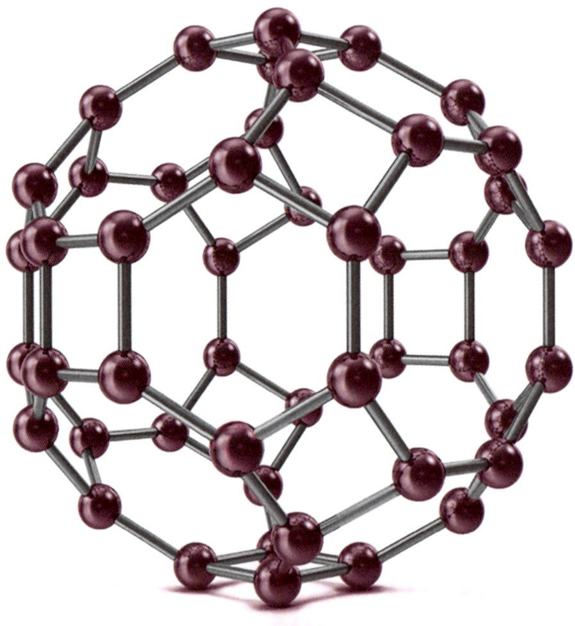

Imagine that each hexagon or pentagon in the structure is actually a story, a view, a perspective from an individual. There are lots of individual perspectives, and they each name and describe the meta-structure from a different and unique angle, reflecting their worldview, which is shaped by their own history, their gifts, their ways of working and being in the world. We can see the stories and different perspectives all linked, and together become inseparable parts of the whole structure. The structure wouldn't be whole if any of the boundaries of the hexagons and pentagons were removed.

We can also see that the stories are illusory: there are no actual pentagons or hexagons that exist independently of the whole. Each individual story exists because of the overall whole, and yet our mind seems to like seeing those smaller shapes. The individual stories are easier to digest than trying to make sense of a complete, dynamic meta-story all the time.

"I initially went to the retreat to connect with this group I'd heard so much about as a business opportunity. As a designer working on purpose-led projects, it was essentially a group of my perfect clients. Nine months later I've worked on multiple projects with a variety of Enspiral ventures and am essentially in partnership with a couple of Enspiralites, building a collective agency. It's been huge for building my livelihood... and I'm gaining so much more than that. I feel like I have a short but deep connection with dozens of people within the community that I can reach out to at any time with a generosity of heart and mind, and that is incredibly valuable to me."

"Enspiral is a loose network of social innovators and freelancers who support each other to practice new ways of working, on matters that matter to them and the world. It's a professional network that encourages you to do your best work. We share assets, resources, ideas, energy, money, and time and make stuff happen together. It's a community of people, mostly in New Zealand, but with members across the world. And it's an ideal of how we wish people treated each other in the world, and sometimes we embody that ideal, and sometimes we don't. But it serves as an inspiration to us all, and to others who hear and learn about what Enspiral is and symbolises in our minds and hearts."

Enspiral consciously holds a meta-story, its identity is collective and the challenge of holding this is perhaps part of what it means to be an Enspiralite. Being part of the whole supports and validates the individual members, and acknowledges interdependence - it gives us something to point to and say "Hey, look at this, there are other ways of doing things, it's not just me, I don't have all the answers, there's a whole network of people doing cool stuff with different views over here".

This is the same challenge we must reflect on for reality itself. Real life, emotion, and the patterns of social relationships are infinitely more complex than the Buckyball's icosahedron shape. There is a wholeness, albeit a messy one, to society and the systems of life on Earth, and it is infinitely more complex than any of the individual perspectives that can perceive of it. What is it to live in this super-complex, entangled society in which we find ourselves in the early 21st Century? Organisations like Enspiral that embrace this kind of multi-dimensionality may just be the perfect training grounds for meeting the complexity of the contemporary world, and the interconnected challenges and opportunities we face going forward.

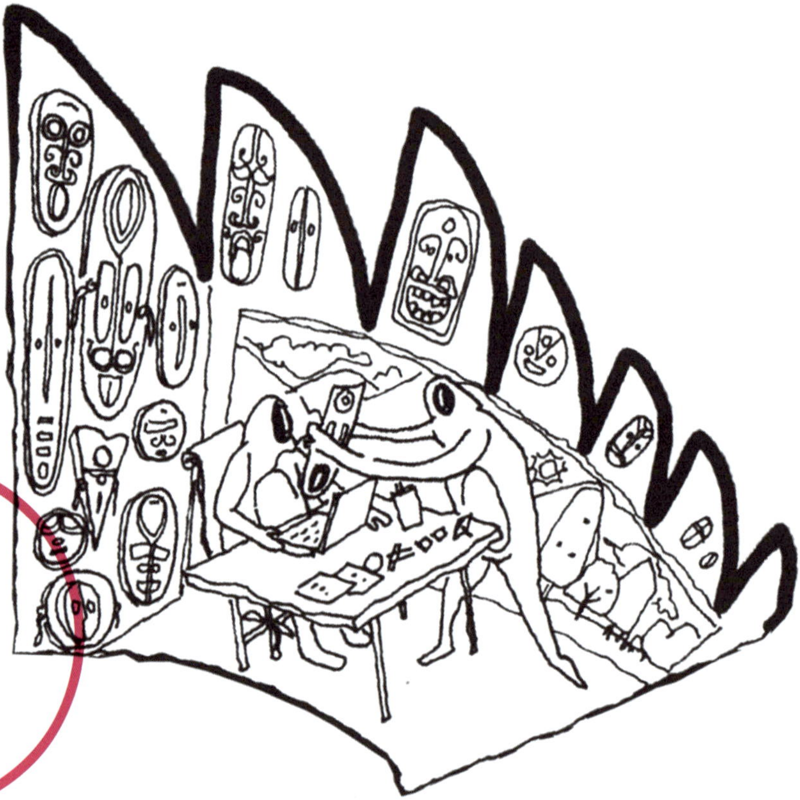

essay.Seven

Finding the stuff that matters

by Chelsea Robinson

"Find your place on the planet.
Dig in, and take responsibility from there."
~ Gary Snyder

To shift the needle you need to shift your mindset

In a world of converging issues, it's natural for the mind and heart to be twisted with questions:

How can you make the biggest difference on climate change?

What if the only thing you feel you can do is plant a community garden with your neighbour?

How can you reduce the rate of suicides in your community with your software skills?

What if the only thing you can think of to do is build a mindfulness app?

How can you strengthen the biodiversity in your region?

What if the only option available is to take a permaculture class?

How can you bring about new forms of organising?

What if you are happy to be a crypto entrepreneur and the only thing you can think of is to experiment a lot with ethereum?

How can you make changes to the way capital moves, the way land and ideas are owned, and do so in a way that creates more equal access to the things all humans need to thrive? What if your first idea is to start a church discussion group on these topics, or a book club?

All these questions are driven by the same impulse: How can I make a difference?

As you try to answer this question, your mind will take you towards a problem or a solution. Where do your questions, needs, assumptions and skills lead you? Do they truly help you find the greatest impact, or do they just help you find your new favourite reddit thread? In a life of service, how do we balance what we have to offer, the opportunities in front of us, and who we could be? How do we come around a table together to figure that out?

Finding the *"stuff that matters"* can be counterintuitive. Discovering an intervention that could really help others requires rigour and discipline, and is a non-linear process. Many of us think our first idea is the best idea. No matter where you start, whether you're a seasoned investor, an artist, an accountant, or a first-time entrepreneur, we all often jump to conclusions and make illogical leaps in our thinking that prevent us from having our intended impact. We get stuck in our subjective reality and don't engage rigorously with the shared reality.

Over the past 10 years, I've had the privilege of working in many arenas of impact work. I've been part of delegations to the United Nations. I co-founded and built a movement called Generation Zero, with 10,000+ active members changing national laws. I led business development in social enterprises, including Loomio.org. I've run social innovation labs and coached innovation for social change in many countries. I've consulted on impact and philanthropic strategy for some of the largest funds ever created. I've seen a useful cross section of impact work. I've been inspired and disappointed at the same time.

People all over the world are working hard to make the biggest difference they can to the issues that break their heart. It is deeply inspiring and gives me hope. However, I've come to believe that the common shortcoming of most efforts is unwillingness of the leadership and teams to look outside of their existing mindset towards learning what could be more impactful. Regardless of who we are and what we have to work with, the more we are able to question and understand our own thinking, the more impactful we will be. I have certainly had my eyes opened to new impact strategies again and again. Hopefully, I can help speed some of your efforts by sharing what I see, and accelerate our communities towards meaningful change.

In this complex world, we cannot assume we know what works, so we must experiment. Issues are connected, and we need to look upstream from what we immediately see and think through how to make a bigger change. We need to shift toward a mindset of system entrepreneurship.

We have recently learned to idolise ethical business practice, and with this new awareness 'social entrepreneurship' has become a strong focus of students, academics, founders, economics and politicians alike.

For example, it is popular to work with the Lean Business Canvas when starting a social impact project. But the matrix of a business plan: customer, problem, solution, doesn't cover the complexity we're facing today. System entrepreneurship is a mindset that takes interconnected, compounding factors into account in the problem solving. Instead of biting off one piece of the bigger picture and commercialising an intervention, system entrepreneurship is iterative, first working with one aspect of the situation, then another, unravelling the ball of wool that has gone unseen by a culture of solving things as separate pieces. It is harder to commercialise, and harder to explain, and harder to define a single value proposition, but it is worth the effort, because the impact of these interventions is so much higher. This new way of thinking can direct you to what matters, and the Impact Canvas can help.

"This little light of mine, I'm gonna let it shine"

Remember: There is no single most valuable thing you can do with your time.

Our lives are winding journeys filled with setbacks, growth spurts, educational moments, and periods of stasis. We are hastened by hope and slowed by fatigue. It's no surprise that in our own personal complexity we struggle to integrate our own worldview. Calculating impact is complicated by not always being at the part of our journeys we consider the 'right time' to invest in societal change.

In my own journey, over and over again I have gone looking for the single most influential role I can play. Each time, I've pursued something specific, as well as looking for what I'm ready to do. So, not only are we each searching for powerful intervention points, we are looking into ourselves for the parts of us ready to shine in this particular chapter of our journey.

The Impact Canvas: a tool to find what matters

The Impact Canvas was born out of my experiences in Enspiral. After running non-profit activist groups for more than five years, I needed to re-calibrate with reality. I had been consumed 100 hours a week (working to solve the climate crisis), which was not sustainable financially or emotionally.

I got involved in Enspiral a couple of years into its development and began learning about using business, cooperatives, and technology for impact.

Building movements to drive policy change had taught me that the world doesn't work the way you want it to. I understood, despite the business books' advice, that even if you show up dressed well, with ambition, insight, and confidence, people don't always listen to you. There are entrenched corporate and political interests. This kind of training helped me keep my clarity of focus on being real, retaining the somewhat naive optimism of the startup community. I felt curious. While aware of the risks, I felt a curiosity around the idea that technology and community could change everything.

We were able to create magic and learn a lot from the diversity of ideas in our community. I learnt about validation, design thinking, customer development, bank account creativity, ownership structures, and more. I shared what I knew about democratically run organisations, with rotating leaders who facilitate consensus; the importance of having a strategy for impact agreed on by all; and how to draw an influence map and build rapport with institutional stakeholders for systems change.

Out of all this, the impact canvas came to life. I believe community organising, activism, and entrepreneurship are the greatest forces of our time. Let's combine them to ignite our sense of agency.

The Impact Canvas is a worksheet of questions to answer as a team. It helps build a shared purpose and strategy for your socially or environmentally impactful project by connecting the big picture with a starting point that's unique to you.

Guide to the Impact Canvas

This tool is designed to help small teams, especially founding teams, find their mission and discover how it serves the bigger picture. Whatever your project is, this tool can help you make your assumptions explicit and test them. This could benefit a community, school, or software startup. Whatever your thing is, you can have a go with the canvas.

The Impact Canvas will summarise your impact strategy and the assumptions baked into it. It's about exposing the mental model you have for how change happens, and your role in that. You will need to articulate your hypothesis about how what you are doing contributes to creating the world you want to see. Even if you have already thought about this before, think about it again with your team, and with more rigour. It's important to know: Why are you doing what you're doing, and what are you hoping will happen because of it?

Find the mechanism of reasoning between your vision - the world you want to see - your mission, and your contribution to creating that world. Map how your method of interfering with reality will lead to changes in society. Make it explicit, so your team is in alignment and you can test if it works or not. The end result should be something like this: "We believe that by doing X and Y, we will create Z effect in the world, and this will lead to ABC changes, which will enable our vision".

One of my projects at Enspiral was LifehackHQ, a social innovation lab focused on finding and intervening in systemic factors to help young New Zealanders flourish, and help reduce suicide rates nationwide in the long term. As a social lab, we coached teams to identify prototypes that might enable this vision within their regions and communities.

We needed an educational tool to help our teams understand that ideas are not the most important part of impact work. Impact needs to be considered on multiple levels, addressing the root causes of community issues, surfacing the ecosystem of existing organisations, and what unique talents each can bring to bear. The canvas helps you to be a mindful changemaker, rather than to rush in assuming you know how to fix everything.

IMPACT CANVAS

1. Examine Assumptions	2. Define the problem	3. History of the Problem	4. Your Vision	5. Ecosystem & Partners
Start here List your assumptions about how change happens	How do you currently define the problem?	What historical patterns have affected this issue in the past?	What is your vision for a future?	What are others are doing about this problem already? Other organisations or stakeholder groups.
I assume these problems exist because...	What are some of the root causes of this problem?	What are some new insights on the nature of the problem?	What key societal milestones must be reached for your vision to become reality?	What relationships with other organisations could you build on?
I assume right now that the core levers for change are...				

6. You and Your Team		7. Your Impact Hypothesis		
Your strengths, personally or as an organisation	What unique value can you contribute that others can't? Brainstorm some interventions you could uniquely offer	What is the clearest way to state the issue as you understand it now?	What is the intended area of intervention?	What metrics can you measure to test if these ideas are effective?

7 Step process

Here are seven steps to work through with your team or thinking partners. Imagine these as prompts for conversations that could take place over time. One meeting per week for six weeks, or perhaps a full immersion weekend to dive in and focus. Be prepared for divergence of ideas in your team. Addressing differences at this stage will allow you to question your impact at meaningful levels. If you put your best into it, you will come out with a clarity of purpose, a reason for your shared direction, and an easy starting point.

0) Know what you want to change

Know what you want to shift before you start this process. Identify an issue area such as child poverty, youth depression, elderly care, native species protection, privatised fractional reserve banking, or anything else. At this stage you can be broad.

If you have already narrowed your issue into so much specificity that there's no room for finding deeper issues, such as 'lack of vegan lunch options in schools', then you need to zoom out a little. A very narrow problem area only allows you to agree with yourself. You can test this by trying to turn your problem statement into a solution by removing 'lack of'. In this case, 'Vegan Lunch in schools' is the assumed solution. Try shifting your sense of the problem to describe the qualities that are wrong, for example: 'kids are hungry or eating poor nutrition food in schools, which is affecting performance'.

The closer you get to describing the thing you want to change, the broader the problem will feel. Try something like: 'Poor school performance and health of five-to-ten year olds in Chatsworth'. This does not assume you know why problems exist, or that school lunches are not vegan enough. This is a good starting point for further exploration.

What change do you want to see? In what area of society?

1) Recognise your assumptions about how change happens

Many people use their current worldview to diagnose a problem. A school teacher who wants to increase the environmental awareness in their school might start a series of educational workshops to teach more people in the community about plastic. This is an 'educational' theory of change, where the assumption or underlying belief is that people will behave differently with more information. An economic theory of change would explore a different angle. Assuming instead that if you want society to make better decisions about plastic, making non-plastic options cheaper and more desirable will result in behaviour change. Both examples show problem-solution logic heavily biased by the worldview of the person thinking it through.

Ask yourself how you think an issue was created, who has power and who doesn't, why you believe the problem still exists, and what you believe needs to happen to make a difference. Notice that you may be making assumptions because of your worldview. Work with others to help you notice this.

2) Deeply examine the problem you are trying to affect

I asked a young woman from a low income community to explain why she was focusing on educating parents in her area. She saw youth issues as caused by a lack of parenting and values in parenting. During the conversation, we explored further the conditions facing her community. We uncovered that dire unemployment and the lack of government investment into infrastructure (including schools and public transport) may also be contributing to a general lack of support for young people transitioning from childhood to independence.

The assumption she had made, that it was the parents' fault, was a popular belief at that time, emphasised by the narrative of the government. Educating parents could have massive benefits, but it was important for her to realise the bigger picture: cycles of poverty perpetuated through investment decisions and institutionalised racism.

What logic leaps are you making? What are you leaving out of the picture? Ask yourself how you would define the problem you're trying to address. Try to capture it in one sentence. Ask yourself what is causing this problem. When you name causes, ask yourself "What is causing that cause?" Follow the links of causality to improve your understanding of the system that is making this issue occur. Get input from other people to understand whether our thinking aligns with the way others see the problem, especially those affected by it.

3) Investigate the historical context of this issue

Whether it's local history or global history, looking back can help you look forward. Consider the history of democracy in various countries.

How was it won? Was it only through protest? Or through changes in economic structures?

The invention of the credit union (mutual banks) was a way for the working class to amass financial power and become part of the ownership/investment class, and thus become politically influential. When we look back at the history of the United States we see how wealthy families influenced policy and electoral campaigning during the post-world-war and civil war rebuilds. The United States today is still shaped by the decision making of those times, and philanthropic industry is still heavily influenced by those families. Looking at these histories shows that an initial understanding of a problem like 'there's not enough funding for progressive political parties' is really better thought of as 'the role of money in politics has shaped where we are today and the unmitigated contributions of wealthy families in democratic election processes needs rethinking'.

Exploring past examples of social change (positive or negative) can help us to understand the dynamics of society and come up with new definitions of the problems we seek to solve.

Pause: notice any new ways of understanding the issue. What new ideas have come to you since you dug deeper into the root causes of the issue? What new insights emerged from examining history that have changed your assumptions and initial hunches?

4.a) Articulate your vision

Clearly state how the world looks when you've succeeded. It's as simple and as difficult as that. Do not state a solution in this vision statement. Describe what your community or the world is like when your deeper vision for the world is achieved.

4.b) Name the steps or milestones

Name the steps or milestones that indicate you are moving the world towards your vision. These are likely to be big-picture milestones that you do not have direct control over, like 'the price of oil makes globally transporting goods less economical than local production and consumption', or 'there is a national review of high school curriculums and how history classes portray slavery and colonisation'. Milestones can act as a pathway for you.

Take care not to write a to-do list. This is NOT a list of actions; it is a list of positive symptoms that the world is recovering from the illness. They are signs that the issue that you are working on is healing, shifting, or changing. What are those signs?

5) Explore your ecosystem

You are not alone. Map other organisations that are helping solve the issue, and look into how your interventions or ideas line up with or duplicate what they're doing. What can they do that you can't? What's better left to them?

When we were working on LifehackHQ we decided not to work directly with anyone younger than 18. Instead, we worked with people who supported under-18s. We also decided to be interdisciplinary and live between sectors, as very few entities were doing that weaving work.

What have others got covered that you don't need to do?

6) Identify and claim your unique strengths

List your unique strengths as a person or as an organisation in the context of this issue. Do you have first-hand experience with one of the problems in the web of issues you're facing? Do you have more access to money and resources than others in the sector?

In Generation Zero, we realised that being young was a key strength when building a movement around intergenerational justice. Even though other organisations of much older folks were saying the same things, in the eyes of the media, moral messages about what Earth we're going to inherit meant more coming from the mouths of babes.

What do you have that no one else does?

7) Articulate three sentences that help you:

Summarise what you have learnt about the issue and what you're going to try.

- **What are you here to address?** Name the issue clearly, based on your problem and vision exploration.
- **What are you going to try?** Name your best guess at a good starting point intervention, based on looking at what others are doing and what is your unique contribution.
- **What will you track?** Name how you might measure whether the intervention is effective/impactful, based on milestones in the short and medium term that you hope to see.

Do it.

The role of community in amplifying impact

Communities can be very good platforms for shared action, but not always the best format for focused work on issues out in the world. Helping a community like Enspiral or LifehackHQ to focus on an outward-facing impact strategy can be very hard. Communities are often made up of people who want support emotionally or financially, and not always folks who are committed to rigorously challenging and evolving their belief systems to find solutions. Although communities make a direct impact on the lives of those involved, they can be very self-absorbed. A demanding amount of discipline is needed outside your own beliefs and stories of how the world works.

Enspiral itself is not producing deliberate external outcomes. The most direct units of impact are the projects that people organise themselves around. However, the community is a very important primordial soup for increasing everyone's capacity for impact. This is the essence of becoming a platform for impact: combine passionate people, a trickle of money, high risk tolerance, and good intentions. If you can sustain yourselves, have events, build relationships, and work together, then you'll get thoughtful, awesome projects. Humans are innately creative and across our lifespan we iterate towards our highest calling. Wherever people are at when they enter your community, if it's diverse enough, they will find their place and get busy.

Educating each other is a fantastic way to help a community achieve more impact. How do you help people find impactful work? We ask ourselves whether Enspiral should judge and measure if we were making enough impact, or simply hold space for growth as people figure it out. Perhaps we should just focus on building Enspiral itself, and have more and more working groups that experiment with processes and a clear value proposition for members? This is a constant tension.

If I could go back and do Enspiral again, I would institute more intentional learning systems so we could constantly integrate new information about the nature of impact. Most of the work of making a difference is grunt work, implementing the vision one day at a time, but you'll grunt in the wrong direction if you don't stay oriented on the map and adjust the compass. The experimental nature of the Impact Canvas and the idea of setting up a hypothesis and testing it to determine what works is the kind of culture I would implement if I could go back in time and use it without community when everyone was just getting started. Events held regularly enough to see progress could be places to challenge each other to show what's working and what's not. This can be done together and with feedback loops like this you can expose blind spots.

A lot of the work of making a difference is unlearning and reshaping your ideas about how the world works. You need to allow your ideas about what impact is to evolve with input from others. In Enspiral, we have wondered if is not the splash of the rock being thrown into the water that matters, but the ripple that shifts the water long after the rock has disappeared.

Humans are not very good at understanding ripple effects, compounding effects, and long lead times. That's why we're struggling with climate change, lack of retirement savings, and health issues caused by short-term lifestyle choices. But we can learn to see non-linear effects of interventions. What better context for this re-education than a supportive peer learning environment, like a chosen community of folks working together to make good go faster.

Safe travels

There are no silver bullets. You need to start where you are, but invisible assumptions can block you from creating the positive effect you want to have. You can take a good first step if you start by examining your own thinking and rigorously experiment using the Impact Canvas.

If you are part of a community, or building community, remember that communities are two main things: cultural echo chambers, and accelerators. What culture do you need in order to create impact? What culture do you want to avoid replicating? What culture do you want to echo and mirror to each other over the years to come? A culture where everyone is held accountable for whether their ideas are actually creating good in the world. A culture where people are willing to be proved wrong enough times to find what's right. A culture where you help each other find what matters.

What do you want to accelerate together? Stuff that matters.

Read the full E-Book filled with facilitation advice and deep examples at IMPACTCANVAS.CO

#ChangingTheFuture

Greed
Generosity
is infectious.

You are a virus.

Be a good one.

#

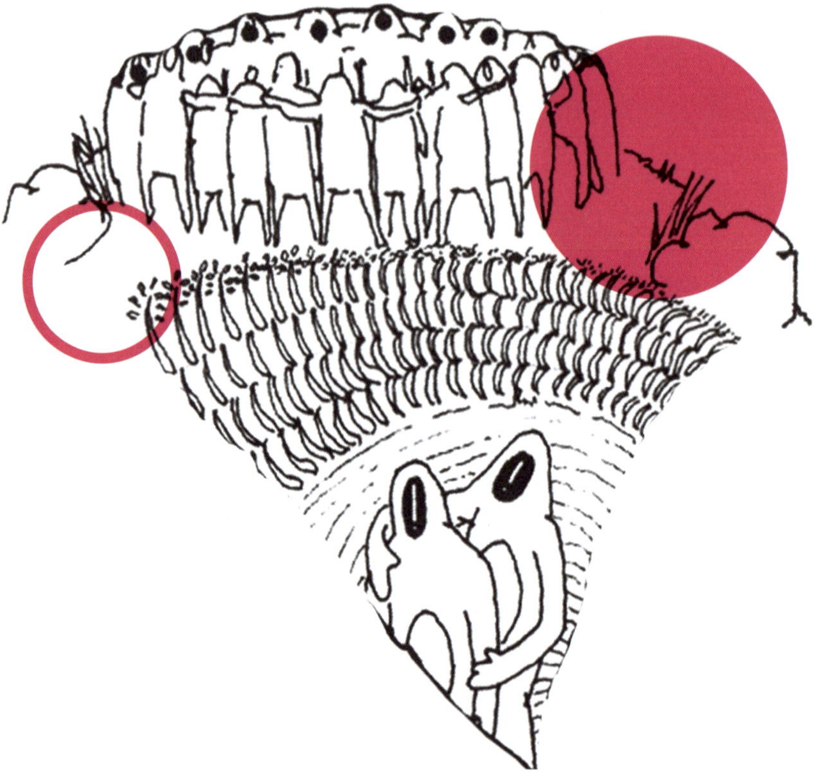

essay.Eight

Out beyond consensus there's a field: I'll meet you there

by Richard D. Bartlett

"Out beyond ideas of wrongdoing and rightdoing,

there is a field. I'll meet you there." -- Rumi

I've been relentlessly focused on one thing for nearly seven years now. Since the Occupy Movement at the end of 2011, all the strands of my life have woven together into one coherent rope. I've been participating in, facilitating, studying, writing about, designing software for, building a company around, and teaching methods for **collective decision-making.**

My thinking has developed a lot over that time, so I want to share some of the most potent lessons I've picked up along the way. I'll introduce some cutting edge practices in group decision-making, and explain why I usually focus on the subtle issues of culture, power, and social psychology rather than the particulars of various voting protocols. But this is a story, not a textbook, so I'll rewind first and introduce myself…

Hi, I'm Rich

My name is Richard Dennis Bartlett. Born in 1984, raised on a farm in the Wairarapa, a rural district outside of Wellington, New Zealand. My family is Christian, and originally from Western Europe, but we've called ourselves 'New Zealanders' for a couple generations.

Until I was 27, I never really thought about how decisions happen in groups.

Growing up, the same decision-making model was in operation across all the different aspects of my life, starting from my home, school, and church, continuing on through university, and then into the workplace. All these groups were governed by the logic of hierarchy, modelled after theocratic dictatorship. Call him God or Dad, Teacher or Boss, at the top of all these groups there's a single source of all authority. If he (it's usually a 'he') is a benevolent dictator, he may parcel out some of that authority to subordinates ('priests' or 'managers'). But regardless of how much power he distributes, as the ultimate authority, he always gets the last word. Group conformity is maintained by the selective application of his approval and punishment.

Because my experience was uniform across all these different groups—my home, church, school, etc. I barely even noticed it. I was like a fish who didn't know the word for water. That all changed in 2011 when I got swept into the Occupy Movement and caught my first glimpse of a world without dominator hierarchies.

Turn on, tune in, drop out

I've been telling people 'my Occupy story' for seven years, but I don't think I've ever come close to expressing the significance of that brief period of intense personal growth. It's effing ineffable, like trying to talk about an amazing psychedelic trip. I reach for words like 'expansion, awareness, interconnection, dissolution' and most polite grown-ups gently back away. Indeed, for a lot of people these days, "Occupier" holds about the same meaning as 'tripper': a kind of naïve optimist who wants to change the world but can barely organise a picnic.

I'll ask you to put those associations aside for a second, and just focus in on one aspect: the method of coordination. Remember that for a couple of months, there were nearly 1000 camps in cities all over the world, extending practical hospitality to anyone who showed up, offering food, shelter, and meaningful conversation, producing media and running libraries, medical centres, and universities. This movement emerged on every continent, without a centralised authority or organising committee, and reached global scale within a couple of weeks. Inside each camp, all the practical day-to-day operation of village life was organised along non-hierarchical lines. Nobody was in charge.

We gathered each day to sit in the 'general assembly'. This circle was open to anyone who wanted to participate in day-to-day decisions about camp life, or debate the more philosophical questions. This was my first experience of collective intelligence, where the patient application of deliberative process, empathy, and creativity brought us insights that no individual could discover on their own. There were times when I felt like a single neuron in a collective brain. In the bootstrapped collective intelligence of the general assembly, I started to sense the enormous potential we have when we're coordinated in the right way. For the first time in my adult life, I felt hopeful, like we might actually have the capacity to design solutions to the enormous challenges of 21st century life. As my friend Lucas says, the climate crisis is an "all hands on deck" scenario; we need collaborative methods that mobilise and harmonise the creative capacities of all of us. We need groups that are greater than the sum of their parts.

I'll readily admit that it was flawed and messy and temporary, but the Occupy experiment left with me with the conviction that mission-driven decentralised organisations can vastly outperform profit-driven hierarchical forms.

Occupy also showed me that there's a lot more to power-sharing than simply saying you want to share power. Even with a shared commitment to collaboration: we have to unlearn our hierarchical conditioning, learn new habits, build new skills, invent new language and organisational forms.

I guess the most honest way to put it is that Occupy gave me a sense of personal mission. Now I'm like a dog with a stick, chewing on the knotty questions of self-organisation:

What would it take for us to govern our shared spaces, projects, companies, institutions, and countries without coercive power structures? Can we replace domination with deliberation?

Or to put it more bluntly: ***Can society work without bosses?***

The Occupy camp in Wellington's Civic Square was my first laboratory for exploring these questions.

Deliberating in the general assembly each day was such an intense education. Negotiating with other people, trying to find agreement about how we should organise our little village, I learned that the most important thing I could do was **listen**. Not just listening to rebut, listening to understand, *where are you coming from? what do you believe? what do you value? why do you think like that?*

When I truly understand somebody's position, I can make a proposal that they can agree with. It's not about being clever, having the best ideas, or being right, it's just about listening, being flexible, and looking for solutions that satisfy as many people as possible.

That listening skill is something I treasure to this day. Whenever I'm confronted with an opinion I disagree with, if I can summon the energy to take a compassionate view, I always find new insight. On my good days, I tell myself, *"assuming this person is not wrong, stupid, or bad, what could I learn if I share their perspective for a moment?"*

While I had this lovely inspirational time at Occupy, it was also kind of a disaster. We discovered the limitations of the open-air general assembly format. We learned how difficult it is to govern a public space, especially when you're making decisions with random people, some of whom are drunk, or intentionally disruptive, or just passing through and sharing an opinion without any commitment to the community. I learned that consensus only works to the degree that people care about each other. We tried to include everybody, which sounds good in theory, but it was painful to discover that including some people inevitably excludes others. We learned that community is defined by its boundaries.

As our camp disintegrated, a few of us Occupiers met with some of the folks from Enspiral. In retrospect, it seems extremely fortunate that we found another self-organising community experiment, at just the right time, just a few blocks away. Pretty soon, we shifted our research project from the open air lab of Occupy into the co-working space of Enspiral.

A club for pragmatic idealists

I found that Enspiral had a lot in common with Occupy. Both communities were obsessed with large-scale systems change, guided by the twin motivations of impending collapse and utopian possibility. Both blamed hierarchical domination as the root cause of the economic, social, and environmental crises that define our century. Both emphasised participation, collaboration, collective intelligence, self-efficacy, and self-determination.

Enspiral introduced me to something new, though: instead of the protest posture, I met a more subtle strategy, less like boxing, more like martial arts. Acknowledging that business has an outsized impact on society, they decided to use the tools of business to work for socially beneficial ends.

Our little band from Occupy were welcomed with open arms (literally). We were given space to work and encouraged to test our hypothesis that self-organisation could be a robust principle for coordinating productive groups. Our idealism was greeted with enthusiasm, and balanced with a dose of pragmatism.

"Yes, your vision of changing all of society is really great...
and also, what little piece are we going to work on this week?"

The two most common phrases I heard in the early days were "that's a great idea!" and "how can I help?" The hospitality I experienced was so extraordinarily open, it didn't take long before I started referring to Enspiral as "us".

In retrospect, I see this as Enspiral at its finest: a patchwork community with an enormous abundance of generosity and ambition far outstripping our material resources. These are people who have stared into the void, acknowledged that civilisation may be approaching collapse, and consciously chosen optimism, creativity, and solidarity as our best strategy.

The love child of Occupy and Enspiral

Having been equally inspired and frustrated by our experience in the general assembly at Occupy, we started a software project to take the pain out of collective decision-making. We call it 'Loomio', like a loom for weaving the threads of individual perspective into a tapestry of shared understanding.

The software is very straightforward: it's an online discussion forum like any other, enhanced with facilitation tools that support deliberative decision-making. You can poll opinions and vote on proposals. There's nothing really hi-tech about it, no machine learning, or artificial intelligence, or algorithmic genius. It's a deeply human process: group members come together to discuss shared problems, talk through options, and collectively agree on the best solutions to try. It's designed to be open and flexible, so it is used by people in all sectors of society, from government departments, to cooperatives, NGOs, informal networks, and decentralised companies. Wellington City Council, who wanted us removed from their front lawn when we were occupying the city square, hired us for our deliberation expertise a couple of years later.

As well as building software, we've also built a company structure that embodies our values. We're a worker co-op, which means the workers have the ultimate say over the company direction. The software is open source; we think of ourselves more as *stewards* than *owners* of this common resource. Our constitution prioritises positive social impact ahead of profit, so we are legally locked onto our mission: *to make it easy for anyone to participate in decisions that affect them.* We've still got a way to go before the revenue model is really thriving, but with a couple hundred paying customers we can see a path to economic sustainability in the near future. I'm so relieved to say we've done it in a way that guarantees our self-determination, and I'm so grateful to the crowdfunders and impact investors that have supplied the million dollars in funding it's taken to get us here, and to the superhuman commitment of my colleagues.

It's a great privilege to get to work on my guiding questions every day: How do we work together as equals? How do we collaborate without anyone being in charge? Can we run an effective enterprise without a rigid chain of command? These are still open questions. On our 5th birthday I sighed with relief, "Yep, we've survived at least". I know we've created a tool that supports the work of thousands of impact-driven groups around the world. But our reach is still pretty insignificant compared to the big digital platforms, so it'll be a few more years before I'll be ready to claim with confidence, that yes, it is possible to out-collaborate dominator hierarchies.

When you have a lot of ideas about how the world should be different, building a company is a great opportunity to test your thinking. My opinions about groups and decisions have evolved a lot since 2011!

Making the cut

Because I was so used to being bossed around in previous workplaces, when I had the chance to set up our own company I was fairly obsessed with the idea that nobody should be excluded from decision-making. So when we started out, we did nearly everything by consensus. I believed at first that it would always be worth the effort to negotiate and deliberate, seeking the widest possible agreement: sure it takes longer, but I figured we would always get better decisions by involving more perspectives.

I have to take a quick detour here, because 'consensus' is a very confusing word. If you look it up in the dictionary, you'll see 'consensus' is commonly used in place of 'unanimity'. By contrast, if you read any consensus decision-making handbook, they'll be quick to point out that you can make consensus decisions *without reaching unanimity*. Consensus process is about including everyone and using dissent to improve the proposal until everyone can live with it. That doesn't necessarily mean that the proposal is going to be everyone's first choice. We're aiming for as much agreement as possible, but unanimity is not required.

These days, I think of consensus less as a decision-making method than a bonding mechanism. I understand why Quakers regard consensus meetings as a kind of spiritual practice. I treasure all that time we spent listening deeply to each other, negotiating patiently, opening up to the possibility that others may know better, letting go of the need to be right, learning to put the collective good ahead of my personal interest, and being reminded over and over that I can only ever have an incomplete understanding of any issue. These are some of the qualities about myself that I value the most, and I attribute them mostly to the sustained practice of consensus decision-making.

It was surprising to discover this irony: consensus brought us together, but the more our team bonded, the less we needed consensus. Once we built a foundation of strong relationships, we became much more willing to delegate. I learned to trust that my colleague will do a good enough job without my input.

The word 'decide' has Latin roots meaning 'to cut off': it's a process of elimination, cutting off possible options until there is one left. You can think of a decision as an exercise in simulation and prediction. It starts with a problem: *the office is too hot.* Then you generate a list of possible solutions: *I could open the window, turn on the air conditioning, or close the shades.* Then there's a simulation process "if I choose solution X, I predict the outcome will be Y". Finally, you evaluate these possible outcomes and pick the one that looks most attractive.

When you run this simulation and prediction exercise in a group, complexity rapidly escalates. More brains generate more interpretations of what the problem is, and more possible solutions to consider. Then you have a bunch of different people each running their own simulation. All our simulations all generate different results, and we all have different values, so we're evaluating the simulations against different principles: *I need to feel cool at work, so I can be productive. My sense of well being is tied to my sense of productivity. So we should switch on the air-con. Whereas maybe for you, you need to feel like we're being environmentally responsible—it's part of your identity. So we should choose the most energy-efficient option.*

You can see how this is a good way to get to know each other: even the most insignificant decision can be a gateway to our deepest needs, values, and principles. However, the important part is that, until the decision is implemented, *it's all a simulation.* We don't know what's going to happen until it happens. It takes a lot of energy to get everyone's simulations to align, but all that effort might not get you to the right decision. We can only know the outcome of a decision by observing what happens after it is implemented. So these days, my focus has shifted slightly, from being good predictors, to being good *learners.*

By the way, this explains the productivity gains of Agile management over up-front planning. Agile focuses on rapid iterations: you get to action as quickly as possible, and share the results. In this way, you improve your predictive capability by looking backwards together, rather than putting a lot of energy into describing what we think might happen in the future.

I'm still a big believer in consensus as a method for building collective identity, personal development, forming a shared purpose, agreeing on your principles and norms, setting objectives, and making significant decisions, like who should join our co-op. I just don't think it is the right tool for a lot of tactical decisions. The cost is high, and the methodology keeps you oriented to predicting rather than learning. In our context, once we'd built a lot of trust and shared understanding within the team, consensus seemed like a waste of those extraordinary resources. Many of us felt we wanted more freedom to act without seeking agreement first.

The good news is we're entering a golden age of collective decision-making: these days, we have a toolbox full of different methods. I'll look at just two of them here (advice and consent), to start mapping out the space beyond consensus.

Advice process

In 2014 Frederic Laloux published an influential book, Reinventing Organisations, which popularised a decision-making method called the 'advice process'. I usually paraphrase the advice process into three bullet points:

1. Anyone can take *any* decision…
2. if they're willing to be *accountable* for the outcome...
3. and they first *seek the advice* of people with expertise and people who will be affected by the decision.

Notice it says "seek the advice of", not "get the agreement of". It's about gathering input, listening to diverse perspectives, and then *making your own judgement call.* This gives you access to most of the collective intelligence of a consensus process for a fraction of the cost.

Personally, I would only rely on the advice process so long as there are a bunch of other organisational mechanisms in place, e.g.:

- A firm agreement about purpose (e.g. quarterly objectives, or principles of behaviour), so everyone is heading in more or less the same direction.
- A method of evaluating decision outcomes together (e.g. regular retrospectives), so there's an opportunity to learn from good and bad decisions.
- Pro-active measures to support relationships (e.g. one-on-one meetings, peer mentoring, conflict resolution), so differences of opinion stay within the bounds of healthy disagreement and don't mutate into unhealthy conflict.

If you have structural supports like these in place, then the advice process can be a huge efficiency multiplier.

I was recently introduced to an extraordinary example: The Borderland is a week-long festival in Denmark where everyone is invited to co-create the event. All day-to-day decisions are made by advice. They've adapted their own version of Loomio, so people can participate online, before they meet physically. I met Hugi Ásgeirsson, one of the key organisers, a few weeks before the 2018 festival. I was surprised to find him relaxed and happy, despite a major organisational crisis. Just six weeks out, it looked like they would have to cancel the festival, as they lost permission to use the original venue. But because they have the culture and the technology for decentralised decision-making, the whole community mobilised to find a new location in record time, with specialised volunteers completing all the bureaucratic hurdles to make it legal and safe. In a traditional organisation where information is centralised, the leaders are busy making decisions and mobilising people to respond, and their capacity is limited. In a self-managing network, decisions happen in many different places simultaneously, while the leaders are busy maintaining whole-system context and steering attention towards any gaps.

Consent

The second method that's gaining popularity recently is called 'consent decision-making'. If consensus aims for maximum agreement, consent is 'no objections'. There is an enormous difference between those two!

I first encountered consent decision-making through Sociocracy, an organisational philosophy with roots dating back to 1851. In more recent years, it has been gaining traction as more and more organisational designers, facilitators, and consultants turn on to the transformative power of this simple method.

In a consent decision, you're not asking everyone "is this the best thing we can do?" Instead the question is, "is this likely to do harm?" Sociocracy people use this phrase "good enough for now, safe enough to try".

For step-by-step instructions for how to make consent decisions in meetings, check Samantha Slade's blog post 'Generative Decision Making Process'[1]*. They developed this method with our friends at Percolab. It's a remix of Holacracy's 'Integrative Decision Making', enhanced with some facilitation subtlety from Art of Hosting.*

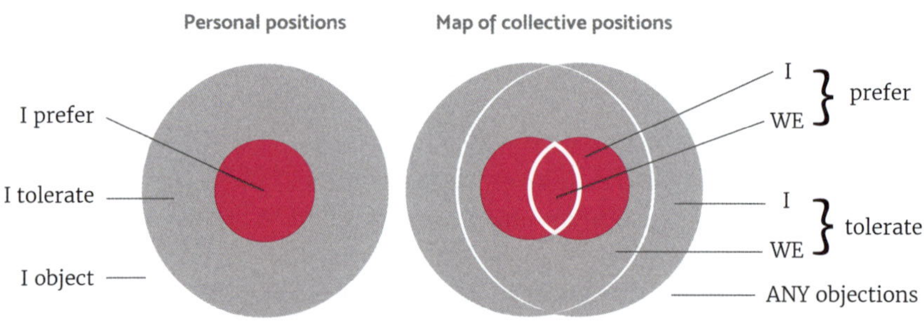

1 https://medium.com/percolab-droplets/generative-decision-making-process-cf0b131c5ac4

One of the common complaints against collective decision-making is that it can quash individual initiative. Someone starts with a cool idea, but then you have to make compromises to satisfy the most conservative group members. By the time the idea has made it through the 'design by committee' process, you wind up with a mediocre proposal that nobody loves.

Indeed, I've seen the demotivating effect of this dynamic in play at Enspiral. We have not fully developed the habit of distinguishing 'consent' from 'consensus', and we frequently confuse consensus for unanimity. So when I have a new idea, I unconsciously slip into marketing mode, aiming to convince everyone that *this extraordinary breakthrough proposal will solve all our problems overnight!* This approach inevitably leads to one of my colleagues adopting a critical posture: *"yes but what about…"*, and before you know it, we're in a long-winded negotiation. By the time we get to agreement, my energy is exhausted, before we've even implemented anything.

Now we're learning to introduce ideas in a different way, not with *"does everyone agree this is the best possible thing we could put energy into"*, but *"I want to try this thing, does anyone think it will do harm?"* The attitude shifts towards personal agency over unity, and towards small iterative changes over large-scale renovations.

Binary thinking is the enemy of collaboration. Consent decision-making opens up space for creativity, by drawing our attention to the terrain between 'yes' and 'no'. When I work with in-person groups, we visualise this terrain with a Venn diagram distinguishing preference (I love it), tolerance (I could live with it), and objection (no way!).

You can immediately see that the space where everyone's preferences overlap is very small. If you're aiming for consensus, it's going to take a lot of negotiation and compromise to get there. With consent, the solution space expands to allow all the tolerable options, so there's much more room to play. You still pay attention to people's objections; nobody is forced to accept a decision that violates their principles. At the same time, this method develops our capacity for tolerance, a value that can only be strengthened with practice.

Crucially, we have noticed that **people are much more willing to make concessions after their preference has been acknowledged.** It's common to see deliberations get stuck in a frustrated state, where everyone is simply advocating for their preferred position. If the deliberation does not have enough structure, it can be very hard to keep track of everybody's position. We get anxious: *maybe you haven't heard me, so I better repeat myself or raise my voice.* First I need confirmation that you understand my position, then I may be willing to put it aside and go with your proposal. This can be supported either with a facilitated process *(let's go around and hear what everyone thinks)*, or visual aides like the Venn diagram, or software like Loomio.

How to change the world in three easy steps.

I wish I could tell you there's a brilliant method or a simple technology that makes collective decision-making easy, but after seven years of searching, I'm convinced that we're never going to get to 'easy'. Humans are hard! Most of us have so much training in individualistic, top-down, authoritarian ways of working together. Our experiences in hierarchical dominance cultures have formed our core beliefs and expectations in ways that are incompatible with collaborative environments. I don't believe there is a shortcut, a simple step-by-step manual for letting go of ego, developing compassion and empathy, or a 'how-to guide' for embracing uncertainty.

So I'm not aiming for 'easy', exactly, but I'm optimistic that we're making iterative improvements as a species. I think tools, methods, ideas, and stories can function like prosthetics, helping us to walk with a little more confidence, speed, grace, and strength. I've seen new decision-making protocols help groups get unstuck. We have solid evidence that Loomio users are more satisfied with the governance of their groups.

In my personal journey, my biggest breakthrough came with that first consensus decision-making circle at Occupy Wellington. As I've matured, I've learned I don't need to stake my identity on one decision-making tool, any more than a carpenter identifies with only their hammer.

I don't believe in a one-size-fits all decision-making method. Mature groups define a set of different methods for different jobs. My favourite example right now comes from Gini, a self-managing firm in Germany. Their decision-making stack (mandate, advice, consent) is elegantly explained in Manuel Küblböck's blog[2] "How we make decentralised decisions". At Enspiral we have "4 different classes of decisions", and the expectation is this will change in time.

2. https://blog.gini.net/how-we-make-decentralized-decisions-ccd2de61b8b2

If I had to choose one decision-making technique or one technology that's going to change the world, I would guess we haven't invented it yet. These days I'm most drawn to what co-ops activist Doug Webb calls "post-consensus cooperative decision-making". Just the word 'post-consensus' is awesome; to me it implies that *yes, absolutely you should learn how to do consensus, and have that personal development experience where you learn to listen and negotiate and reduce your ego. But you can do better than using consensus for tactical decisions!*

What matters to me is that we try, we fail, we try again, and we fail better the next time. The more we can share what we're learning, the better our failures will be. I honestly don't know if we'll develop and adopt new collective decision-making infrastructure in time to avoid World War III, but I got to tell you, it feels great to try.

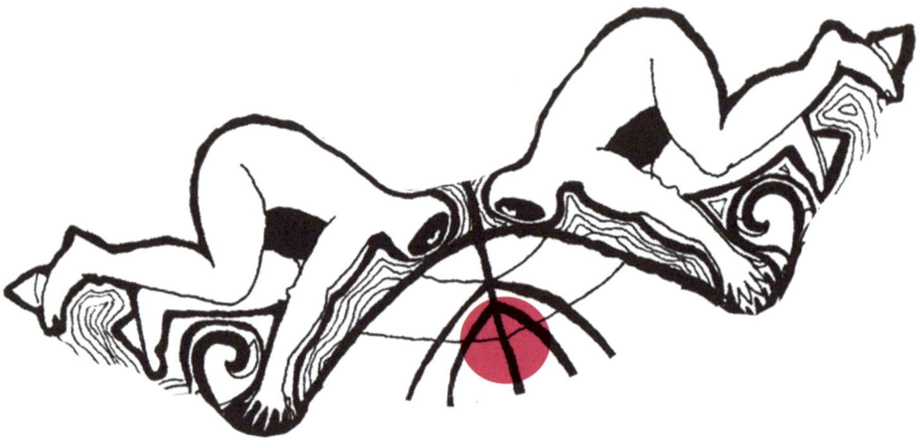

essay.Nine

Start with I

by Kate Beecroft

Start with I[1]

What does it mean to cooperate with other human beings? What does good cooperation look like, how can it exist alongside competition and what does it mean for us as individuals? Learning how to cooperate in a way that feels good means we need to look at our different ego states, neuroses, and funny little human traits that make sharing and cooperating hard. We need to do inner work. This chapter is centred in my practical experience of figuring out how to wind down my ego (read: how not to be an asshole) in community.

This is an integral part of new organisation thinking and parallels my own journey. I was going along a path that seemed perfectly normal - trying to beat others in work and life, trying to compete in a system that rewarded winners and made competition and coercion seem perfectly normal. At school, at university, in my first jobs - oppressive hierarchy and zero-sum behaviour was normal. These systems brought out some negative traits that weren't good for me or others.

Joining and co-creating a different kind of community in Enspiral allowed me to bring out another side - one that could be compassionate and empathetic, listen, cooperate, and share - while still building businesses and growing professionally. Over the past six years of being involved with Enspiral, I've learned the value of working on and with yourself. I've also learned what that looks like in community - and how it leads to more collaboration, cooperation, and self-management.

1 The title of this chapter is partly inspired by a piece by my colleague Michel Bachmann called 'Start with Who' https://medium.com/@michelbachmann/start-with-who-15b8857ed718 which was in turn inspired by the Simon Sinek approach 'Start with Why' https://startwithwhy.com/

Self-management is an approach to work that prioritises autonomy and self-development alongside alignment with others. It allows a system to operate without a command and control hierarchy. It is a vital component in creating the caring and healthy work environments we need to address the complex challenges we are all facing.

A key learning is that it's not that easy to leap from an environment and system that promotes antagonistic behaviour into a cooperative one without making some effort to understand yourself. This is a process everyone coming from hierarchy into collaborative community has to undergo. We have to unlearn the coping mechanisms that served us in competitive environments.

This essay explores the possibility that:

1. Healthy structural change might be possible if more work-based communities begin, grow, and flourish.
2. Without individual level personal development, we risk repeating the same unhealthy patterns, undermining efforts to effect change at a system level.

System change? Sure, to what end?

Imagine, if by some precipitous opportunity, we suddenly found ourselves in a social and economic system that, by design, enabled and promoted cooperation, equality, and fairer access to resources for all.

What would happen? Would we immediately bring back zero-sum, anti-cooperative behaviour? Has our neoliberal capitalist economic system, built on scarcity and competition, bred this into us? Would we destroy this new system?

This has happened before. Many well intentioned revolutionaries aiming to overthrow sick systems quickly became dictators. Egos, political manoeuvring, and competition to stay on top create black holes into which would-be heroes quickly fall. The very notion of 'smashing systems' (often used in marxist and anarchist circles) brings with it a forceful kind of change - setting the foundations for a forceful system.

Instead, we need incubators for people thinking about new systems to first experience a culture of care where slowly their own personal transformation can take place.

This is not some 'New Age' abdication of responsibility for class struggle or a position that things are 'not so bad' and we just need to be nicer to each other. Our global systems and structures need to drastically change, but they cannot without change in the culture that sits beneath them.

Know thyself... in a community

In a crowded, rapidly urbanising world, many of us have lost a connection with traditional, place-based communities. We are seeking new 'communities' where we can experience genuine belonging and care. One place that these new communities are flourishing is in the world of work. New constellations of relationships - centred around a common theme, project, or interest - are emerging, connecting up the increasing numbers of people working outside the traditional employer/employee dynamic. Over the last ten years, there has been an unfolding of communities and networks of this type around the world. Organisations like Ouishare, Open State, Outlandish, SandBox, Impact Hub, SMart are all great examples of people who are experimenting with new ways of working together. At the same time, within many traditional companies there has been a flurry of interest in how to move beyond pyramid structures that are reliant on command and control to get things done.

Emerging as a key tenet of this new approach of work are principles of self-management and autonomy. Although there is much interest in the tools and processes of how this is done, there is much less is said about the personal development that must accompany it. Whether old or new, individuals populate systems and companies - and the things we build are reflections of our inner worlds. Therefore, while communities and networks are indeed one part of a macro-level solution that can help us tackle the enormous challenges we face, we must not forget to consider the individuals within them. How we are in ourselves, and how we care for each other.

Me - in the Enspiral world

Enspiral is a community and a network where people are building tools and products with societal impact. We are trying to do this according to principles of decentralisation, openness, transparency, trust, autonomy, and without old-system hierarchy. There's not a lot of money here. There is not a lot of security. There is a lot of chaos. Everything is fluid. Everything is in constant motion. There are no job descriptions or rules.

There's nothing really keeping us together. The choice to be part of the community needs to be made again, every day.

I entered Enspiral when I was 26, after completing a Master's Thesis in Governance Theory and Political Science. I worked briefly in the public sector, before starting a small business and foraying into business development for one of New Zealand's largest social enterprises. I was feeling pretty alone and experiencing extended periods of 'low mood'. I had been steadily acquiring and integrating aspects of 'zero-sum' behaviour necessary to get ahead in old system organisations and in the world outside. I was a bit tired of scheming and learning on my own and needed a way to connect to other people outside of the options mainstream society was presenting.

Luckily, in the same city were a bunch of entrepreneurs, ostensibly working on big structural problems by building apps and social enterprise businesses. I thought that by applying my mind to these really hard problems with like-minded people I would begin to feel better about myself.

Until I encountered Enspiral, I felt like an outsider in most of the groups I was part of. This isolation affected my ability to accept myself and others around me. One of the key ways this showed up was that I was angry that people couldn't seem to understand there were absolute wrongs that we all must accept and fight. Some of our worst characteristics and behaviours are drawn out by a modern organisational culture that makes it seem like the only option available to us is to compete, win, and dominate.

> *If the drive to emotional growth continues to be unattended, and perhaps even unknown to us, it can short circuit our whole lives in a bid to be heard. Fed up with waiting, it may simply throw us into a paralysing depression or lock us into a state of overwhelming anxiety. By breaking us in these ways, the frustrated, stymied drive is trying to be interpreted and accommodated. What it lacks in eloquence and focus, it makes up for in persistence and strength.*[2]

In many ways, the totally confusing nature of Enspiral, and my inability to 'master it' (e.g. quickly accrue social capital and power) spun me into a very hard journey of self discovery. I came for the 'structural thinking and entrepreneurial approach' but I was not showing up with the behaviours. Nor, I came to realise, was this the name of the game. I was

2 The School of Life. CHAPTER 4.SELF: EMOTIONAL SKILLS The Drive to Keep Growing Emotionally

initially attracted to the idea of doing business for good, but I found a much more challenging, rewarding, and transformative journey than I ever imagined.

As dryly eloquent Enspiral Member Teddy Taptiklis famously put it at the Enspiral Retreat of 2017, we are a 'pack of strays' who have somehow found each other. This is a feeling shared frequently in Enspiral - it's a bunch of lost souls looking for others thinking and acting in a different way.

The people I first met were a curious mix: entrepreneurs, activists, and professionals who were asking big, ambitious questions. They were thinking at a level I had never encountered before, both structural and systemic. People were confronting questions like, 'How might we change the way we make decisions?', 'How might we change the food system and make it more local and sustainable?', and 'How might we improve youth mental health in New Zealand?' It might seem ludicrous, but the attitude was: "Yeah these are big problems; let's just get started and see what we can do." The mixture of naivety and bravery was refreshing. To me, it's linked to an attitude New Zealanders have for giving things a go. That Enspiral started in Aotearoa New Zealand, and specifically Wellington, is not a coincidence.

> *"It's true you cannot live here by chance, you have to do and be, not simply watch or even describe. This is the city of action, the world headquarters of the verb."*
> Lauris Edmond on Wellington, The Active Voice, 1994

One of the biggest lessons I learned at Enspiral was how to better interrogate myself and my work. When I first joined Enspiral I was working with Joshua Vial and Rohan Wakefield, the co-founders of Dev Academy,[3] doing public relations and marketing. Every time I wanted to do something, or write something or even when I had 'an idea' I would check with them first.

The feedback was a pretty consistent "What do you think?", often followed by a the 'Five Whys' process, one of Joshua's favourite techniques for helping people think for themselves. This experience gave me confidence, as well as useful tools for interrogating my work. Over the next couple of years I went from being unsure about my own abilities and skills to embracing a 'lean and entrepreneurial" approach - trying things and being ok if they failed. I also learned a lot about sharing my

3 An Enspiral venture - a training school for developers with a focus on diversity and communication (devacademy.co.nz)

my full self. The first few 'Check Ins' I took part in brought up feelings of deep anxiety at the thought of telling all these people what was truly happening in my brain and body. I thought it was essential to prove I was competent by seeming strong, secure, and unruffled in order for them to trust me enough to work with 'serious stuff'. In actuality, when we connect with the ever-changing, irrational, emotional inner worlds of ourselves and each other, it is much more likely that we can trust each other to communicate what we need and how we can help.

I went on to work with several Enspiral initiatives. As well as Dev Academy, these included Bucky Box (software for food cooperatives), the Low Carbon Challenge (an accelerator programme for low carbon businesses), Lifehack (tackling youth mental health via digital technology and immersive programmes), EXP (an agency for experience and programme design), and Cobudget (the Enspiral built-tool for collaborative resource allocation). A few of these system-changing ideas have made a small rip in the fabric of society - most have been marginal. But over the years, the long game of Enspiral has begun to emerge: a place to prototype experiments in self management and the collaborative, participatory potential of groups.

When Susan Basterfield, an early influencer of the Teal movement[4], joined Enspiral in 2015, it became clear to me what Enspiral was all about. It was a petri dish for behaviours, practices, tools and processes for self-management - potentially far more important and systemic than building software applications or a boss-less freelancers' collective. Self-management brings depth to our work. Rather than merely sharing ideas, we reflect and model practices that enliven our theory of change.

There is nothing particularly magical about the Enspiral community or the people in it. Nor is the concept of 'community' anything new at all. That humans need to be surrounded by others, to survive, grow, and flourish has been proven again and again by people all around the world. Groups anywhere can do this. Being in community is something that we all know as humans. Our work now is to bring it back into our productive workspaces.

In a system where relationships are primary there can be no hiding. Lis-

4 When applied to organisations, this paradigm views the organisation as an independent spirit with its own purpose, and not merely as a vehicle for achieving management objectives. Teal organisations are characterized by self-organisation and self-management. The hierarchical 'command and control' is replaced with a decentralised structure consisting of small teams that take responsibility for their own governance and for how they interact with other parts of the organisation. Assigned positions and job descriptions are replaced with a multiplicity of roles, often self-selected and fluid. People's actions are guided not by orders from someone up the chain of command but by 'listening' to the organisation's purpose. See Reinventing Organizations Frédéric Laloux, 2014

tening, compassion, a well-tuned sense of how people are feeling, and an ability to ask for what you need are essential to self-organisation. Our existence depends on relationships. When we admit we don't know something, or that someone's else's idea is better, or that we're scared and in pain, or that we feel alone, we start to create the conditions where trust can grow. Moreover, at Enspiral many of us rely on each other for livelihood as well community relationships - we are in this business for the long haul. If humans really, truly need each other they will build strong and flourishing communities[5].

Practices for the challenge of dealing with yourself

Inner work and individual practice

What does it mean to do 'work on ourselves' or 'have our personal practice'? To me, a starting point is understanding how we react to different phenomena or situations and what we do about it. Individual self awareness and ongoing development is not new. The ancient Greeks at Delphi inscribed 'Know thyself' in the Temple of Apollo.

No one else is responsible for your experience

One of the hardest parts of being in of a self-managing system is the realisation that no one else is responsible for your experience. Accepting this is as refreshing as it is scary. It means walking away from being the child in a parent/child dynamic, which exists when you think someone else is responsible for what happens. You cannot have a temper tantrum - you need to grow up and be an adult[6] - I came from an environment where you ask permission before taking any action. At Enspiral, the reverse was true: think for yourself, seek advice if necessary, act, measure the outcome, repeat.

This position helps adjust to whatever life throws at us - we are responsible for how we choose to react to any situation.

5 Charles Eisenstein compellingly makes this argument in his book Sacred Economics, 2011. ISBN: 1583943978

6 For theory on ongoing development Robert Kegan is a great gateway. See: The evolving self: Problem and process in human development. (1982). Cambridge, Massachusetts: Harvard

Figuring out and sharing your boundaries

Knowing your boundaries is essential to being part of a fluid system. It involves spending time figuring out what drives you, what triggers you, what enlivens you, what you avoid, and what leads you to shut off or lash out. If you spend some time figuring this out, and learn to work with what you find, you're off to a good start. When boundaries are continually eroded or crossed there is a high risk of burn out or frustration.

An example: I have a strong resistance to late night calls, and an even stronger resistance to early morning ones. I will take one late night call a week, and in my team we are making a collective agreement only to work with people based in time-zones that suit our working patterns. I've learned that I need to be clear about this in order to bring my best self to my work.

Putting forward boundaries and calling out when they're crossed is still an ongoing struggle for most people, particularly those who have worked in systems where those boundaries are often eroded by someone with more power. It's also hard in a self-managing system. Requests can come with an urgency that can railroad boundaries. For these reasons it's worth supporting this practice with team retrospectives and tools like the Colleague Letters of Understanding[7]. It requires an ability to state needs and to listen to others' needs as well.

Having boundaries is crucial for working in a self-organised, collaborative way. This goes all the way to boundaries about who we are as individuals. I haven't lost the innate 'Kate' things. I still have a penchant for sometimes saying exactly what I think, telling unenlightened jokes in meetings, and holding strong to my absurdist life philosophy that flows into making work as unserious as possible. But I am more aware of it.

Group practice

Collective intelligence and 'getting out of the way'

Across Enspiral, we have a strong commitment to hearing all sides. The behaviour of deeply listening and honouring all voices means that more stories and ways of being are present in the group. This is what builds collective intelligence and makes creative solutions possible. People see

7 Colleague Letters of Understanding were prototyped by The Morning Star Company - a fully self managing tomato processing plant in California.

that their contributions are not just welcomed, and listened to, but are actually a fundamental part of how the group makes decisions.

For this to work everyone in the community has to go through a process of learning how to truly listen. This is hard. This is where modelling and leadership comes in. I have been guilty of not truly listening and riding roughshod over someone by ignoring their contribution and skipping to the next point. I have been in tense situations with colleagues where I have not deeply heard their perspective or tried to understand what they were truly saying. I have also experienced being called out (in a gentle way) on this type of behaviour. For instance, when someone circles immediately back to the perspective that I just ignored to ensure that person knows they were heard, I learn something.

Another important part of valuing all voices is addressing privilege - the systemic ways that some voices are heard more than others. Men like Sam Rye (a community builder and designer) and Mix Irving (an educator and open source software developer) have been leaders in demonstrating how to 'get out of the way'. Under patriarchy, men and people from privileged cultures and backgrounds can take up more space because cultural patterns support this. Getting out of the way means acknowledging when our privilege allows us the stage, and using this to invite other voices in. Strong, explicit social contracts or 'Agreements'[8] enshrine the importance of prioritising diversity. At Enspiral, other examples include Māori scholarships to Dev Academy students, childcare at retreats, funding for mental health counselling, work on conflict resolution proccsses, and asking people exhibiting sexist and racist behaviour to leave the community.

Giving and receiving feedback

In my experience this is the hardest part of being in a self-managing community and team. Opinions and theories on how to do it (or whether to do it at all) vary.

Personally, I think some of the best ways we learn about how we are, and how we're impacting others is by deeply listening - tuning in to ourselves and the reaction of those around us. If you're going to do a formal feedback process - ask for consent and whether the other person is ready for it. My colleague and cofounder Francesca Pick pointed this out to me once. I thought I was practising radical candour by calling out a be-

8 Refer to the diversity agreement in Enspiral Handbook https://handbook.enspiral.com/agreements/diversity.html

haviour that really triggered me as it happened. She was not in the mood to receive my feedback. We agreed that if I was going to give feedback I would check in first on whether it was a good time.

Throwing in the spanners

If Enspiral were a place of groupthink, I wouldn't have stuck around for long. There are some champions of honesty and divergence in our midst who encourage us to bring our best game, not rest on our laurels, and to keep pushing for a new level of quality.

Sometimes a Loomio conversation is seemingly going smoothly and everyone's in 'convergence' (or agreement), and then someone like the wonderful web developer, systems thinker, and anarchist Craig Ambrose throws in a challenge or direct disagreement. In doing this, he helps us see the big gaps in our thinking, and elevates the discussion to a new level. This takes both individual bravery and group trust. Divergence helps integrate differences and weave coherence. It's hard. We haven't always done it well, but it's critically important.

Culture is the behaviour that makes up the day-to-day. People who may think that Enspiral is a big lovefest, where everyone is nice to each other all the time are wrong. If they could join one of the meetings of our team, mouths would drop at the hilariously straight-up way we get to the point. At Enspiral, people are respectful, kind, generous, and often quite silly, but people are not always 'nice'. This mode of communicating is codified as 'radical candour'. It needs to be modelled, respected, and practiced all the time. To be challenged is healthy for development of the self and ideas. And learning that your own truth is welcome (as long as it's presented in a non-violent way) creates confidence.

Taking off the masks

A core practice across Enspiral is the 'check-in' - instrumental for collective vulnerability. Checking-in is like breathing at Enspiral - every meeting or gathering at Enspiral starts with a check-in, which is a specific question like 'What surprised you in this last week?' or a more general 'What's on top?'.

The first 20 'check-ins' I participated in brought up feelings of deep anxiety in my stomach. I thought it was essential to prove I was competent by seeming strong, secure, and unruffled in order to be trusted enough to work with 'serious stuff'. In reality, when we can connect with the ever-changing, irrational, emotional inner worlds of ourselves and each other, it is much more likely that we can trust each other to communicate what we need and how we can help.

Enspiral Dev Academy lunches are a practical example of continually taking the mask off. Everyone (25-30 people) is invited to take one minute to say whatever is most important. This could be sharing the pain and heartbreak of unrequited love, a tale about the annoying logistics of moving, or an amazing anecdote about a customer or user. Anything goes. The challenge it to show up and be seen as a whole human. The purpose is to deepen relationships and trust.

> *"Some of the the greatest intimacy and community we have or fail to have is with our colleagues at work. And because we spend so much time at work and it so defines us, our souls, the light and darkness of our souls, is on display at work."* ~ Krista Tippett https://onbeing.org/

Facilitation and hosting

A practice and pattern that cannot be overstated in helping groups to function and individuals to thrive is facilitation. It's a pretty crazy thing that in any given call, or meeting, or at a retreat, a majority of Enspiral members can facilitate the meeting or gathering to a very high standard. A high standard means the meeting flows, people are heard, no one person dominates, divergence is handled well,, decisions are made, actions are noted, and people connect with each other and have a good time.The facilitator is an 'unopinionated space holder' - facilitating an outcome, but remaining unattached to what it might be. .

As Joshua says in the first chapter of this book, a lot of what happens at Enspiral is copying, changing, and sometimes improving existing practices. With facilitation and hosting, we draw use, and copy a lot from many forms of group process, including Māori kōrero, Art of Hosting Conversations That Matter, Non-Violent Communication, Theory U, Liberating Structures, and Open Space Technology.

Agreements and social contracts

Self-management does not mean anarchy in the workplace. In a self-managing system, a group of people who want to get something done together need to co-create a series of social contracts to commit to how they show up. Known at Enspiral as agreements, (available online at handbook.enspiral.com) these provide the scaffolding for the base level values or principles of any group. Agreements define boundaries. If a contract is co-created within the group and collectively agreed upon, it ensures the group has a way to call out and address transgressions.

In here, with us

Humans thrive in community. In light of the dissolution of many old forms of social and religious organisation, workplaces have emerged as a dominant organisational structure. The workplace is where many people meet their need for the continual presence of other people - to learn with, to build things with, to be challenged by, and to love and trust.

Self management is an organising system for autonomy and cooperation. A crucial part of self management is moving from a a system where zero-sum behaviours offer the biggest payback to one where we can simultaneously act in our own best interests by acting in the best interest of others.

My own experience of adult personal development, and community development at Enspiral speaks strongly to me about the potential for self-managing communities to be the place where people can grow and flourish, and learn how to move past damaging behaviours. Since I joined Enspiral, I have worked on my tendency to be judgmental. I have been challenged on my privilege, being unkind (sometimes being sarcastic and trying to get a laugh at the expense of others) and my lack of generosity (looking how to achieve my own ends at the expense of the group). Through feedback mechanisms and learning to show up as person full of broken bits, idiosyncrasies, and sometimes irrational reactions, I was able to see how I let myself be triggered, selfish, uncommunicative, and sometimes mean. I learnt how to listen. These learning opportunities have been essential to my self-development and ability to collaborate.

On the face of it this 'looking inwards' is not radical. On other levels it really is. It's refusal of the notion that the problem is 'out there' with 'them'. An image that often comes to my mind when thinking of 'them' is a circle of men in black suits in a boardroom on the 23rd floor conducting the dark arts of neoliberal crony capitalism. Let's think instead of ourselves and the people in here, with us.

If organisations big and small adopted this way of being, and many individuals could undergo this journey, we might start to make the world anew. Perhaps it sounds crazy that this is my theory of change, but I believe this is part of a bigger paradigm shift. One where we build systems that nurture our ability to cooperate, collaborate and aid our development. Perhaps we can find a better way than command and control systems for building amazing things that may actually help us solve some of the deeply scary challenges on our doorstep.

> *"Being human is not about individual survival or escape. It's a team sport. Whatever future humans have, it will be together."*[9]

The opportunity we all have, regardless of the work we are doing and where we do it, is to take up the forever unfinished work of being our best selves in service of our communities, and to find our pack of strays who can do it alongside us.

9 Douglas Rushkoff, Survival of the Richest, Medium, July 8, 2018. (https://medium.com/s/futurehuman/survival-of-the-richest-9ef6cddd0cc1)

#ChangingTheFuture

anyone **can...**

Two of the most dangerous and powerful words in your organisation, and in our world.

These words have the power to enable.
These words have the power to transform.

How do you use these words in your organisation?
How do you use these words in your world?
How do you back them up with action?

- ...get involved in setting the budget
- ...decide their own working hours
- ...contribute to our strategy
- ...directly contact anyone else
- ...join the board meeting
- ...start a new project
- ...recruit new people
- ...select their own salary

#

anyone
can...

somebody
should...

nobody
does...

#

essay.Ten

21st century leadership

by Silvia Zuur

The world of work that I entered in the 21st century looked very different to the world my parents entered in the 20th century, or my grandparents before them. I didn't embark on a one-career life like my Granddad, who was a veterinary surgeon for his whole professional career. I'm not going to progress in a linear fashion up the ladder of one organisation—assistant, manager, executive. My world of work, and how I work, looks very different.

At the same time, the organisations I have worked in also look different. They are not ruled by command and control. Money is not the key motivating factor. A job title that has the word 'leadership' in it does not bestow that automatic right upon me. In these organisations, leadership is about who I am and what I do, rather than a role that I step into.

I've been navigating new organisations and new ways of working for the last 10 years, and I've learnt that they require a new type of leadership for both the organisation and people to function and thrive. This is my reflection that **those who step into this form of leadership cannot rely on the tools of the past.**

This chapter is for those of you who are trying to solve big problems, perhaps by building organisations. More specifically, organisations with non-hierarchical ideals exploring new ways of working, looking at problems that may not have existed before, and solving them in ways that have not been tried before. This means the type of leadership you are required to step into is also new.

This is leadership in amorphic contexts; where the organisational infrastructure of the 20th century is not (your) reality. You are stepping into unknown territory. Looking to the past gives little guidance for the future, because the landscape and paths in front of you have not been explored before. The organic structures around you are fundamentally different to the pyramids of the past.

This leadership of the 21st century arises out of you and grows out of the respect of your community.

What qualities make a new leader?

Who are these new leaders? What are they like? Reflecting on my own experience **the number one quality is to be curious.** An innate inquisitiveness is needed to do this work. A wish to know why things are the way they are and an unwillingness to accept the status quo, or to accept the current reality as a given.

We grow in the direction of the questions we ask
~ The Appreciative Enquiry process

I'm talking about a form of curiosity that goes beyond what you can Google. It's a type of thinking which **learns how to ask non-Googleable questions.** It invites innovation and encourages growth. It's a form of innocence and playfulness that we knew as children but seem to lose as we grow older. It's a willingness to meet another human where they are at, and get to know them beyond how they first present. It enquires into why people show up for work, and what actually motivates them beyond the surface appearance. An effective leader of the 21st century is able to see others around them as experts of their own experiences, and help people to grow into their own power.

A curious leader also needs to manage their supply of empathy. Empathy gives an ability to step back and not judge instantly. Empathy, in this style of leadership, is about asking: What was the context that made someone act in a certain way? What is their story that has given them this worldview? This can be tough on those Friday afternoons when the world seems to be conspiring against you!

Colleagues have pointed out to me how often I ask the question: *But, what about the humans?* The reason I ask this is it's crucial to understand how decisions affect people, especially those on my team and those I am trying to serve. What might be the unintended social consequences of my behaviour? Leading in an emerging paradigm means you don't know the solutions, but it also means you might not know the negative ripple effects of your work.

When I stepped into co-leading Dev Academy, a web development bootcamp, a bunch of change was needed. Neither the organisation nor the people working on it were thriving. Unfortunately, in retrospect, I forgot to ask the 'what about the humans' question enough. Lack of time and resources put pressure on the situation, and even though I feel like we made the best decisions in the moment, if I could do it again I'd ask that question more often.

The last quality is a leader's ability to give and receive feedback. **Feedback is about being willing to reflect and accept being wrong,** as well as a deep curiosity to learn more about oneself. I can recall two impactful times when I've received feedback that was less a critical analysis of my behaviour and more a reflection on my patterns of being and working.

Firstly, a colleague Bart once told me: *Silvia, you have an incredible network and bank account in the trust economy. Your bank is overflowing. It's time to cash some of that in.* He woke me up to the unsustainability of my excessively altruistic behaviour. I needed to give and receive, deposit and cash out, in equal measures, or I was going to burn out. This was an uncomfortable truth to wake up to. I've never been that good at asking for what I need, and my need for independence can make me fearful of asking people to support me.

Secondly, at a retreat, a group of women reflected to me how much of my entrepreneurial work has been tidying up after other peoples' ideals and false promises. I knew I had done this one or two times, but having it named and fed back to me made me reflect on my deeper pattern of behaviour and the anxiety I sometimes feel working in the entrepreneurship space. Learning the art of receiving feedback is hard, but so is the art of giving it, so I felt proud when an Enspiral contributor recently posted this: *Much appreciation to Silvia for your mastery of the art of feedback. So specific, insightful, and useful. Your feedback has stuck with me over the years, and it matures with time.*

Enspiral: a mixed leadership journey

Enspiral was my leadership initiation experience. But no one in Enspiral ever gave me the title of 'Leader'.

Enspiral both accelerated my leadership and dampened it. It provided opportunities and encouraged me to really ask myself what work mattered to me. Enspiral allowed me to experiment, and it was a place to play. The unformed chaos called on my creative problem solving skills.

I could stumble into a meeting of the Board of Directors and ask myself "What might a new way of being a director look like?" Enspiral encouraged me to dream of a better world and supported me to work in service of creating it.

So, how has it stopped me? There were times when I wanted to step into leadership, but I was confronted by a culture of everyone needing to have an equal voice that everyone had to listen to. This tended to dampen my own voice at times, because I was unable to stand in my own expertise and trust myself even if we were exploring a topic where I had the most context or skill.

There's also the paradox of working with people who knew me so well. Sometimes people saw the old me, the administrator and facilitator, when it was actually time for me to lead. There was no clear way to step out into a new role. With no clear rhythm nor hierarchical process to navigate, it was hard to change my identity and share how I had grown.

I encountered an assumption that non-hierarchy is always a good thing. Non-hierarchy can both build or squash leadership. When unhealthy, it can cause us to get mired in grey, rather than enabling a spectrum of skills and possibilities. In non-hierarchical spaces, leadership needs to be earned, claimed, and sometimes even fought for. And then, after claiming it, every single act needs to renew your leadership on a daily basis.

The leader's journey

In Joseph Campbell's book, The Hero's Journey, he describes the archetypal journey of leaders through the ages. I've found it useful to help make sense of my own leadership journey. Nicanor Perlas refined this journey into a four step process: The Call, The Trial, The Illumination, and The Return. These four steps form the foundational arc of how one might embark on this new leadership journey. I'll share some of the insights and tactics I have gained, and reflect on the journey.

1. Call: how it all begins

As Perlas suggests, everyone's leadership journey begins with a Call. What was the Call that woke you up? That you could no longer ignore? What was the experience that altered your biography forever? It might have been meeting a person, reading a statistic, or hearing a talk.

Was there an injustice communicated to you that made **you wake up to realities beyond your lived experiences?**

Sometimes it comes as a knock on your door from Gandalf, or being offered the red pill or the blue pill in the Matrix. But more often than not, it's less clear. Something happens that makes you realise there is potential inside yourself that has not been awoken, which demands that you answer the Call.

It's 3:23 in the morning
and I'm awake
because my great great grandchildren
won't let me sleep
my great great grandchildren
ask me in dreams
what did you do while the Planet was plundered?
what did you do when the Earth was unravelling?

surely you did something
when the seasons started failing?
as the mammals, reptiles, birds were all dying?

did you fill the streets with protest
when democracy was stolen?

what did you do
once
you
knew?
~ Drew Dellinger

When this shift occurs, there is a tilt in the Universe that means you can never go back. You cannot go back to not knowing. No longer can you ignore the need that you have woken up to. These moments that call us into action, when we step into leadership, are often unexpected. Instead of doing what you want, you now do what needs to be done.

You may only recognise that moment when you look back. That was the case for me. Enspiral was my leadership journey, and it's only now, when I look back, that I realise this. I did not enter Enspiral with leadership ambitions. They unfolded through a suite of experiences and events that I woke up to and stepped into. For example, every Enspiral retreat has been such an opportunity and invitation. It's an opening to serve the community in a tangible, practical way. Over the last seven years I've co-organised six of the retreats and helped with five others, and each time my sensitivity for the leadership required in this space has increased.

Conflict in communities like Enspiral are another clear call on new leadership. As someone who actively avoids conflict, it has been moments of conflict that have propelled me into leadership more than anything else. The art then is to work out if it is a conflict that only hurts me, or something that is damaging the community.

The motivation for stepping up is different for everyone, yet I am sure it has nothing to do with a new job title, pay band, or permission bestowed upon you by a manager. It's an awakening inside yourself, a realisation you can, and must, do something.

2. Trials: the challenges of organisational leadership

Leadership is not easy, so often the moment you commit yourself, you realise: "this is a way bigger problem than I ever thought." Stepping into leadership is like opening a Pandora's Box that you can't close again. As Perlas says, it's the Trial that comes after answering the Call. The core Trials I've faced while building new organisations have been within the themes of compromise, power, health, responsibility, and relationships.

Compromise

Ideas are great, but reality is never that simple. Leadership often requires creating a new reality, and accepting its imperfections.

As soon as you begin to turn ideas into reality, the compromises begin. The marketing budget is not quite big enough. The week is just not long enough. Your team has its own ideas and implementation strategies. **Reality has a rough way of chiseling away at the perfect idea.** Through the concessions inherent in compromise, it's easy for organisations and leaders to lose integrity. The million micro-decision made daily can lead us down an unintended path.

Suddenly, you find yourself publicly standing for something that is no longer perfect. You need to represent the imperfect reality that you have created.

In the second year of leading Chalkle, the startup I co-founded in 2012, I received a nomination for the Women of Influence awards. This was a surprising and wonderful honour, but it came at the time when my original co-founder had left the business, I did not have a strong team around, and I was starting to have doubts if I even had a business model. I discovered how sometimes the external image displayed has a disconnect to the internal experience, which gave truth for me to this quote: *Don't compare your insides with other people's outsides.*

Power

These compromises often apply to the ideals of non-hierarchy, which can look great on paper, but in reality may be quite a different experience. The disconnect is around power. **Power is like dust in a house: it settles and accrues in the corners.** Power is never spread evenly in an organisation. If Power is not addressed or named, it will gather in unnamed places. An explicit dictatorship may be better than an implicit power structure. Hidden power may invite a perception of equality, where you can sit around a table with a verbal agreement of all being equal, but a newcomer may notice that everyone seems to listen to one person more than others. **This creates a confusing situation for anyone trying to join, and a frustrating situation for anyone trying to lead.**

The clearest example I could think of here was my experience of being a director of Enspiral Foundation Ltd. The community agreement is that this role does not hold additional power, except in exceptional circumstances. Yet I found the experience to be quite different. We were not all equal sitting around the table. If a decision involved a brand risk or a financial risk, I could not help but have the director voice on in the back of my mind. I know that impacted my behaviours. Negative legal or financial consequences, would land in the directors laps. How could I ignore that?

Name power. Address the power. It is never equal.

Health

Budgets, payroll, employment contracts, strategies comprise the **backbone of a traditional organisation.** As leaders try to improve how these elements are implemented in the 21st century, it's easy to ignore the positives as you eliminate the negatives. This can lead to idealistic new organisations being more unhealthy than more traditional, pragmatic, ones. New organisations may throw out perceived bureaucracy, but also the useful structures and systems.

Often in these unhealthy organisations, the most pressing symptom might appear to be the balance sheet, but I've found that the true illness is likely to be much deeper in the core of the organisation. Keeping an organisation healthy is much like keeping a human being healthy. It is our responsibility as leaders to ensure the health of all these systems. An organisation needs a heart beat and a rhythm. Money should flow like blood, not bleed out through cuts and wounds. Communication needs to circulate through the nerve system and keep the toes and fingers informed. An immune system needs to maintain integrity, of the mission and the people. A skeleton, a structure, needs to holds it all together.

Responsibility

In an organisation I fundamentally believe that **if everyone is responsible then no one is responsible.** In organisations with goals of non-hierarchy, I've found that you need to spend more time understanding power, accountability, and support, when you cannot rely on a hierarchical structure to provide these. Fluid, forming systems may be all well and good while the sun shines, but what about those rainclouds? It's those stormy times, when 'everyone' is responsible for the overspend on the budget, or 'everyone' was meant to look after that person who had a tough time at the retreat, or 'everyone' was meant to deliver on that contract, where I have struggled the most to navigate leadership. It's the times when a sense of responsibility is not matched by explicit mandate to act.

In Enspiral, this has been the hardest in terms of caring for people and managing the Enspiral brand. When we worked on removing the hierarchy in Enspiral, we originally removed the structures of care and "everyone was responsible" for caring. This meant that I found myself, initially unconsciously, feeling responsible for all of the caring for the community. If someone was unhappy, I took it personally. At the same time, if I heard complaints about Enspiral rumouring through the Wellington ecosystem, I took them on as my responsibility to fix. But, for both of these situation this was not the community agreement, nor my role. Two interventions solved this situation; developing a stewardship system and the Catalyst roles.

Whose Job Is It Anyway?

There was an important job to be done. Everybody was sure that Somebody would do it. Anybody could have done it, but Nobody did it. Somebody got angry about that, because it was Everybody's job.
Everybody thought Anybody could do it, but Nobody realised that Everybody wouldn't do it. It ended up that Everybody blamed Somebody when Nobody did what Anybody could have done.
Author Unknown

3. Illumination: what have I learnt?

I've spent a lot of the last seven years "doing what needs to be done". I could weave a narrative about fixing organisations, solving problems, and tidying up other people's messes, a story of serving the community and building the commons. But is that the only story? Was I truly selflessly serving?

I could tell a different story, about gathering social capital. Maybe I do the work because I'm 'Little Miss Fix It'. Maybe I like to feel important and be in the middle of everything. Enspiral created opportunities that fit my skill set and helped take me where I am today. In other words, it served me.

The former is about an individual serving a community, and the latter is about a community serving an individual. Both narratives are true. It's in this paradox where the true art of navigating self-leadership and community leadership emerges.

Enspiral has been built by thousands of acts of leadership by hundreds of people, and it has created new opportunities for all of us. This work was never a logical decision for me. The hours spent, the tears cried, the words written on Loomio never made sense in isolation. Yet I helped create an ecosystem for hundreds of people to find the work that mattered to them. **We built a network that now serves beyond us.**

Those that build the house are built by the house
~ Koro Bruce, Tapu Te Ranga Marae

Tending my relationships

Relationships are not an infinite resource; they need to be cared for and fundamentally respected to be sustained. An organisation of five people is a web of 20 potential relationships. This can be tended to simply, but grow to 10 people and you suddenly have 90 potential binary relationships. It is your role as leader to tend that web, and under-estimating the complexities will ultimately belittle your work.

It's not paychecks and job titles that hold the new organisations together. Money and status were the currency of 20th century; in the 21st century it's relationships. Yet so many of our 'heroes' appear to pay little attention to relationships. So many idolised people seem to have forgotten their families, and so often the work gets hidden behind egos. The hero story misses the relationships, where their power is actually manifest. Campbell might talk about a hero's journey as a path to be traveled, in the stages described by Perlas, but what I've realised it that it misses the complexities of the relationships that propel each leader forward. **A leader does not journey alone.**

Staying balanced and grounded

On my 33rd birthday I got a lemniscate, also known as the infinity symbol, tattooed on my ankle. It's a symbol that represents the two most important things I've learnt: balance (both sides of the lemniscate are equal) and groundedness (reminding me to keep my feet firmly on the earth).

As a leader, 'balance' for me has many different facets. It's about maintaining integrity so that your head, heart, and hands are balanced. Balance is when your body feels healthy, when you have had the amount of sleep you need, and eaten the right food. Balance can be found in conversations—am I truly listening or just waiting to speak? So often leaders spend their time talking, but talking and listening needs to come in balance. Balance is about finding the stillness in the storm. It's about walking the tightrope of expectations and pressures.

Groundedness is about coming back to reality, not floating off into an egotistical hyper-competitive world. Groundedness asks you to come back to yourself, and constantly be present to why you do this work in the first place.

For me to be a leader in any context, I need to work hard to hold myself to account and stay grounded. I've gone through extreme waves of workaholism—living and working with your co-founder and moving your startup office into your home is not a good way to create balance!

Happiness is when what you think, what you say,
and what you do are in harmony.
~ Mahatma Gandhi

I have found a good way to check in on remaining grounded and balanced is:

1. **Head** - How much time do I spend thinking? Did I join the last strategy meeting? Have I spent some time on a whiteboard with a colleague recently?

2. **Heart** - How much emotional labour have I taken on in my community? Did I host the last community potluck? Have I had a coffee with one of my colleagues recently and asked how they are?

3. **Hands** - When did I last physically create something? Have I gone for a walk or a hike recently?

Personal well-being

On this journey of navigating leadership I've had some critical learnings about my own wellbeing.

I am part of a group of nine women who are my core colleagues in life and work. They are not my direct co-founders or business partners, but we work in similar ways, in similar contexts. They are people who empathise with me on my journey, but have enough distance to be objective and bring me perspective. We have made a commitment to each other to meet every three to six months to share our challenges, our joys and our learnings.

Having a home base is crucial for me. I need to be able to potter, make bread and kombucha, clean a cupboard, or sit on the couch and knit for a whole afternoon. Home is the place where I can selfishly be me. When your leadership is founded on service, it is crucial to have a place where your only concern is your own wellbeing.

It's been pivotal for me to find moments to clear my head and not think about work. When work is not just a nine to five job, it becomes harder to turn off my brain and allow perspective to bring me fresh courage. This might be a 30 minute walk around the block, a whole afternoon at the beach, or a month in the Alps making cheese! No matter what I am doing, I have never regretted a wander in the woods.

Finally, my mental wellbeing has a very strong correlation with my inbox. I've realised I need to set aside a decent amount of time to clear it. In busy times, this takes the form of a daily calendar slot.

Community navigation

Alongside commitments to myself, I also need clear strategies to lead organisations and communities sustainably.

Clarity is my most important tool. As soon as something feels unclear, my alarm bells go off. Clarity is needed in tasks, responsibilities, relationships, and accountabilities. It's not just about needing to lock everything down. Clarity can also be gained by acknowledging that something is unclear. Just as long as we are all on the same page! Lack of clarity about my responsibilities leads me to worrying about everything!

I've spent a lot of time learning how to create organisational systems that help hold people to account. On a basic level this looks like clear weekly rhythms, names associated with tasks, monthly retrospectives, and transparent budgets. The goal is to not centralise information in my brain. I love setting up external processes because they hold people to account better than me turning into a human task tracker.

Lastly, what are the 'No's' you need to voice to empower your greater 'yes'? Finding these help me stay true to my commitments and maintain my integrity. A friend once gave me the feedback of feeling frustrated at me for saying yes to the things that are shiny. She asked me if I was being strategic, or just opportunistic? I realised that the more I grow, the more opportunities come towards me, and the more I need to learn to say no. It all comes back to finding the balance that allows me to thrive and therefore the organisation to develop.

4. Return: bringing it all together

The way I show up and strive to lead with integrity probably looks different to your leadership. But there are some things all leaders of the 21st century have in common.

We need to look forward to define the leadership of the future, instead of perpetuating patterns from the past. No matter the context, I encourage all leaders to foster curiosity and empathy inside of themselves. They need to ensure the Integrity of their own deeds and those of their organisation. They need to learn the art of giving and receiving Feedback in a way that furthers learning and relationships.

I once read that: *Courage is acknowledging fear, but acting in spite of it.* Those moments when we step forward as leaders are acts of courage. We shouldn't idolise courageous leaders, but we do need to acknowledge the fear that they have overcome, even if we can't see it.

Leadership is hard work. There are so many challenges, in the world and within our organisations. The organisations we build will not be perfect. Along the way, we've all had to make a million decisions, some of which may have led to something suboptimal.

But perhaps the hardest task, and most important, is simply recognising each other on our unique leadership journeys. We are all at different stages. Some of us are just starting, awakening to a Call. Some of us are confronted by Trials, tripping up and falling, stumbling into hidden power structures, or navigating the complexities of people and relationships. Some of us may have just had that 'aha moment' of Illumination we were waiting for. As each of us move forward on our ever-unfolding paths, we need to remember to see each other, recognise the journey, remind each other to stay balanced and grounded, look after ourselves, and not to say yes too often.

Enspiral has been my context for the last seven years. It has represented the deeper 'why' of my work. It's provided me with colleagues, friends, flatmates and co-founders, and a place to stand and grow. It gave me an opportunity to answer a call.

My journey has been an experience of leadership in the 21st century, where leadership is not assigned by authority. **Leadership in the present century arises out of individuals, and grows out of the respect of their community.**

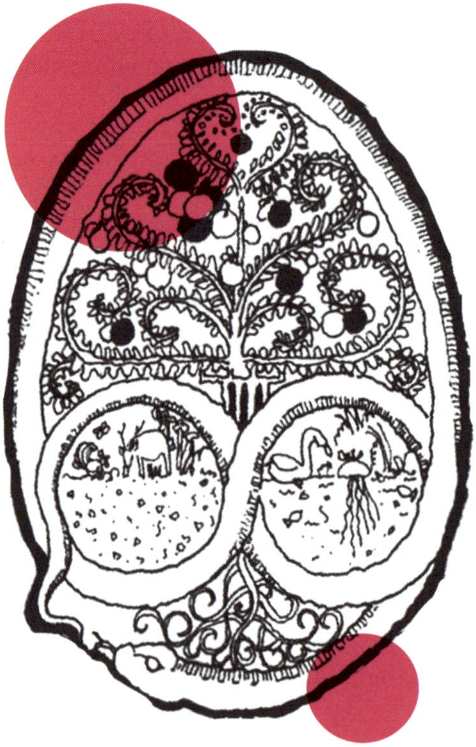

essay.Eleven

In service of change

by Damian Sligo-Green

This is the story of how we built a worker-owned ecology of professional services businesses. With a background in business development and sales (financial services for mom and pop businesses and SMEs) I joined Enspiral early on in its evolution. I didn't set out with the intention to build community-orientated business but I always had the drive to effect positive change in the world. Enspiral is the place my real learning journey began. What follows is an outline of that journey, and of some key phases in Enspiral's story so far.

The Enspiral I joined was mostly made up of programmers, activists, and early stage startups. The majority of the livelihood in the community was (and still is) drawn from professional consulting work - mainly software development and programme design/facilitation. The challenge of working out how to structure and support multiple freelancers working together as a distributed, self-governing, and autonomous agency was central to the formation of the whole Enspiral system. Over the past five years I've been developing, iterating, and evolving the model alongside others. While lots has changed over that time, the same central questions have persisted:

How do we do interesting, meaningful work as peers?

What are the patterns, skills, tools, and structures that allow us to do this while continuing to progress individually and collectively?

How do we grow resilient, effective, and sustainable organisations, anchored to strong social purpose?

Enspiral Services - connections, contracts and co-evolution

I worked in a corporate for a few years, before the mind-crushing rigidity, lack of growth opportunities, and absence of purpose led me to self-employment and managing a small business. This was just after the Global Financial Crisis and it was a challenging time to learn the basics of business. While finding some commercial success, I quickly became lonely, and found that my work wasn't delivering the positive change I craved. I was ambitious, searching for purpose-driven collaborators, and hungry for meaning in my work. As it happened, so was Enspiral.

At that time, Enspiral Services was the economic heart of the community. In short, it's where the money was made. It played a pivotal role as the feeding and breeding ground for new relationships and opportunities to emerge. It came to be within Enspiral Space, a shared co-working space with accessible pricing and professional meeting rooms. Inside this space, collaborating freelancers, activists, and entrepreneurs were drawn together to work, share, dream, and scheme on new projects, tools, and new possibilities. Enspiral Services facilitated meaningful value exchange - contracts and collaborations. These were the bundles of energy that bootstrapped the community. Without these, we wouldn't have gathered the financial wherewithal that allowed people to stick around and cultivate deeper interpersonal connections. It was these deeper connections that enabled us to develop the collective problem-solving capabilities that made so much more possible.

Legally, Enspiral Services was a Limited Liability Company with no special constitution and a single director/shareholder, Joshua Vial. It was founded as Josh's private consulting agency and as the kernel of a bigger vision developed, he began to invite other developers and later, project managers and salespeople into the fold. All of these professionals shared the intent to make a positive impact in their work. With the magic ingredient of facilitation added to the mix, this technically proficient head and hands gained a heart. Many freelancers were used to working on their own or with small groups of trusted collaborators. Enspiral Services played the role of 'the agency' which was able to project a larger presence, tell a common story and win bigger jobs. It accrued a surplus of money in a common pool instead of diverting that surplus to shareholder owners or directors.

Viewed through an evolutionary lens, it's important to note the environment in which Enspiral Services formed. Enspiral Services came to be in Wellington, Aotearoa/New Zealand. Wellington is a densely packed (but small) capital city with a population of around 150,000 people. It's easily walkable and has a highly connected, educated, and relatively mobile labour pool. It's the seat of central government and key government agencies, host to two universities, has a progressive city council and is home to a diverse mix of corporate, IT, and creative organisations. Wellington is a highly connected hub in a nation of five million people, with a relatively strong social safety net, low corruption, and a culture that encourages humble self-starters to 'make a go of it'. Thanks to the openness and support of Wellington City Council, we were able to gain access to meaningful, innovative work - even without much of a track record. Having the backing of a Council that was willing to take small risks and committed to creating opportunities for cross-sectoral collaboration was a massive boon.

Like Enspiral, Enspiral Services was never one thing. It evolved in response to its changing environment and underwent several distinct phase changes. With my own distinct bias, I've attempted to give colour to these phases and their attributes in the tables and commentary that follow. Its first iteration can be best described as a Freelancers' Collective. Initially, Enspiral was mainly made up of programmers (Ruby on Rails and PHP), project managers comfortable with technical projects and sales & customer development people. Contracts were developed for clients near and far (thanks internet!) and with a good market price for skilled programmers coupled with low operational overheads (laptops and wifi) we generated a good surplus. As time and Wellington spun their magic, a wider set of professionals were drawn into the Enspiral vortex. Lawyers, accountants, designers, and activists joined and wove a more diverse and dynamic community.

Enspiral Services 1.0 - The Freelancers' Collective

(circa 2010 - 2014)

A loosely held group of freelancers handpicked and organised by a hero-leader, but over time, increasingly self-selecting. In Enspiral's own words (circa 2010):

'Enspiral isn't a regular sort of company... You call the shots... We offer opportunities, not jobs... We look for people who can be world class... Changing the world is our passion'

Ownership	Single Director, Single Shareholder
Structure	**Hero-leader:** charismatic salesperson who leads business development and internal talent recruitment - was also the sole company director and bore the legal risk of the enterprise. **Operational Conductor/s:** Internal administrator/s making sure key systems work (accounting, invoicing, and freelancers getting paid) was done and that contracts etc were in place. **Contractors** The individuals or teams designing, programming, or coordinating the specific projects and contracts.
Governance	Governance was lightly held and somewhat opaque, resting mainly on the shoulders of the sole director.
Business model	20% of invoices billed to clients went to the middle. This covered insurance, accounting costs, core operations and began to generate a collective surplus. Deciding what to do with it then became part of the challenge.

Pros & Cons of the Freelancers' Collective model

What was great

- Community building
  - Bootstrapped an economic community and kickstarted the whole network.
  - Fostered new working relationships and opportunities.

What was difficult

- **Accountability and transparency**
  - A resistance to developing fixed roles and structures meant poor individual and organisational accountability.

  - Operations and decision-making lacked transparency - power lived in informal silos, slowly building wider uncertainty and distrust.
  - No processes for due diligence around proposals, contracts etc.

- **Strategy and systems**
  - No clear strategy beyond, 'do good work, do it well' - the system was trying to be everything to everyone.
  - Work was often high value but short term.
  - The 20% rule wasn't well suited to all circumstances. Some people could bill less for their time, some projects were for organisations doing meaningful work with small budgets.

- **Delivery**
  - Heavy reliance on key salespeople to develop leads. Relationships and context lived with those people - not with the organisation.
  - Increasing variety of services being offered (software development, design, facilitation, event planning etc), which made communicating the offer a huge challenge.
  - Lack of ownership and a shifting labour pool meant less consideration for continuity of service and prioritising long term customer needs.

- **Professional and personal development**
  - Adapting our mindsets and approaches from working in hierarchical (agency quashing) organisations to this new environment.
  - Inadequate focus on behaviours, relationships, and systems that enabled individuals to grow professionally and personally.

Outcomes

- People developed a new appreciation of the challenges presented by 'flat' organisations and the myriad challenges associated with collaborating in a non-hierarchical way - especially those of governance, self-management and accountability.

- For most, a long journey of personal awareness and growth was kick-started - building new capacity to listen to and understand our own needs, limits, and edges along with those of our peers.

- People left to pursue more time-tested organisational models and ownership structures that separated ownership and risk from security and a paycheck.

- An appreciation of the need for clearer boundaries and systems for easier coordination and collaboration.

One size doesn't fit all

It's worthwhile reflecting on some of these challenges: **a resistance to developing fixed roles and accountability structures and the mindsets and approaches adapted for working in hierarchical organisations.** As the number of people working through Enspiral Services increased, working out who was doing what and for whom became less clear. This increased the need to create standards and accountability structures - which led to some resistance. I believe this resistance reflected an aversion to roles-as-hierarchy arising from time spent in hierarchical organisations or under the thumb of horrible bosses. These environments also bred mindsets that rewarded measurable execution and for the most part, discouraged organisational innovation and change. This created an awkward paradox as people didn't want the fixed roles and accountability structures, but they also didn't know how to operate effectively without them!

Other challenges presenting in this phase included:

1. People weren't invited to Enspiral to be told what to do.
2. Enspiral Services was a simple system with a simple story which worked well when it was small and closely knit, but became more difficult as it all became more complex
3. The system was still working itself out - making parts of it rigid seemed like an impediment to evolution or change.

Whatever the reasons, a wider cultural aversion developed towards attempts to standardise or homogenise anything. As you can imagine, this meant change was slow, messy, and painful. The pain of this slow messiness, coupled with the growing body of freelancers and breadth of services being offered, allowed small teams with more specific propositions to naturally coalesce and this catalysed the next phase of evolution, **teams.**

Enspiral Services 2.0 - Teams (circa 2010 - 2014)

Teams formed as the whole collective grew too big and unwieldy. Natural collaborations began to emerge between small groups of freelancers, coordinated around their own vision, brand and group processes. The 'one collective' model evolved to enable more variety in the organising forms and services on offer in the market. This allowed different teams to form and set their own course, with eyes and ears open to opportunities for collaboration with other teams.

Ownership	Single Director, Two Shareholders
Structure	Different teams formed with different core values, offerings, internal agreements, and membership protocols
Governance	A 'Core Group' was formed which included representatives of each team and the company directors. The group coordinated important decisions that affected all teams, including decisions around: • shared services • financial flows • accounting, risk mitigation, and governance issues • individual and community needs • the coordination of collective activities A process for light quarterly reporting was also established *but not always followed*
Business model	The percentage contribution to the centre became increasingly variable, from 20% down to 0% in some circumstances. This depended on the scope of the project, the health of the team, and increasingly, the perceived value of Enspiral Services.

Pros & Cons of the Teams model

What was great

- Teams differentiated their offerings, building their own brands and presence in the market.
- Both teams and individuals developed a greater sense of collective need, intent, and the sustainability of their venture.
- Teams prioritised the internal health of their members, seeking ways to support each other financially and professionally.
- Some collective costs were shared, including accounting and legal fees.
- It was easy for teams to form because freelancers were already contracting through the parent company.

What was difficult

- **The complex structure**
  - Like a bunch of new startups, except it was easier for people to walk away due to lack of rigour around ownership, legal responsibility, and continuity of service.
  - More murkiness - it was sometimes hard to see where the responsibilities of a team ended and those of the parent company began.
- **Finance**
  - Collective investments didn't have a commercial edge, and sweat equity didn't translate to viable livelihood.
  - The differing value of services and varying contribution to the centre saw a gradual decline in collective funds. This ultimately diminished the sense of abundance and had an effect on participation in the network.
- **Communication - internal and external**
  - Often difficult internally between teams with so much time spent winning and delivering work.
  - Customer care was under-resourced and some relationships were neglected.
  - Some freelancers continued to operate independently - a challenge for internal visibility and risk management.
  - Higher barrier to entry for new people - existing working relationships were already well established and context increasingly expensive to communicate.

Outcomes

- People took real ownership for their own needs, becoming more aware of their own strengths and weaknesses and gaining a sense of what they needed to learn/develop.
- Many also got pretty fed up with the constant change. Not everyone had the patience, stamina, or life circumstances to support variable incomes or working on stuff that matters but doesn't pay.
- Many individuals opted to leave and work with more traditionally organised companies

Small parts, loosely held

What followed was a stage of collective inertia. As a 'fix' we didn't go far enough to deal with the challenges of our collective operating model. We weren't prepared to make the hard breaks and new commitments necessary for an alternative - so we formed teams inside the collective but kept the same underlying infrastructure. This was intended as a temporary measure to keep things streamlined, while retaining the benefits of shared overheads and collaborative budgeting. However, many of the challenges outlined above persisted. Furthermore, the wider Enspiral network and its diverse body of ventures had begun to grow - exciting, but a challenge in itself. We had also moved into a new co-working space that didn't have the same good vibes as the original Enspiral Space, which had a negative effect on the overall culture.

There was a gradual decline in rhythms, energy, and enthusiasm for Enspiral Services and what it had once represented to the community. Too many people had spent too much energy for too little reward, trying to innovate something that was no longer fit for purpose. The business was in decline and in early 2016, we began winding down the collective consulting model. Instead, we began to move towards something new that better served the many talented consultants and their multifaceted offerings. We called these Livelihood Pods.

Pods[1] have their own lineage. They were prototyped within Enspiral Dev Academy (EDA) based on the lessons learnt within the larger network. Within EDA[2], self-managing teams had control over their own budgets and managed their own capacity. While it was a good idea in principle, this specific implementation lacked the transparency and sense-making mechanisms to operate effectively. Co-dependent pods can't operate in silos but independent pods can. They can also connect up with each other for mutual benefit and meaningful value exchange given the right circumstances.

1 'Pod' is just a made up word for a small, member owned company

2 EDA is an Enspiral venture that trains junior programmers with workplace ready skills using a bootcamp model

Enspiral Services (is dead) - Long live Livelihood Pods (2016 - current)

No two pods are the same, but there are commonalities. Within Enspiral, we've identified two distinct varieties of pod: **Income-pooling** pods and **Eat-what-you-kill** pods. Both varieties share the following attributes:

- Companies with few people <12 (that intend to stay small)
- Intended to serve the human beings within them and operate as a high trust 'professional family'.
- Have a sense of longevity beyond just a contract or project.
- Operate in a high trust environment, aiming to cultivate a healthy ecosystem of complementary collaborators (pods, ventures and freelancers) in their neighbourhood.

Ownership

Different arrangements across different pods (companies). Many look like worker co-operatives with member-directors and equal shareholding. Most are Limited Liability Companies Some contract or support non-members to deliver specific work or projects.

Structure

Most pods are small consulting companies selling time, and consist of three to eight people. Many have suggested pods could support up to 12 people.

Income pooling pods

- One created a hybrid remuneration system that pays members a basic income, a daily rate and a percentage of hours billed.
- Another agreed on a set monthly rate for members regardless of individual consulting income generated.

Eat what you kill pods

- Share overheads, a brand, and run different virtual accounts for directors and projects.

Governance

Governance tends to be separate from operations and is divided between directors. Often delegated to those who are best suited or inclined to dealing with the specific domain based on skills or interest.

Business model

Varies according to pod. As above most of these are consulting companies, selling labour and materials at a professional rate.

The modes and methods of pods differ significantly here.

- Some require that members do all of their consulting through the entity and use a percentage of sales to pay for common tools and marketing.
- One works like a professional membership organisation and charges members a monthly fee for professional support and shared services. It also operates as an entity-in-waiting for projects that don't have another natural home.
- Others are shared consulting vehicles with a variety of revenue share arrangements but may also incubate early stage products.

Pros & Cons of the Livelihood Pods model

What was great

- Variety. Pods enable a wide variety of forms and configurations that suit the needs of those they serve (clients and members).
- Adaptability. Because of their size and the lower cost of communication, disseminating information can be faster and cheaper.
- Security. Smoothing off the financial highs and lows of boom and bust freelancer work.
- The development of deep interdependent working relationships with a small group of peers sets the foundations for high-trust working relationships.
- Safe environment to develop the direct and considerate communication skills.
- Increased resilience across the ecosystem and siloed business risk. One failing pod won't drag the others down with it.

What was difficult

- Less easy to collaborate 'internally' as agreements between pods become agreements between legal companies, rather than between individuals.
- Requires more effort to maintain collective rhythms, culture and communication between the pods. Each pod tends to focus on its own world rather than the wider community.
- Harder to keep collective intent aligned and translate it into clear strategy.
- More difficult to support personal development - small companies can't facilitate the needs of juniors as well as larger companies can.
- Reliance on on self management and the professionalism of the members involved.

Outcomes

- Members take greater ownership for their own work and how it impacts collective outcomes - the potential risk and reward are greater.
- Some pods have wrapped a significant portion of their unique offering around tools and methodologies that have been developed within the network (eg Loomio, Cobudget) and continue to live in symbiotic relationships with those tools and ventures.

The journey continues

If I was to plot my professional journey (along an emotionally charged timeline) it would look something like this:

Corporate	**Self-employed** (the beginning)	**Self-employed** (Part II)	**Freelancer Collective**	**Livelihood Pod**
"Man, this sucks"	"Woo! This is great!"	"This is hard and I'm lonely"	"Wow this feels better but is hard and confusing"	"This is amazing and hard but totally worth it"

I've come full circle from working in a complex, specialised hierarchical organisation to working in a complex, specialised member-based organisation. From the outside, it might not look that different, but on the inside it's made up of peers who support and respect each other as equals, hold each other accountable and actively cultivate shared ownership and responsibility.

In a similar way, from the outside, an interdependent group of 'Livelihood Pods' might look no different from any other group of 'normal' collaborative small businesses that align strategically to better serve their clients and build opportunities. Organisations that value the whole by considering and aligning to the needs of all their stakeholders are the kind of entities we're fostering. We're not doing this just because we want to do great work, we're driven to create a more abundant, kind, and considerate way of doing work that matters.

So much of my own journey has been facilitated by the gifts of peers and mentors who knowingly and unknowingly have shared their hard-fought insights and skills with grace and generosity. I don't think Enspiral would have persisted without the ethos of gift-sharing at its heart. Whether it came packaged as open source technology, retrospectives, facilitated group sessions, or a hug at the right time, this makes up the abundant and generative interpersonal commons that underpin our community.

The future of this growing ecosystem of Pods looks bright. Talented people are showing up, giving their all and sticking around through the hard times. We're getting better at doing what we do and we're cultivating a healthy culture of mutual support - balancing explicit value exchange with a genuine intent to see each other succeed. As connected, self-governing, worker-owned teams with deep trust and aligned intent we stand on solid ground. From here, we can do better work, together.

Where to from here?

by Lucas Tauil de Freitas, john gieryn,
Charley Davenport and Phoebe Tickell

Lucas is sailing with his 13-year-old daughter just off the coast of the Coromandel peninsula in New Zealand. He is suspended perfectly in the present moment and knows that he'll relive this again and again. The scent of garlic and fennel waft from a big wok in which john's cooking cabbage to add to a big soup he'll share in a Food Not Bombs vegan community meal in Portland, Oregon. In Barcelona, Phoebe's got a glint in her eye as she facilitates a group of people from across Enspiral, Ouishare and other sister networks, in the first manifestation of a 'network of networks'. The sweet and dry smell of pine rosin permeates Charley's cello from a hillside house overlooking the airport in Wellington, New Zealand. The music of a Bach cello Suite dances through Charley's mind as he responds to messages in Enspiral's helpdesk.

Across the world, Lucas, john, Charley and Phoebe share a hopeful smile as the newest Enspiral Members.

Two weeks later they gather at Enspiral Summer Fest in New Zealand along with about 60 others. The four of them discover a bonfire still burning after wandering out of a deep dive group discussion. Topics such as "what does it mean to enspiral?" or "what could Enspiral look like in five years?" are not unusual in these annual meetings.

Charley comments: "I love hearing this conversation unfold with new folks and the warmth of understanding that is reached."

Lucas chimes in: "Yes, I do too – having these conversations is one of the best ways we let people into our practices – open-sourcing them as a number of other communities do – and cross-pollinating."

Charley adds: "We don't fence ourselves off being in Enspiral. One of its design features is that it interacts with other circles and parts of your life."

john says: "In Whitman's words, "...I am large, I contain multitudes." In bringing our whole selves we each show up coexisting across many circles and interpersonal relationships."

"For me," Phoebe adds, "it's like a lens through which I interact with reality. The ways of being and doing I practise in this community inform the way I show up and work in the world."

Charley throws another log to the fire, which emits orange sparks – dancing and disappearing into the night sky.

john says: "Thinking of new folks, though, you can't change someone, nor can you really help them; rather you walk the journey with them in mutually transformative and adaptive ways. That is, solidarity – not charity. Everyone has a unique voice and gift to add to the whole if we can see them as peers, as we do when seated in circle."

"Beautifully said john," Lucas replies. "This really resonates with me. It impresses me that for 40 years I had never thought of charity or transformative reality. I was part of a fast prototyping workshop for Auckland Council. We invited local communities together to rig pop-up workshops out of scaffolding and help people fix things – electrical work, plumbing, crafts – and we would invite people in to help each other. This was my opening door to Enspiral, eventually meeting Rich.

My main takeaway from this was that no one likes to receive charity: they like to work together to solve problems. They said 'only the hood can help the hood.'

Phoebe, john and Charley are listening intently as Lucas continues: "Not just experts should be heard here. Close-knit teams perform much better than a team made up of experts."

Charley says: "Yes, this is one of the main things that brings us together at Enspiral: the vision of the future. Contributors, Members and others here, there's no distinction between us in this respect. We're all focused on placing that first brick of utopia."

"The idea of Enspiral triggers people's dreams.' Phoebe adds. 'I've seen Enspiral inspire belief in a better future, one where we get to solve our own challenges. This is one of our biggest assets: a living idea. The work is what we do from the realisation that another future is possible. And manifesting that future takes working together in a completely different way."

Lucas says: "I'm fascinated by utopia. Some people think it's a no place; a place that doesn't exist. Some people see it as a place yet to be discovered or an ideal. My favourite understanding of utopia comes from an Argentinian filmmaker Fernando Birri. A student asked him: "what purpose does utopia serve?" Fernando responded: "In order to understand the purpose of utopia, you have to understand where it is: it is in the horizon." It's the nature of utopia."

Phoebe adds: "Yes – we walk ten steps towards them and they move ten steps further away. The role or purpose of utopian ideas like Enspiral is to keep us walking. To give us a course to steer. Enspiral is like the north star. It guides people through the night."

Lucas concludes: "It's like a lighthouse. We get excited by these questions and in the pursuit of reaching utopia, we realise the questions and answers have changed."

"What do you hope Enspiral will be like in the future?" Charley asks.

"For me," Phoebe responds, "Enspiral represents both the future, and the present. It's the future in that anyone can make Enspiral into what it will be – it is a living lab for new ways of being, doing and working together. It's the present in that being part of Enspiral calls me into deep presence and awareness – of who I am, how I want to be with people, how I want to show up in the world. It's the power of an idea. It's the power of a shared intention. It reminds me that the quote by Margaret Mead is in fact real: "Never doubt that a small group of thoughtful, committed citizens can change the world; indeed, it's the only thing that ever has."

Phoebe continues, "it's a reminder that a more human world is possible. It's a rebellious 'no' to the status quo. It's an earnest attempt at hacking the normal way we work in society. It's a prioritisation of the important parts of being human. And it's a reminder that together we can create islands of sanity, networks of trust and hope, and new organisations that practise what they preach. In Enspiral, it's the being, and not just the doing, that is important." john adds another log to the fire and says: "I agree. I think there's an opportunity for purpose-driven communities like Enspiral to create conducive space for people to unfold their unique gifts – to develop their capacity in relation to others, to a wider community, and to a purpose that transcends that community. In courageous spaces we can better support people to see the potential that resides in our differences, and the value of others. This capacity will support us to hear and tell new or ancient stories that are currently marginalised by the hegemonic narratives. These shared visions may be one key in moving our communities towards change that is sustained and longed for, collectively. Lucas, Phoebe and Charley get in closer to the fire.

"I love the idea that we'll be more diverse and have deeper connections," Charley agrees.

Phoebe reflects: ""I think that if in five years, Enspiral were still nourishing all of us and nourishing us to do our best work, that is "enough." At the same time, we can continue the work to make more spaces that are not echo-chambers. Could we push towards engaging with the bottom billion? When do we have a responsibility to recognise "the world is burning," and look at how we act in response to that? As we look into the future, we're going to be seeing more and more chaotic and uncertain situations. How could networks of resilience help prepare and respond to disasters? How could the Enspiral model be used more by the disenfranchised?"

The four of them are now holding their hands up to the fire as they try to balance the heat and the cool night air.

Charley bounces off, "This is really interesting to have your and john's perspective here, side by side. It seems in our future vision of Enspiral there's two different patterns of change: deepening and scaling."

Phoebe says: "Yes, maybe we don't really need to get any bigger but at the same time there might be replications of us – Enspiral circles in San Francisco, Europe or elsewhere – and ways of sharing resources and know-how between those circles."

Charley says: "Exactly. And john, it seems your aspirations and hopes for us in the future are about the deepening: being more inclusive, having better connections to different areas and with each other. Doing more of our best work."

Phoebe adds: "Sometimes I notice people seeing Enspiral as an "elder" – a network with a rich history of stories, artefacts, and tools. How can Enspiral mentor new and fledgling networks? How do we make sure that we document our stories and tools well?

"I think that's one of our roles as Enspiral members, and something we need to be aware of," Charley says. "Stewarding how these stories are told and preserving the integrity, while at the same time observing and accepting that evolution and change, itself, is one of the features in our way of being."

Phoebe says: "Something else to consider is: what if Enspiral came to an organic death? What does graceful death look like in Enspiral? What could emerge from the decomposing soil of Enspiral if we did let it go? And… if "Enspiral" died, would what Enspiral really is disappear? It's the relationships, and they live on, the seeds continue to be sown, the spores continue to spread."

Silence. The fire flickered as the four looked to one another for a deep moment.

After consideration, Charley spoke: "I think I would be okay with that. This is one of the things JV has said that stuck with me: if we disbanded the formal company and took away the digital tools, systems, and our collective practices, what remains is our relationships. For example, when you look at something bright like this fire or our faces and look away: what you see is an afterimage. What would be left of Enspiral is memory and knowledge. Perhaps that's the acceptance you have to have coming in as a new Enspiral Member. It's a pattern of living, which means that it could die – or not, while you're here."

Phoebe concludes: "Maybe that's a new pattern we could take forward, regularly asking ourselves: "Does Enspiral still feel alive to you?""

Further silence. They have a collective yawn, which is followed by laughter at their shared sentiment during this time: full of warmth, trust, and invisible nurturing. Off in the distance other bonfires burn, emitting streams of changed matter, and sparks that dance into the night sky, indistinguishable from the distant stars.

Our buzzwords: Unpacked

by Susan Basterfield, Hannah Smith and Anthony Cabraal

When groups of people work, live and grow together they create language. It happens organically. Jargon is something that helps people belong; adopting the lexicon is part and parcel of adopting a community identity. It enables 'the in' to feel 'in together', but for those who are 'not in', it can be a barrier to understanding, suggest an exclusive, insular culture or simply be really annoying. Enspiral is no different, so we've had a go at creating a guide to some of our (currently) most commonly used 'buzzwords':

Buzzword — How you might hear it — What it means

Bootstrap

"Let's just bootstrap this until we're confident it works."

Not sure what it's got to do with boots, but essentially this means funding a new business or initiative using internal resources. Often used to describe the process of earning money from one client or venture and then spending the surplus on new ideas.

Catalyst

"She's a great catalyst, so full of ideas, and excellent at seeing connections between things"

A nebulous job title covering a broad spectrum of leadership activities that serve the greater good. May include starting new initiatives, connecting people and opportunities, coordinating and codifying things that need doing, and supporting those who are doing them.

Check-in

"Let's all check in quickly before we get started. What's on top for everyone just now?"

Inviting everyone in the room to speak at the beginning of any meeting or gathering. Brings all the voices in right from the get-go and makes it OK to talk about anything going on that might affect how we are 'showing up' (see below). See also 'check out'.

Check-out

Let's do a quick check out - how is everyone leaving the session today?

As with 'checking in' (see above), a process that invites everyone to say whatever they need to say before a 'container' (see below) closes and a meeting or gathering comes to an end. Often quick and lighthearted.

Container; create a

"You need a strong container to have that conversation properly."

No, it's not a small box. But it kind of helps to picture one. When we talk about creating a container we mean demarcating safe, comfortable, and productive conditions for a particular conversation or activity to take place. Closely aligned with 'holding space' (see below).

Cross-pollinate

"I love how much cross-pollination goes on at Enspiral between all the teams and ventures"

Copying the bumblebee (sort of), cross-pollinating is taking ideas from one team or group and sharing them elsewhere in the eco-system (see below). Often occurs at gatherings when multiple groups are having connectable conversations in close proximity.

Eco-system

"They aren't really in the community, but are definitely part of the eco-system"

Borrowing from nature again, this is used to describe the whole landscape of interconnected people, projects, and companies relating to a specific community, idea or conversation.

Followership

"We don't celebrate followership enough!"

Less talked about than the act of leadership, but no less important. Best described as offering active, visible support to someone who is taking a lead on something eg agreeing to show up to a first-time event and making it known to others. Something we love to practise and encourage at Enspiral.

Harvest

"Who's up for harvesting everything we've discussed today?"

No, it's not picking apples from a tree - 'harvesting' generally means to collect and write up all the big ideas or actions from a discussion, workshop or gathering. A harvest might look like mind maps on big pieces of paper, photos of post-it notes on windows, or notes on an online document to be shared. No Enspiral gathering is complete without a harvest of some sort.

Hold space

"Thanks for holding space for us so beautifully on this retreat."

The act of creating and maintaining the optimum physical and social conditions for other people to do what they need to - to meet, converse, decide, debate, explore - without seeking any specific outcome. Space-holding is a key skill amongst Enspiralites.

Land

"What she said really landed with me."

When a statement or articulation of an idea hits home, and feels newly meaningful. Often accompanied by a sense of relief and/or new energy - like an aeroplane touching down at the end of a long flight.

"How did that land with you?"

Inquiring into someone's well-being when presented a new or surprising bit of information or feedback.

Retreat

"I'm really looking forward to the retreat and to chilling out together for a couple of days"

A few days when a group intentionally spends time together away from the work environment. With Enspiral this usually involves good food, great conversations, a fire and, at some point, dancing.

Sense

"My sense is we're really close to something here"

Something unnamed, a thought or process that hasn't quite landed (see above) yet. Something being sensed is still a bit fuzzy; sometimes an idea or insight that's not quite fully formed.

Sense-check

"Can we all just stop and do a quick sense-check on this?"

To interrogate an idea or proposition in a different way or from a different perspective. Sometimes articulated as "what are you noticing?" Surprising how easy it is to overlook this one.

Show up

"We need to keep asking ourselves how we want to show up"

Showing up at Enspiral doesn't just refer to going along to meetings or parties - although we do plenty of that. It also refers to being conscious of the mindset we bring to a project or activity - being open-minded, reflective, gentle, or considered for example.

Stewardship, stewards

"He seems to be struggling. Let's check he has a steward to help him through the bumps"

This is a big warm blanket of a word that covers a range of supportive, peer-to-peer behaviour. Normally established as a formal connection between two people who are also part of a larger group.

Surface

"In this session let's try and surface what's really going on here."

To voice assumptions, tensions, ideas or feelings that might be present or underlying but not clearly expressed. Better out than in might be another way of putting it.

Unpack

"Sounds complicated. Let's try and unpack it a bit"

Sometimes it's not just suitcases that are heavy. Social tensions, complicated pieces of work, and confusion in teams often need to be broken down and discussed. 'Unpacking' looks like pairs or small groups talking through challenging situations with care and consideration.

It takes a village...

Enspiral is the collective force behind Better Work Together.

The thinking and efforts of this community over years of hard work and learning together is the reason this book exists. It has been shaped by many minds along the journey and grew from ideas on a whiteboard to the book you hold in your hands.

We are deeply grateful for the invisible support from everyone who helped champion and nurture this work, both within the Enspiral community and from our friends working alongside us all around the world.

Production team

Anthony Cabraal had the original vision, and together with Susan Basterfield coordinated all the content as producing authors. Natalie Sisson joined as the third member of the core team to kickstart the project and drive a successful crowdfunding campaign. The deft editing support of Alanna Irving and Hannah Smith stripped away the noise and sharpened the language. Creative director Renato Inácio went above and beyond to express the collective, creative spirit of this work, and together with illustrator Mukund Iyer transformed text into a wonderful piece of art..

Co-authors

Nine long-time Enspiral members took time away from busy lives building companies, growing communities, and delivering impact to step into the role of co-author, writing the essays in the book.

Contributing authors and supporting forces

Enspiral is a community full of supportive, talented, proactive people who are open to experiments. The following humans contributed to the project in various ways: leading pieces of content, contributing time, ideas, providing critical eyes, and perspective or financial support.

Billy Matheson
Gina Rembe-Stevens
Doris Zuur
Lucy Carver
Nick Laurence
Nanz Nair
Theodore Taptiklis
john gieryn
Phoebe Tickell
Lucas Tauil de Freitas
Charley Davenport
Mix Irving
Anake Goodall
Mary Jo Kaplan
Nati Lombardo
Sarah Houseman
Charmaine Myers
Sandra Otto
Mario Kaphan
Manel Heredero
Albert Cañigueral
Miki Kashtan
Manuel Küblböck
Marty family
Zuur family
Nadine Isler
Lani and Hugh Evans
Ronan Harrington
Dominique Snyman
Lisa Gill
Joriam Philippe
Douglas Rushkoff
Doug Kirkpatrick
Colin Basterfield
Hannah Smith
James Mansell
Helen Sanderson
Frederic Laloux

Catalysts

Six organisational catalysts backed this project with funding and made the whole thing possible. These organisations actively contribute to growing the power of community in our world.

DAOstack

DAOstack is a platform for decentralised governance that enables collectives to easily self-organise around shared goals or values. DAOstack is sometimes called an operating system for collective intelligence, or a Wordpress for DAOs – 'decentralised autonomous organisations' - which use blockchain-based governance protocols to convert human input into efficient, effective decision-making.

The Genesis DAO (funders of this project) represents an experiment in allocating resources using decentralised governance protocols that have the capability of scaling to organisations of infinite size.

https://daostack.io

Namaste Foundation

Namaste Foundation exists in service of a peaceful, just, and regenerative world. The organisation is an expression of solidarity with many movements. They serve the common good through understanding, collaboration, and relationship.

https://www.namaste.org/

Space Base

Space Base is co-creating a global Space Ecosystem to serve entrepreneurs in emerging space industries - starting in New Zealand.

Their goal is to provide access to training, networking, technical services, and investment opportunities where they are needed most.

http://spacebase.co/

Bamboo Creative

Bamboo Creative is a digital agency based in Wellington, Aotearoa and a part of the Enspiral network. We help develop good ideas into great ones and design engaging, meaningful experiences for end users. A diverse team of designers, developers, storytellers and product strategists, we're committed to working as peers on projects that help people connect with themselves, each other and the wider world.

http://www.bamboocreative.nz/

The Philtech Initiative

The global open Philtech Initiative was established in May 2018 to cultivate sustainable and efficient purpose-driven organisations aimed at solving root causes of world problems by prioritising their social and environmental impact over the traditional 'increase profits at any cost' approach.

Philtech Initiative originated from Rybakov Foundation, a private philanthropic organisation founded in 2015 by Igor and Ekaterina Rybakov with headquarters in Moscow, Russia. It's supported by hundreds of entrepreneurs, philanthropists, futurologists, researchers, visionaries, creators, and journalists around the world.

http://philtech.global/

Peerdom

Peerdom offers a curated marketplace of collaborative tools, business models, legal structures, and best practice recommendations from which teams can pick and choose to craft fulfilling, engaging workplaces founded upon integrity.

The Peerdom model is easily applied to founding new or transforming existing companies, as it simply describes a procedure for how peers work together in a financially sustainable and fair organisation that is owned, operated and managed by its own workers.

https://peerdom.org/

Co-authors profile

Richard D. Bartlett has been cultivating the Enspiral garden since 2012. He co-founded Loomio, an open source software tool for collective decision-making, and The Hum, offering practical guidance for decentralised organisations. Rich is passionate about co-ownership, self-management, collaborative governance, and other ways of sneaking anarchism into respectable places.

Susan Basterfield is catalyst and convener, helping individuals and organisations release potential through participatory organising, exploring her hypothesis that our transition into what's next will be brought about by and through community. She is a prolific writer and speaker, and has shared her experiences from India to Korea, Canada to Chile, Sweden to Australia, and most places in between.

Kate Beecroft is a strategist, facilitator, process designer, and business developer who has been launching trainings, designing, and hosting events and consulting with companies on the principles of self management. She is based in Europe and is co-convenor of Leadwise Academy and co-founder of Greaterthan, a venture in service of people and organisations at the forefront of radically new organisational models. Her dream job is to be a bibliotherapist.

Anthony Cabraal is a creative producer, writer, and business owner who has helped many Enspiral initiatives start and grow since 2012. He serves as an advisor to several startups, and loves to get new ideas off the ground - including driving the creation of this book. He is based between Wellington, New Zealand, and Melbourne, Australia.

Sandra Chemin has been passionate about innovation, experimentation, and learning by doing all her life. She is the co-founder of the first digital agency in Brazil, sailing around the world with her family, co-founding a school designed for social inclusion and as the founder of futureyou.be, helping organisations and individuals create the future of their work. She is a sought-after speaker and is based between New Zealand and Brazil.

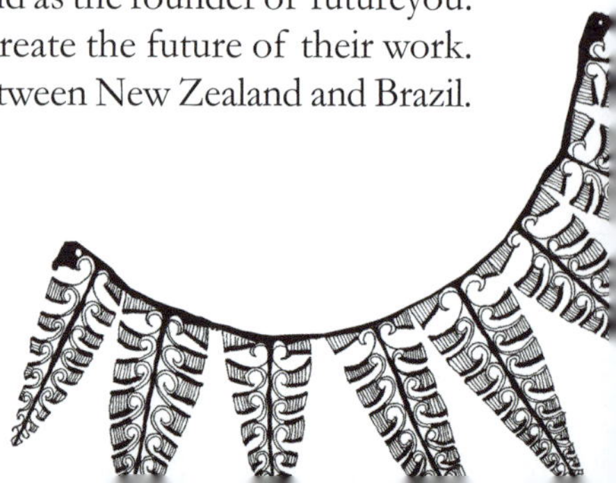

Alanna Irving joined Enspiral in 2011. She was co-founding executive director of the Enspiral Foundation, and co-founder of Loomio, Cobudget, and other open-source technology tools for deep collaboration. Alanna is an expert in bossless leadership, deconstructing and reconstructing money, governance, and ownership for a radically cooperative future. She lives in Wellington, New Zealand. More: https://alanna.space

Joshua Vial is the original founder of the Enspiral collective and has worked on many ventures and projects since then, most notably Enspiral Dev Academy. As a programmer, entrepreneur, facilitator, and educator he works in the space where technology, deep purpose and systemic change meet.

Francesca Pick is a driving force in several international collectives such as the Ouishare network. Her work is focused on community building, new organisational models and participatory governance. She is based in Europe and is the co-founder of Greaterthan, a venture in service of people and organisations at the forefront of radically new organisational models.

Chelsea Robinson is a systems change strategist who has been instrumental in building and leading organisations including GenerationZero.org, LifeHackHQ.co, and Loomio.org. She lives in San Francisco and continues to expand her impact and influence with a focus on philanthropic strategy and non-profit strategy. More: chelsearobinson.me

Damian Sligo-Green brings a living systems lens to his work, paying special attention to the deeper needs of people and planet. He's energised by working with others on projects that shift mindsets and behaviours and ultimately facilitate action. He's based in Wellington and works through Bamboo Creative, a digital agency within the Enspiral community.

Silvia Zuur brings people into the heart of all organisational change work. She has been growing Enspiral with a focus on educational ventures, transformative events, and healthy organisational strategy since 2012. With more than a decade of facilitation experience, she is comfortable pacing the main stage of an event, sorting logistics out the back, or scheming and dreaming new ideas. An adventurer at heart, she has based herself in Wellington.

References

We've made every effort to acknowledge sources and provide links to original work, and the original sources of the thinking that we build on in our work. Below you'll find a generalised list of websites that are referenced throughout this work. Our intention is to continue to grow this list of resources on the website: **betterworktogether.co**

https://handbook.enspiral.com

http://loomio.coop/

https://en.wikipedia.org/wiki/Council_circle

http://greaterthan.works

https://teamhuman.fm

https://shareable.net

https://forumforthefuture.org

https://amanitas.cc

http://theleanstartup.com

http://www.reinventingorganizationswiki.com

https://en.wikipedia.org/wiki/Open_Space_Technology

https://onbeing.org

https://www.holacracy.org/governance-meetings

http://www.ottoscharmer.com/theoryu

http://www.morningstarco.com/

http://www.artofhosting.org/

http://www.liberatingstructures.com/

https://www.cnvc.org/

https://devacademy.co.nz/

http://www.lowcarbonchallenge.nz/

http://www.exp.agency/

https://cobudget.co/

https://lifehackhq.co/

http://futureyou.be

http://thehum.org

http://www.impactcanvas.co/

http://www.generationzero.org/

http://www.self-managementinstitute.org/

http://www.reinventingorganizations.com/

https://www.ehf.org/

https://www.newfrontiers.nz/

https://www.ouishare.net/fest

https://www.ouishare.net/

https://holochain.org/

https://www.scuttlebutt.nz/